D0889779

Bill Cohen's 1972 Campaign for Congress

Bill Cohen's 1972 Campaign for Congress

An Oral History of the Walk that Changed Maine Politics

Edited by
Christian P. Potholm II,
with Jed Lyons

Introduction by the
Hon. William S. Cohen

ROWMAN & LITTLEFIELD
Lanham • Boulder • New York • London

Published by Rowman & Littlefield
An imprint of The Rowman & Littlefield Publishing Group, Inc.
4501 Forbes Boulevard, Suite 200, Lanham, Maryland 20706
www.rowman.com

86-90 Paul Street, London EC2A 4NE

Distributed by NATIONAL BOOK NETWORK

Copyright © 2022 by The Rowman & Littlefield Publishing Group, Inc.

All rights reserved. No part of this book may be reproduced in any form or by any electronic or mechanical means, including information storage and retrieval systems, without written permission from the publisher, except by a reviewer who may quote passages in a review.

British Library Cataloguing in Publication Information available

Library of Congress Cataloging-in-Publication Data available

ISBN: 978-1-5381-7092-2 (cloth)
ISBN: 978-1-5381-7093-9 (electronic)

♾™ The paper used in this publication meets the minimum requirements of American National Standard for Information Sciences—Permanence of Paper for Printed Library Materials, ANSI/NISO Z39.48-1992.

Contents

List of Photos

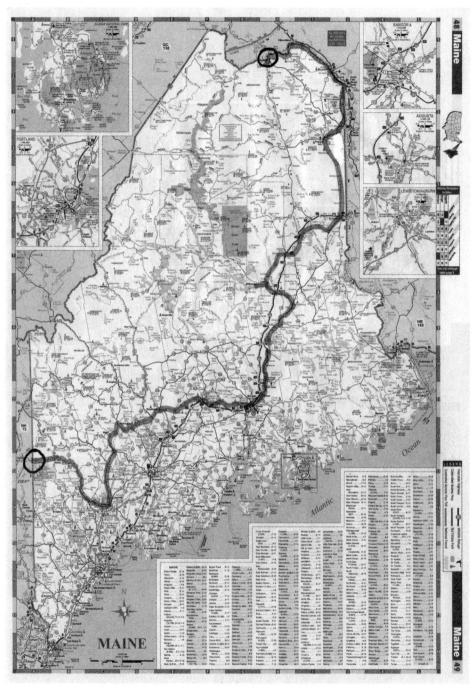

Route of the 650-mile walk from New Hampshire to Canada.

PREFACE

WHEN BILL COHEN DECIDED TO RUN FOR THE 2ND DISTRICT CON-
gressional seat in Maine in 1972, he was 32 years old and was serving
as the newly elected Mayor of Bangor, the state's third largest city. The
2nd District comprises some 80 percent of the state's geography and
runs from the New Hampshire border to the Canadian border, basically covering most of the rural areas north and east of the populous
southern Maine coastline.

Bill asked his longtime friend and Bowdoin College fraternity
brother, Christian P. Potholm, to manage his campaign. In 1972, Chris
and his wife, Sandy, had just moved to Brunswick, Maine, where Chris
had been hired to teach in the Bowdoin government department. Fast
forward 50 years and Chris is retiring from Bowdoin in 2022 after a
distinguished teaching career, authorship of twenty books, and a second
career as Maine's leading expert on campaigns, polling, and politics.

I was an undergraduate at Bowdoin in 1972. I had taken a couple of
courses from Chris and we had become close. He asked me to work on
the campaign that summer as one of the advance men on Bill's 650-mile
walk across the state. That summer was memorable in many ways, not
least of all because of the opportunity to spend literally months in the
company of Bill himself. We had a good, lighthearted relationship with
a lot of banter on the road and in the evenings when we would enjoy the
hospitality of complete strangers who put us up for the night, fed us, and
arranged impromptu gatherings of friends and neighbors who came to
hear Bill speak around a campfire, in a living room, or in the backyard. It
was magical to watch Bill effortlessly connect with everyday Mainers and
to hear their earnest and heartfelt questions and comments.

We had some humorous experiences that summer, many of which are recounted in this book. In New Smyrna one day, someone suggested that Bill jump on a horse. As photos were being taken, the horse bolted and off went Bill, who was not a trained equestrian. Luckily, another horseman took off after him and managed to grab the horse's bridle and save Bill, who was holding on for dear life. In Houlton, we learned that campaigning in a drive-in movie theater at night isn't a very good idea. And there were many funny moments as we negotiated our sleeping arrangements each night in the homes of the gracious families who volunteered to host us along the way.

As Chris Potholm explains in the Foreword, the 1972 Cohen campaign was historic for its revival of the Maine Republican Party that had become moribund, old, and out of touch. A remarkable number of future GOP statewide officeholders volunteered on the campaign. Most of them were either still in college or just out of college. Future U.S. Senator Susan Collins was an undergraduate at St. Lawrence University in 1972. Another future U.S. Senator, Olympia Snowe, was married to her husband, Peter Snowe, the President of the Maine State Senate who tragically died in a car accident a year later. Jock McKernan was in between his senior year at Dartmouth and his first year in law school. We played frisbee that summer on the walk. Jock went on to become governor of Maine and became Olympia's second husband. Bob Monks, running for a Senate seat in the 1972 primary against Margaret Chase Smith, lost his race, but, as you will see in this oral history, Monks played an outsized role in Bill's campaign and in many more future GOP victories.

After Bill was elected, I spent two college summers working for him as a legislative intern in his Washington, D.C., congressional office. In 1975, I helped start a small book publishing company in a Washington suburb. Chris became our consultant and was instrumental in guiding our early efforts. In 1976, I volunteered to work for Bill at the GOP national convention in Kansas City where I met my future wife, Blythe. When we were married, Chris and Sandy came to our wedding and Chris served as an usher. One of our two sons, Ted, was a student and teaching assistant of Chris's at Bowdoin. Ted also worked as an intern for Bill at the Department of Defense. Over the past 50 years, I have had the good fortune to have published many books for both Chris and Bill, as well as for Bill's wife, Janet. Our lives have continued to intersect in many meaningful ways.

I have always wanted to publish an oral history of the 1972 Cohen campaign. Now, 50 years later, we are finally doing it. Bill, Chris, and I spent over 20 hours on Zoom calls in 2022 during which we interviewed each other and many of the individuals who were instrumental in the '72 campaign. Their memories five decades later were sharp and vivid and brought us all back to that remarkable summer and fall when a handful of inexperienced but passionate supporters came together to help elect a young, neophyte, but very determined Bill Cohen.

Bill's election was a seminal event in Maine politics and it rescued the Republican brand from extinction. Today, Susan Collins is the sole Republican in the Maine delegation. Will there be another young, aspiring GOP contender in the future who takes the party by storm? If so, it will be no more surprising than Bill Cohen's improbable come-from-behind victory in 1972.

I want to express my appreciation to my longtime executive assistant Jackie Zirn, who labored long and hard on this project, and to Senior Executive Acquisitions Editor Jon Sisk, who shepherded the book into print so expertly. Jon, now living in Maine, has been a valued colleague for 35 years here at Rowman & Littlefield. I also wish to thank our esteemed colleague Elaine McGarraugh for her assistance on this book.

Jed Lyons
President & CEO
Rowman & Littlefield
Advance Man, 1972 Cohen for Congress Campaign
June 2022

FOREWORD

ON A LOVELY JUNE DAY 50 YEARS AGO, TWO YOUNG MEN SAT IN THE Brunswick commons and ate hot dogs. Bill Cohen and I, close friends, fraternity brothers and fellow summer police officers, were discussing his possible walk across Maine's 2nd Congressional District that summer as part of his campaign for Congress. The idea had been brought to me by Bob Loeb, a student in my class who lived in Illinois and who told me about Dan Walker's successful walk to the Illinois governorship.

After I enumerated the various pros and cons, Bill asked if I really thought it was a good idea and could he do it, saying, "Are you sure?" With the hubris of youth and secure in the knowledge that I didn't have to do the actual walking, I replied, "I'm sure." Bill nodded, "I'm sure, too. I can do this."

Six hundred fifty long miles later, he had.

To appreciate the situation facing Cohen during the summer of 1972, some context is in order. Although Maine's Republican Party had dominated the state's politics from 1854 until the 1950s, the Muskie revolution reversed the state's political history. By 1972, the Democrats controlled one Senate seat, the governorship, and both congressional districts. Only Margaret Chase Smith held major office and she was 75, frail and hampered by the heart attack of her chief confidant and operational leader, General Bill Lewis. She would be defeated handily by Bill Hathaway for that remaining GOP Senate seat in November. Without Cohen's success in the 2nd Congressional District (CD) election of 1972, the Republicans would have been swept from all the major elected political offices in the state of Maine.

Winning in the 2nd CD was no easy task at that time, either. This sprawling jurisdiction was 73 percent rural and the largest district east of the Mississippi. Moreover, by 1972 the 2nd CD had become behaviorally heavily Democrat with their candidate Bill Hathaway, winning by huge margins since 1964 with victories of 62, 57, 56, and 64 percent, respectively. The Republican Party was also widely perceived as being the party of plutocrats and corporations with little interest in working men and women, and the party itself seemed unable to mount effective campaigns in the 2nd CD or statewide. Reeling from its losses and split between conservatives and moderates, the party would not be able to provide much meaningful help or strategy.

In that context, the idea of a walk across the state that summer had some obvious appeal—especially to two political neophytes.

It had never been done in Maine.

Remember that, in those days, summer political campaigns were desultory and sporadic, often limited to cameo candidate appearances at state fairs and Fourth of July parades. Most campaign efforts didn't start in earnest until Labor Day. Pundits said voters weren't interested during the summer: "Everybody is at the beach or at camp." TV and print coverage was limited. TV advertising by individual candidates, moreover, was very limited and often confined to October, and we had virtually no money to do that in any case.

But we did have a young, vigorous, athletic candidate who could be counted on to become very competitive and see the daunting task through. The son of a baker and familiar with the demands and pressures of blue-collar life, he also could and would identify with the people he met along the way and relate to their struggles and needs. Bill Cohen could make history and in doing so, win a seat in Congress. I knew he was as competitive and tough as they come.

Having such a single focus, we thought, could give Bill visibility at a time when there was little going on politically and when the press was bored and looking for stories. Today there is a 24-hour news cycle with a constant bombardment of news; newspapers and their role in political campaigns, however, have experienced shrinking circulation as interest in the print media has diminished greatly.

But in 1972, newspapers *were* the coin of the realm in terms of political coverage. They even had reporters assigned specifically to politics and they would send reporters out to cover stories—not as today, where newspapers mostly rely on press releases and Tweet feeds. The working press, not only from the dailies but also the weeklies, we thought, would come and walk with the candidate for an hour or half a day or a whole day and trudging along, they would have to acknowledge the authenticity of the effort and share, at least in part, in its arduous nature. They would then tell the story of The Walk to their readers.

We didn't see how The Walk strategy could miss in getting Bill the press to get his name recognition up with his opponent, the Democrat Elmer Violette who had already run statewide for the U.S. Senate against Margaret Chase Smith (losing 41 to 59 percent in 1966).

Of course, we had no idea about how arduous the whole walk would be and how labor intensive it would become. It turned out you couldn't simply have the candidate walking alone along the road looking like a lost or even purposeful hitchhiker or homeless person. You had to constantly publicize it in advance and in real time as it progressed. Campaign walks turned out to be very hard work and not just for the candidate, for they depended on clever and dedicated field people making correct daily decisions on the spot. A tremendous responsibility was on their shoulders.

As this oral history affirms, Bill Cohen would have a set of outstanding advance teams lining up stayovers a week ahead and stayovers the day before, and there were two cars, one ahead and one behind with signs that read "Bill Cohen Ahead: Honk and Wave." Listen to the voices in this collection, though, and you will hear how effective their efforts were and how much fun the participants had. But a huge amount of work went into the whole process, far more than we anticipated that fine summer day in Brunswick.

Not only was the walk far more arduous than we had first imagined, but we made it even more difficult. I have always felt guilty for insisting that the candidate spend each night in a real Maine family's home, eating and sleeping in their house. I didn't calculate that the candidate, after walking 18 or 20 miles a day, would simply want to eat dinner and crash into bed. Instead, he would end up having to be the center of attention far into the night before starting things all over again the next day. Try as they might, the field people could not shield him from the ongoing attention and being kept up far into the night discussing the issues.

These field people not only made the walk of William Sebastian Cohen possible in the form that it eventually took, they also helped him to win the races for their individual counties as they established their grassroots efforts that helped to change the perception of what Republican candidates were, presenting the party with a new, young, vigorous, energetic candidate and his hard-working volunteers. Long after Cohen had moved on to new locations, his field people would double and triple back to those people to keep the enthusiasm alive.

As many of the contributors indicate, the 1972 walk eventually turned out to be seminal and much duplicated as a campaign tactic/concomitant strategy. The walk would end up being a campaign staple for a new generation of Republican candidates. Dave Emery adopted it first, then did Jock McKernan, followed by Olympia Snowe, and finally Susan Collins. In the process all utilized it and projected the same moderate, youthful Republican personified. For four decades that moderate, youthful image would be the overriding legacy of the Republican Party in Maine.

The essence of Cohen's campaign slogan, "The Man the People Found" also became the staple for the subsequent image projection of moderate, young, energetic candidates more attuned to the voices of blue-collar workers and especially small business employers and employees. In truth, this all had echoes of Margaret Chase Smith in her prime, identifying with that same demographic cohort and stressing independence and self-reliance (and not party ideology) that helped her become the legend she was.

Of course, by the end of the 1980s, these campaigns had been literally run into the ground and lost their utility except for very local elections. Yet, since Susan Collins last utilized the tactic, more than a dozen or more candidates—Republican, Democrat and Independent—all came to my Bowdoin office asking if I thought they should do "A Walk" and how to do it.

Invariably I tried to discourage them. "How about if I call it a "Trek?" countered one. Another proposed that "a combination of walking and jogging would be different and I'd get in great shape." Still another was enthusiastic about "biking" across the district alone with a sign on his back. I was unable to dissuade this lad and the sight of his quite hefty, florescent yellow-clad body pedaling through rural Maine like some gigantic golden bumble bee was undoubtedly highly amusing to many. It also had to be more than a little confusing to observers: "Emma, where are the other riders in this race?"

Today with cell phones, walks would put candidates under constant visual supervision. They would not be able to go into the woods to relieve themselves without being filmed. More importantly, today's candidates have to spend so much time raising money, going to fundraisers, and "dialing for dollars" that they wouldn't have time to walk in the first place. Moreover, with the flood tide of dark money and political advertising by multiple groups—over which the campaign has no control—a walk would be washed away in other images, mostly negative, flooding the airways. A walk simply cannot drive the political narrative the way it did in 1972.

Honestly, politics today is truly horrible in nature and individual campaigns have far, far less control over their messages and content. They are unable to run positive campaigns with any hope of convincing voters, and campaigns cannot, by law, communicate with third-party and dark money entities even to ask them to stop. In 1972, I would say that perhaps 30 percent of the electorate was in play, and negative advertising was a very tiny fraction of the debate on television. Today only 8–10 percent of that electorate are truly in play for the candidate's individual campaign as voters are constantly bombarded with a never-ending barrage of negative commercials, some by the candidates themselves, even more by third parties. Individual campaigns cannot stop the negative campaign imagery even if they want to.

It is a sad time for our Republic.

By contrast, this book is about another era entirely, and that is why it was so much fun to work on this book because politics then simply was more fun and more positive and more interactive than today. This shows in the comments of the interviewees throughout their presentations.

Thanks to Zoom, Bill Cohen, Jed Lyons, and I interviewed participants of The Walk and the 1972 campaign and those who participated in it or witnessed it first-hand and engaged in it. The experience was marvelous. Like the Three Musketeers of old, we were able to sit around a metaphorical campfire and share stories from the past with the contributors. I found it to be most exciting, exhilarating, and fascinating to relive the events of that summer that would prove to be so seminal. It was magical. I really didn't want the process to end, but duties and deadlines prevailed.

The Zoom sessions themselves were free floating and free associating. The mystic cords of memory may have been strained in places as accounts differed, but we have left those memories intact as, over time, we all came to remember things in our own way.

In the process of doing our interviews, we learned a great deal. Contained in the various accounts and reminiscences were some insights that provided illuminating, even startling, revelations.

For example, Bill Cohen's courageous vote to approve the sale of AWACS planes to Saudi Arabia at the cost of considerable political and personal pain is explored by a number of participants, including Bob Monks, the midwife of the modern Republican Party.

For the first time, the role of the Israeli ambassador to Great Britain and Cohen's flight to Great Britain to meet with him is documented; the accompanying dialogue and process has not been reported elsewhere. It is both highly revelatory and of great significance to the history of that region—to say nothing of providing perspicacious insights into the inner workings of the Reagan presidency.

Also, for the first time in print, Bob Monks shares invaluable insights into his campaign to remove the Big Box (whereby a voter could check one box and vote a straight party line ticket). This is the single most important systemic change that made the Cohen Counterrevolution possible because it freed up Franco-American voters (the group most likely to vote a straight Democrat ticket) and put them in play.

Bill Cohen himself shares many intimate and previously unrecorded experiences growing up in the harsh realities of Bangor's Hancock Street in the 1940s, later attending Bowdoin College and pursuing his early career in law and his early concerns for social and criminal justice. Bill also illuminates his drive to succeed and the very real challenges and adversities he experienced on The Walk and the 1972 campaign, the "all or nothing" political experience that would determine his future for decades to come.

Among the many college and high school students who participated in the campaign and The Walk, some important voices are heard for the first time. A number of the most notable ones come from participants from Bowdoin and the University of Maine. They share their considerable and often humorous insights.

Even at a distance of 50 years, the recollections of the Cohen field people remain vital and incisive. Their accounts are worth the price of the book by themselves.

For example, Jim Harrington provides innumerable insights about the activities "away from the ball" of the University of Maine cohort, including Dale Gerry, Gordon Smith, and George Smith, who was Bill Cohen's driver and later became Dave Emery's campaign manager in 1974.

For his part, Dave Emery himself gives the reader valuable information concerning the role Cohen and his campaign played in his own successful runs for Congress. His humorous anecdotes and his sharing of similar memories with Cohen sparkle. The shooting of a naughty groundhog by a farmer he was chatting with is but one of the highlights.

More importantly, Emery indicates how The Walk went from being a campaign tactic to becoming a tradition as it was translated to Maine's 1st CD.

And Peter Webster supplies invaluable background as to how 1st District Republican and Democratic leaders viewed Cohen and his campaign, highlighting as he does the roles of the Verrill, Dana law firm, Harry Richardson, Roger Putnam, and the late Mert Henry. Mert Henry remains the grand old man of Maine Republican politics, his impressive leadership in Maine running as it does from Margaret Chase Smith through Susan Collins.

Bob Loeb, the astute Bowdoin student who first suggested to me a walk as a campaign tactic and who would subsequently go on to play a major role in the Cohen campaign, also gives us valuable insights into how the campaign played out in real time and his important activities on Bill's behalf.

Another overarching theme that emerges from the interviews was the considerable importance of a number of Republican state senators, not just in various campaigns but in the foundational legislation of the people that shaped the Maine we know today.

Joe Sewall, Harry Richardson, Dave Huber, Sam and Don Collins (uncle and father of Susan Collins), and Bennett Katz were all instrumental in working with Democratic governor Ken Curtis to first pass and then sustain the Maine state income tax.

They also worked to pass Maine's vital oil convenience act and successfully thwarted Curtis's ill-advised proposal to put an oil refinery on the Maine coast at Eastport. Parenthetically, their actions show how in the 1970s the Republicans were often at the forefront of major environmental issues, opposing Muskie's support for downgrading the water quality of the Prestile Stream in Aroostook County with an infamous potato processing plant and the huge, proposed Dickey Lincoln hydroelectric plan that would have flooded the St. John Valley. This volume also underscores their influence on the Cohen campaign of 1972 and how they contributed considerably to its success.

There are many new voices here, providing exciting and incisive perspectives and important insights. Bill Cohen, Jed Lyons, and I hope readers will be entertained, enlightened, and amused by the collective memories of The Walk and the election of 1972.

A special tribute to the intrepid Jackie Zirn upon whose shoulders the entire production process rested for so long and to Jon Sisk who helped wrestle the final manuscript into publishable shape and especially to Jed Lyons who insisted that these recollections be created and recorded and who edited all the meandering recollections around our metaphorical campfire. Carl Williams and Elise Hocking also deserve much credit for their archival work with the Maine newspapers of 1972.

Christian P. Potholm II
Harpswell, Maine
2022

INTRODUCTION

The Honorable William S. Cohen

AFTER A LONG CAREER IN THE PUBLIC ARENA, I CONSIDERED WRITING A memoir of sorts, a summing up, by listing ten experiences in my life that were meaningful to me and perhaps might be of interest to others. But I always managed to delay the project, keeping in mind Senator Ed Muskie's maxim: "If you can't improve upon silence, don't."

Ed usually invoked this sage advice just before proceeding to give a lengthy and regaling speech to a large, receptive audience. It was a good joke, but mirth has its merit.

I also worried that whatever I thought was important might be seen as the product of an inflated ego or so cautiously written that it would reflect a mere silhouette of the truth.

Over the years, I preferred to turn to fiction to reveal glimpses of my thoughts while wearing the masks of made-up characters. In short, I've been happy to reserve some interior territory fenced off as Private Property.

That is until now.

This oral history looks back to 1972, collecting and sharing the memories of a political era that was free of the complexities of the digital age. It is the direct result of the inspiration and persistence provided by Jed Lyons and Chris Potholm.

When I decided to run for Congress, I turned to Chris and asked (pleaded with) him to be my campaign chairman. I did so because he was the only person I knew who was brilliant enough to undertake what most thought was "mission impossible."

Chris in turned called upon a bevy of Bowdoin students to volunteer to serve as foot soldiers across the sprawling acreage of Maine's 2nd District.

Key among them was Jed Lyons, a mere lad who charmed his way through life's adventures with the confidence of a man of many more seasons. I never knew whether Jed and the others truly volunteered or believed that a letter or two might be shaved off their grades if they had refused.

And I never asked.

While I am a co-conspirator in reflecting upon the strategies and skullduggeries of the 1972 political campaign, this book would never have published if I had been left to my own devices.

So, first and foremost, I am eternally grateful to Chris and Jed for their enduring friendship.

I am also deeply indebted to all who took the time to share their recollections of their roles in helping to shape a way for a neophyte political aspirant to connect directly with the people he wanted to serve.

I could not have been successful without the energy and creativity of Bob Loeb, Rob Witsil, Cindy Watson-Welch, Peter Webster, Bill Webster, Mike Harkins, and Jim Harrington. Sadly, we have lost the voices of Dale Gerry and his wife Dale whom we affectionately called Dale Boy and Dale Girl. Both devoted extraordinary efforts during the campaign and continued to serve in my offices before they passed away.

I need to express gratitude to George Smith who drove a beat-up van over many of the beat-up back roads in rural Maine to make sure that I arrived on time at every event.

One man who stands out above all others—at six foot six and with an intellect of comparable height—is Robert Augustus Gardiner Monks, known simply as Bob.

Bob was instrumental in encouraging me to run and making it possible for a Republican to reach across the great political divide known as the Big Box. He has been a driving force in insisting that all who wish to hold public office (and in the corporate world) must maintain the highest of ethical standards and accountability.

Finally, I am grateful to our Rowman & Littlefield editor, Jon Sisk, and senior executive assistant Jacqueline (Jackie) Zirn who has spent countless hours herding together all who have contributed to this book. She has set timelines for reviewing the many lengthy conversations and ensuring that they be properly edited in order to bring clarity and precision to our recollections.

Chapter I

Oral History Discussion with Secretary Bill Cohen and Professor Christian Potholm

April 23, 2021

Jed Lyons: Our goal is to produce an oral history of the Bill Cohen campaign of 1972. Not just The Walk, but the whole campaign, primary, general, etc. Let's go all the way back and hear from each of you. Chris, why don't you start on the topic of your family? Give us a little bit of the history of how your family came to this country? That will help us better understand the roots of the two most important figures in the '72 campaign, you and Bill.

Chris Potholm: My grandparents came from Sweden and Denmark at the end of the 19th century. And I was brought up with two immigrant stories. One was on my mother's side. They were very poor. My grandmother worked in a typewriter factory in Hartford, Connecticut. Arrow, Hart and Hegeman was the firm. Twelve hours a day and she had one hard-boiled egg to eat every day. On the other side, my father's father was a skilled carpenter in Denmark. And so when he arrived, he became a master craftsman here. The two families had two different backgrounds, but both instilled a work ethic in me very early on. Bill's upbringing was similar to mine. We were both blue collar, we had food, we had clothes, but we were very definitely blue collar. It was imprinted on me very early that what a man did was work all the time. And what a woman did was work in the home all the time. I was first taken to a job site when I was nine years old. I had a little lunch bucket. And I remember very clearly that I fell out of the second-floor window that first morning and ended up in the cellar.

When Bill talks about his early married years, that resonates with me. I felt a great need to work hard. In 1972, I was teaching at Bowdoin and I was writing a book. I was building my own house and working on the campaign. I didn't realize it at the time, but Bill was the hardest working candidate I'd ever seen before or since. And I think The Walk and everything that happened in that campaign worked as well as it did because Bill, too, had this blue-collar father who had to go to work every day at two o'clock in the morning to make the rolls and I think with the ups and downs of the campaign, without realizing it, that sustained me and I suspect it sustained Bill, too. We had to accomplish the mission, we had to bring home the bacon, we had to succeed.

Jed Lyons: Chris, remind us where your family immigrated to and where you grew up.

Chris Potholm: Both sets of grandparents ended up in Hartford, Connecticut. So I spent the first 10 years of my life in Hartford, Connecticut, living next door to my cousin, Dave Parmelee. We had a very warm, wonderful little circle with my cousin Dave. But at the height of my happiness at age nine or ten, my father came home and said we had to leave our house, we had to leave the city of Hartford, that the Irish and the Italian Democrats had taken control and the unions were in charge, and we had to leave. Now, that turned out to be a blessing in disguise, because we moved to the Connecticut shore. And that meant all kinds of freedom and a whole different world. But that's the story I was told when I was nine or ten. So you know, I grew up with quite a chip on my shoulder. And in the little beach community where we lived, my father was the only manual worker. In fact, at one point, they circulated a petition to make him leave, because he wasn't supposed to be doing manual labor there. And so my childhood, looking back at it, I was bound and determined that I wasn't going to be at everybody's mercy. And I didn't like it in the middle of Sunday dinner when some rich person would come by and not pay my father all the money he was owed. So there was a certain attitude of we're going to succeed one way or the other. Dad was building houses. He and one helper. And I remember very distinctly, he had a timecard. And every day he wrote in it how many hours he had worked and so on. When I went to Bowdoin, I figured that's what you had to do. And I kept track of my hours at Bowdoin. Now, when I'm teaching class, the kids always complain how hard they work. Oh, well, you know, they say five or six hours? Well, I kept very good records. And I was so afraid of failing at Bowdoin, I did 55 hours a week my freshman year. Now, by the time I got to be a senior, it was down to eight.

Jed Lyons: You graduated as Valedictorian of the Bowdoin College class of 1962, correct?

Chris Potholm: I did. I was the first person to go to college in my family. And then my parents said I had to be a doctor. I went to my first biology lab and all I wanted to do was throw up. My first six months at Bowdoin were the most miserable time of my life. I hated every moment of it. And how ironic—I've been there for 55 years.

Jed Lyons: All right, Bill, let's hear your story about your family and how they came over and where they went.

Bill Cohen: My grandfather, Harry Cohen, came from an area that was on the border between Russia and Poland. And it kind of went back and forth between who was in charge of the area over the years. I think he left in the 1890s. He couldn't speak a word of English and didn't have any money. He landed in New York passing through Ellis Island. He didn't stay in New York very long because he couldn't find a job. So then he moved to Boston where he tried to find work without success. Then he migrated up to Bangor. I understand that he started off by owning a single cow that he used to try to enter the cattle trade market. That didn't turn out so well either. Finally, he started a little bakery with his two sons and daughter. My uncle Dick, my aunt Gertrude ("Gittle"), my father, Reuben ("Ruby"). My mother, Clara also helped out.

I didn't know my mother's family at all. She never talked about them or didn't want to. She was from Monticello in northern Maine, a very poor part of Maine. and she came from a very poor family. My dad worked hard at the bakery. He used to gamble at the local Elks club. He also liked to go to dances, and he met her one night at a place about twelve miles outside the city called the Auto Rest Park. He fell in love with her on first sight (he told me she had cheeks the color of apple skins) and married her, which was taboo at that time. She was Irish and Jewish people, including my grandfather, did not want to have their children marry non-Jews. Their marriage was pretty unique at the time. I don't think there was another example in Bangor where a Jewish man married outside the faith (except that his brother followed suit a few years later) As a result, he was pretty much on the social periphery of the rest of the Jewish community.

I was born on the third story of a tenement building on a street called Hancock Street. That's where most of the immigrant families lived. It was one long street filled with immigrants from Ireland, Italy, Greece, Syria, Germany, Lebanon, Russia, and Poland. One black family lived in the neighborhood. It was a tough little street. Even at an early age, you had to show that you were tough. You had to fight with any new neighbor that came into the street, you had to show that you could knock out his teeth. There were no clubs or knives; just fists and feet. They would have little gang fights from time to time. Sometimes the toughies from the west side of the city would come over to the east side. And they would have fights break out.

We lived very close to the Penobscot River. And there was a set of railroad tracks that ran very close to the houses. We didn't come from "the other side of the tracks" because the other side of the tracks was the river. We were just fifty to a hundred feet from those tracks and as close as you could be to the "other side."

Our family lived in this three-story tenement building. There was a meat market on the bottom floor ("Slep's"), a barber shop, and a small store where you could buy candy, gum and small items.

Mrs. Soloby, the woman who owned the building, was Polish. We lived in the apartment on one of the top floors, but there were lots of lumberjacks who slept just above us. When they weren't out cutting trees, I remember that these long-limbed, tough people walked or shuffled back and forth all night.

They drank a lot when they weren't working. Then, on the street, there was a number of what we called "canned heaters." You know, when you want to go camping, you buy a little canister of Sterno cooking fuel. Well, they would take the Sterno, a jelly-like substance, and squeeze the alcohol out of it into a handkerchief. And they would drink that. We would see them lying on the streets, barely conscious. Their faces were bruised, and the purple veins in their noses were about to break out from their skin. And that pretty much was the neighborhood in terms of where I lived.

And then if I walked 100 yards down the street, my dad had a bakery there. It was a small bakery with two stories of dilapidated housing over it where a poor family lived. The bakery itself was a hovel, something that food authorities today would shut down. The bakery was where I spent most of my young years before I went to school.

Jed Lyons: What was the name of it?

Bill Cohen: The Bangor Rye Bread Company.

Jed Lyons: Your mother was Scots-Irish. Do you remember who emigrated? Was it her parents or grandparents?

Bill Cohen: I don't know for sure; she wouldn't talk about it. I have no real history of my ancestry other than my grandfather, who spoke very little English. I remember that he was upset with my father for marrying my mother. Yet, when I came along, he liked me a lot. He used to give me a flour-covered nickel every week. He would say, "Billy, someday, someday you'll understand." Those were the only words he ever spoke to me, "someday you'll understand."

My dad, in all of his years, never made more than $9,000. Even though he worked almost 18 hours a day, 6 days a week. He got up every night around 11:00 p.m. to go down to the bakery to mix up the sourdough. He'd then return home and sleep until 3:00 and then return to the bakery. He would then pour the sourdough into a large mixer and start the process of making, proofing, cutting, and baking challah bread and bulkie rolls.

After I got my driver's license, I would mix the sourdough for him so that he could sleep an extra hour or two.

His brother, Dick, would join him around 5:00 a.m. Dick would primarily bake the bread in a brick oven that was fueled by coal. Dick would spray water from a hose on the hot coals to create steam. It was a pretty grim little place. There were naked lightbulbs hanging from the ceilings, along with fly-catching strips over the work bench. My grandfather and his three children would sit at the workbench and make everything by hand. They didn't have any equipment. They showed me how to flatten out a small piece of dough and then fold a strip with my forefinger over my thumb and then chop the dough with my right hand. I'd repeat the process three times and fold the last piece into the others. If you were to buy a roll in a store today, the roll would look like a sea dollar on top. Today the rolls are stamped out by machines. Dad's were all by hand. They turned out thousands of rolls a day by hand, in addition to rye and braided challah for the Friday night celebrations of the Jewish Sabbath.

Since the bakery was close to the river, there were large river rats to be wary of. They usually had a cat to make sure that none slipped into the store. Unfortunately, there was a pretty constant changing of the guard as the cats became victims of the cars that raced along the street. One rat did manage to make it into the seatless toilet in the back of the bakery where it became trapped.

While my mother and father were working, most of the kids in the neighborhood would play "touch" football on a large swath of rocky soil between two sets of railroad tracks that was just fifty feet from the bakery. Touch really didn't describe the game as it usually broke out in fights. We suffered lots of cuts and bruises from the tackles and punches.

Jed Lyons: Were you treated any differently in the neighborhood because you had a Jewish parent and a Christian parent?

Bill Cohen: No. It was really funny. Most of the other kids were not mixed. They were Irish, Italian, Jewish, Catholic. I wasn't aware of any difference of my split heritage at the time and neither were they. We were all roughly of the same economic class. It was the working class on Hancock Street, the butchers, the bakers, the candlestick makers. One Jewish man was a boot repairer. Two others were butchers. Another ran a junkyard. There was one Italian restaurant, two bars, and Dolly Jack's whorehouse. It was just a block away from what was known as the devil's half acre that was lined with beer joints and honkytonk bars.

In any event, what happened is my dad kept the bakery going. He didn't make any money until World War II. My uncle went off to be in the army and so my Dad had to carry the thing by himself. I would go down there with him. I'd spend a lot of time, he would take me with him in a little bakery truck, a windowless bakery truck other than the front windshield, and he put me on his lap and my legs stuck out through the steering wheel and let me drive that way. So the two of us would go on his deliveries, except when you make a turn, it'd be hard for me to stay in the wheel. But that's the bond we had.

My father wanted me to be raised in the Jewish faith. I don't think it was a matter of religion, but rather one of class and economic status. He was, as best I could determine, something of an agnostic. He attended the Jewish High Holidays, but otherwise, he was not particularly observant. He believed that Jewish people had "superior" study habits and work ethics. He'd note that I would never find a Jew who was not hard working or one who was on the street begging. And that basically was true in Bangor. They all worked except for one man that I recall who was mentally impaired and used to wander around the city selling papers on the street. In his own way, the man was working.

Just as in any other social environment, those who became professionals—whether accountants, lawyers, doctors—lived in a certain area of the city that was prosperous. If you were from the working families, the immigrants, you would live down next to the river. After the war, my father's business started to get better. And we were able to move exactly one mile up the street when I was eight years old. So, I went from living in that tough little neighborhood engaging in fisticuffs to a middle-class, peaceful neighborhood. My dad bought the home for $7,500. My mother painted that house by herself over three times. While we lived there, she'd be up on the ladder and on top of the roof doing all the painting. I remember how proud I was that she was unafraid and was just as hard working as my father.

Jed Lyons: Did you move from one school to a different school at that point?

Bill Cohen: No, I went to the same school, a public school. Until I went to junior high school, the same elementary school. But what I did is I moved from lower class to slightly middle class in that one mile. And so I was now in a real house rather than a tenement house. It didn't have lumberjacks walking over the ceilings type of thing. The apartment we lived in had one bathroom, and we had to wash our clothes in an old washer and sometimes in the bathtub. So it was that kind of living. And all I knew was work. He wanted me to be raised Jewish, so I had to start to go to Hebrew school. And that's where the problems started.

When I was six years old, my dad wanted me to go to Hebrew school. And I spent six years in Hebrew school. I went to public school, and then two days a week I'd go to Hebrew school at the end of the public school classes. I was not welcomed. The rabbis were unhappy with me. I didn't quite fit the appearance of a nice Jewish boy. I had blond hair in my younger years and stood out. They knew that my mother was Christian. I was a "goyim" to the Jewish people, and to the Irish and others, I was a Jew. So I lived in an "in between" world. I rebelled against being in Hebrew school and got into several fights there. Each year, I got the highest grades, and each year, they never gave me the first prize. It wasn't a big deal at first, but when the rejection became routine, I lost interest in trying to please the school officials.

My father was a good athlete in his day and excelled in basketball. He used to take me with him to the YMCA where he played basketball with a few of his Jewish friends. I went to my father and said, "How about if I go down to the YMCA just one Saturday out of the month. I'll go to the

Jewish Community Center (Hebrew school) or synagogue three of the four Saturday services." He said, okay, but just once a month. Well, then it was two Saturdays, and then three Saturdays. Finally, I stopped going to the synagogue altogether. This made the rest of my classmates unhappy because prizes were given to those classes that had the best attendance records. Well, my class never got a prize because of me. So, there was always that resentment. And I used to bring Italian sandwiches into the Hebrew school at night, just to antagonize the other students. Just to flout the fact that I was not a kosher boy. I was about to turn thirteen and was planning to be bar mitzvahed. That was the purpose for attending Hebrew school. While I didn't enjoy the experience, I wanted to make my father proud. Rabbi Saul Brown, a very conservative man, said, "We're sorry Zev (my Hebrew name), you cannot have a bar mitzvah because your mother didn't convert to Judaism." I remember controlling my temper—temporarily. "Now you tell me?" He knew that I was about to explode. He then explained that I could undergo a conversion ceremony.

Such as? They would submerge me in a pool of holy water before a group of the synagogue elders. Frankly, that didn't really trouble me as I was swimming naked at the YMCA pool every weekend. But then he added that they would take a symbolic amount of blood from my penis. That did it. I bolted from his office and ran all the way home without stopping. The first person I met was my mother. I said, I'm not going to do this. I was in a rage. When my father came home, my mother explained to him what had happened. He was disappointed, not so much with me, but with their refusal to tell me years earlier. He said, "Okay, you don't have to." I used to wear a mezuzah around my neck. It was a little gold-plated cylinder with a piece of parchment inside. I went down to the Penobscot River just across from my father's bakery, ripped the mezuzah off and threw it as far as I could into the river. I vowed at that moment that I was never going to go anywhere I wasn't wanted. So that was my first act of rebellion, and I never went back to the school. I did play basketball for the Jewish Community Center in the YMCA church league. But that was the extent of my experience with the Jewish community to that point.

My relationship with the Jewish community became a little more complicated. I was able to join the starting lineup for my high school basketball team when I was fifteen. One night I scored about 28 points in a game and the sports page read, in very large print: **COYNE SCORES 28**. Members of the Jewish community complained to the newspaper that the misspelling of my name had been deliberate and was anti-Semitic. I remember thinking at the time: "So now I'm Jewish?

I thought the error was unintentional because there was a basketball player for the University of Maine team named Dudley Coyne who was a high scoring guard and that the headline writer made an innocent mistake. But I later learned why the misspelling was the cause of concern and controversy. Bangor had a history of bigotry and anti-Semitism. The Bangor Jewish community years earlier had invited Eleanor Roosevelt to visit the city to meet city officials and business leaders. A photograph appeared in the *Bangor Evening News* that showed the people who had greeted the First Lady but refused to identify those standing with her. The oversight was not coincidental. They were all Jewish and the paper did not want to give them credit for helping to secure the presence of Mrs. Roosevelt. The Protestant fathers of the city didn't like Jews and didn't miss the chance to prove it.

Jed Lyons: Is there a large community of Jews in Bangor compared to other cities in Maine, such as Portland?

Bill Cohen: Not compared to Portland, we have a smaller population, maybe 34,000 max in the general area. But, of course, probably 75,000 people total if you take the whole area. The Jewish community went from one level to the next. There were not many gradations. So, you were either the butcher, baker or you are a doctor, dentist, or accountant. You're either on Hancock Street, or close to it, or you were up in a place they naturally called the "Hill." That's just the two classes of people. It's not unlike many other cities. You have the workers and then you have the professionals.

So what saved me when I was young is basically I spent as many days as I could at the YMCA playing basketball for hours, sometimes for 10 hours. I got up early in the morning and stayed until night. That's basically what I did. I became an all-state basketball player in high school.

Jed Lyons: Chris, tell us about your religious upbringing and schooling.

Chris Potholm: I think that we tend to exaggerate some of the things that were of influence. In my particular case, going from the city to this rural area in the summer where all the people came to the various beaches, but in the winter, it was more or less deserted. So from the fall to the spring, the kids like me that were there, we lived a very carefree outdoor life. When I got into high school, you really couldn't do anything after school if you lived in one of these outlying towns because there was no bus or any way to get home except to hitchhike.

My mother was a big influence on me in that she saw education as the one way out of this very hard life where you worked six days a week and then on the seventh, you went to church. We had been brought up in a very strong Swedish Lutheran Church in Hartford with all kinds of dogma and stuff, very close to Catholicism. But when we got to Giant's Neck in Niantic, Connecticut, we went to a very, very liberal old Congregational Church. And there was a wonderful minister, Dixon Hoag. He had gone to Harvard and was a great intellectual. All of a sudden, I began to see religion as something that wasn't from on high, but that people thought about and imagined things and looked at sources. It was a very liberating experience for me.

In my high school, probably two thirds of the kids did not go on to college. I had never heard of Bowdoin until one of my principals from Hartford mentioned it. I owe him so much. Stan Fish, my grade school principal, was a Bowdoin graduate and had me come up to Hartford for a Bowdoin Night. That was an enormous chance to see that I could go there and he was encouraging me to go. Even though I had never heard of Bowdoin, I was quickly told that it was like Amherst and Wesleyan and, you know, little Ivy League and I'll never forget, I came up to Bowdoin for my interview by myself on the train. I arrived and it was snowing lightly and it snowed all three days I was here and I thought, oh my gosh, this is like heaven. The dean of admissions then was a guy named Hughbie Shaw.

At that point, he was the only American ever to have hit a home run in the Olympics. So he was sitting at his desk and right behind it was the bat that he hit the home run with. My grades in high school were, you know, some A's, some B's and I had taken auto mechanics and shop mechanical drawing. Imagine a dean of admissions of today seeing that. Anyway, we're sitting there, and all of a sudden he jumps up and he says, "Mr. Potholm, what would it take for you to come to Bowdoin?" And I said, my Dad's a carpenter. We don't have any money. And he said, "That's done. You have a scholarship." And he came around and shook my hand. Tell that story to the kids of today. Now when they're nine years old they're taking advanced SAT prep. And no dean of admissions today would ever do that. But anyway, I said, geez, gosh thanks, and I got back to my high school and an English teacher said, "Well, have you gotten into any schools?" And I said, "Just Bowdoin." He said "Bowdoin, Bowdoin. What do you want, the moon?" He said he'd gone to the University of Connecticut at night. So to him Bowdoin was a magical school.

The great irony is that I was so miserable my first semester at Bowdoin, I wanted to quit. First of all, in high school, I majored in girls. I mean, I went out two or three times a week with girls, sometimes in the afternoon, like, girls, girls, girls, so at Bowdoin there are no girls, okay? We have compulsory chapel—can you imagine? To this day, I can't go into the Bowdoin chapel and stay for any time. First of all, it hurts your back because you're twisting like this, you can't do that. When you're 18, you could twist and listen. And the other thing was, you know, I wasn't an intellectual in high school but there were all these kids that had gone to prep school and they were reading books for the second time, books that I had never heard of. I remember that I had such pressure on me to succeed. I was so unhappy. And we had the fraternity system, which added a whole other layer of unpleasantness that first six weeks.

Jed Lyons: You were classmates in the Bowdoin class of 1962 and fellow members of the Psi Upsilon fraternity, the same fraternity I joined my freshman year at Bowdoin in 1970.

Chris Potholm: Tell us your story.

Jed Lyons: Well, I will briefly tell my story. I had three immigrant grandparents. All three of them traveled across the Atlantic and then through Ellis Island in the early 1900s. My father's parents came from Ireland, one from the north of Ireland from a small town called Newry in County Down near the mountains of Mourne, one from the south in a farming town called Ballybay in County Monaghan. They were both Presbyterians.

My grandfather had been apprenticed as a tailor in Ireland, but he became a bus driver when he arrived in New York. He drove a bus on Fifth Avenue in New York City for 52 years and became good friends with the Irish American labor leader, Mike Quill, who ran the bus drivers' union. He met my grandmother when she boarded his bus one day. As a working spouse and mother, she worked as a ticket taker at a local movie theater near their home in Brooklyn's Geritsen Beach neighborhood.

My mother's mother was born in London and immigrated when she was about 15. She sold ladies' shoes at Macy's in Manhattan until she had children of her own. My mother's father owned a lunch wagon, basically a diner, in Brooklyn. There used to be lots of diners along the East River serving the workers on their commutes to and from Manhattan. He owned one called the Highland Diner. He had polio so he had to be driven to work; he couldn't walk the several miles from their home in the Cypress Hills neighborhood of Brooklyn. He grew up in East New York, a very tough part of Brooklyn in the early 20th century. My mother grew up in Brooklyn, attended Brooklyn College until the war broke out, and then worked at the Brooklyn Navy Yard during the war.

My parents met before the war and were married when my father, Jim Lyons, returned from Europe where he served in the Air Force. I was born in Brooklyn in 1952 and was baptized as an Episcopalian at my mother's family's church. We moved to Long Island, as a lot of families did, when I was an infant. My sister, Susan, was born there.

My father was transferred to Chicago by his employer, O. E. McIntyre, Inc., a direct marketing and advertising business, when I was 12. Dad opened up the new Chicago office on East Wacker Drive. I went to a large public high school in Barrington, Illinois, with about 450 students in my grade, and had the good fortune to have an inspiring English teacher there named Charlie White. I'm still in touch with Charlie who is in his early nineties. He got me excited about books. I became very interested in the great American novelists. I wound up hitchhiking after graduating in 1970 all over the country to go visit the homes of my favorite authors. I spent a few days at Walden Pond to reread Henry David Thoreau's books, I went to New London and found the bar where Eugene O'Neill wrote *The Iceman Cometh*, went down south to where Thomas Wolfe wrote *Look Homeward Angel*. He was about six foot six, and he wrote on top of a refrigerator. All of these wonderful visits to the haunts of my favorite authors got me more interested in reading than ever. I became an English major, and I'm sure that's why I got into the book publishing business in 1975. I've been at it now for 47 years.

Like you, Chris, I was unhappy my freshman year at Bowdoin. I had applied to transfer to Hampshire College. I was miserable my freshman year for the same reasons you were. After going to a school with 450 students in my high school class, I was now at a college with just 650 boys. And I thought, "What a stupid decision I've made. I gotta get out of here." But you, Chris, talked me into staying. I'm glad you did. I loved Bowdoin after that first year.

Let's hear the story of how you two met as freshmen. And why you both joined that particular fraternity. What was the process of being rushed like? Was it in your freshman year? And why did you choose that fraternity and how did fraternities affect your experience at Bowdoin?

Bill Cohen: My dad wanted me to go to the University of Maine. He wanted me to play basketball where he could be in the audience. He argued I should go to the University—which coincidentally would be less expensive, and I could live at home. I didn't know anything about Bowdoin. David Carlisle, a former teammate on the high school basketball team, was in his sophomore year at Bowdoin. He thought that I could get a better education at Bowdoin. Out of curiosity, I attended a game between Bowdoin and the University of Maine at the Orono campus that was just eight miles from our home. I saw Brud Stover play that night and was really impressed. He was a real classy guy. He lettered in football, baseball, and basketball. He was a quarterback in football and a guard on the basketball team. Just a terrific athlete.

Dave Carlisle arranged for me to meet with Frederick Newman, the chairman of the Eastern Trust and Banking Company, who was a Bowdoin alumnus, and he also encouraged me to go to Bowdoin. I said that I couldn't afford the tuition, and Mr. Newman said that he would arrange for help. I was offered a $500 scholarship, theoretically for my academic record at Bangor High School, but I suspected it was because I had been named to the All-State basketball team my senior year. I accepted the scholarship at Bowdoin, and almost immediately found myself in over my head academically. As Chris said before, most of the students had been to prep school. I was a good student in high school simply because I had a pretty good memory in those days. I never really applied myself to study things analytically. All I wanted to do is to go over to the YMCA and play basketball every weekend. So, my image of myself was pretty limited. When I went to Bowdoin, I was encouraged to join a fraternity house. At first, I said no to the idea. I didn't want to join anything. Well, I was told that I had to be in a fraternity and that I'd regret missing the social life if I remained an "independent." That's when David Carlisle said that I should come over to the Psi U fraternity because there were a lot of good guys there that I would like.

I went to Psi U and after a few days of being "rushed" I regretted my decision. I didn't like having to engage in game playing. And when I found that upper-class students could demand that I drink some foul substance, hold it in my mouth while I crawled from the top floor to the basement while they were paddling my ass and then be able to spit out the liquid into the fireplace to put out the flames, I almost quit. This is a bunch of bull. I'm not going to do this. I'm not going to recite all the stupid stuff they insisted that I memorize. I'm pretty much at ease being alone most of the time. I didn't want to be a joiner. I stayed there, but not because I wanted to be there.

But then again, it was relief from the dormitory where I had been assigned to live. I was put with two roommates. One was a guy who had a problem with his feet. They had an awful smell. He couldn't control it. It would permeate the room to the point that I was almost gagging most of the time. And I finally just couldn't stay in the room. We had to sleep with the windows open in the wintertime.

I started hanging around with two of the Psi U brothers, a couple of guys named Tommy and Al. They were the two most unusual people I'd ever met. They were rooming together in Hyde Hall. They would wear their clothes for a week and then just toss them into a pile in the middle of the room. And then they began to pile up over the months, their clothes in the middle of the room. When they wanted a particular piece of clothing, they would just pluck it out of the pile on the floor and wear it for that day or week. I was fascinated with this relationship. Al was a pretty decent basketball player, so I did have that in common with him.

We knew that Tommy slept in the nude. Al had gotten sick one night, and he reached across the twin bed to Tommy's and barfed on the sheets and pulled the covers over the sheets. Later that night Tommy came in, took off all his clothes and underwear and hopped into bed. When he realized what he was squirming in, he went berserk. Still, he never got mad at Al. For some reason, he always forgave Al. I would have ended the friendship if anyone had ever done that to me.

One night Al and I took Tommy's mother's car (which was illegal for him at that time because he was on a scholarship) and drove to Portland to hit a few bars. When we came back, we ran into a major snowstorm. We were really late when we finally got back to Hyde Hall and Al said, "Hey, let's park the car over here and tell Tommy we had an accident and the car was wrecked." Tommy was sound asleep. Al shook him awake and said, "Tommy, Tommy, I'm really sorry that we got into an accident coming back from Portland. The car's totaled and the police are outside, waiting to talk to you." Tommy jumped up, as we knew in the nude, and ran outside looking to see the damage to the car. He hit the top of the stairs that were covered with ice, lost his footing and went sliding bare ass into a snowbank. At that point Al started laughing and said, "Sorry, Tommy. We were just kidding. No car crash. No police." These were just examples of the tricks Al played on Tommy, and yet their friendship never frayed. When both Al and Tommy moved over to live in the Psi U House—known then as the Animal House, because that was where most of the athletes lived and where the wildest weekend parties were thrown—I decided to join them. The decision did not contribute to my academic well-being.

My grades were slipping, and I was convinced I would flunk out. Just to prove how poor my judgment was, I decided to join four of my classmates and drive to Florida for spring break. We were looking for sun, fun, and women. The best of plans went awry. We arrived in Fort Lauderdale and headed for the beach.

The place was loaded with 30,000 students and the men were all muscled out and tanned and the girls were beautiful. We didn't stand a chance. We spent a fruitless night at the Elbow Room and Omar's Tent and someone came up with the brilliant idea to fly to Cuba. So, we drove to Key West and paid $10 for a flight to Havana. Well, Havana was still wide open. It was 1959, "El Anno de Libertad" according to all the signs posted over the city. Castro had just taken over the country. We stayed and partied for three or four days and then my four friends headed back to Bowdoin. I decided to stay for another week. I had planned just to remain for another few days, but I ran out of cash and couldn't pay for a ticket back until I met another American who loaned me the money. I hitchhiked home but made the mistake of going through the Everglades. That is another story.

Anyway, that's how I ended up going to Bowdoin and joining the Psi U house. I met some great guys who I still stay in touch with, including Chris, of course, who would play such an important role in my future.

I was not close to Chris at the time. I envied and admired him as the smartest man in our class. Chris became well known to everyone from the beginning. He had taken a typing course in high school, and that skill became important. The one thing that Chris did after every class, was to go over to his room or the library and type up his notes. And then he would add all the stuff he had been reading on the side. So, you had the lecture itself, plus all of Chris's research. And being an entrepreneur, he sold his notes. Of course, I couldn't afford to buy them. So, I'd have to get them secondhand from somebody else a week later. But I kept thinking, what's going on with Chris's notes? How can I keep up with him?

Jed Lyons: What a great story. Chris?

Chris Potholm: When I got to Bowdoin there was this library with hundreds of thousands of books. And I remember Thomas Wolfe had said he would go to a library, and he wouldn't read every word, but he'd rip through it and say, "Well, I gotcha, now I got you." And so a lot of times, I'd be in the Hubbard stacks, you know, just kind of making up for lost time. Nobody would believe the stories that Bill just told, but they're 100 percent true. If they watched the movie *Animal House* they would see Bowdoin of the 1950s and 1960s—it took me 10 years to believe that that was actually Dartmouth because everything that happened in that movie, every single thing, was part of our Bowdoin experience.

Every Saturday night, when you're sitting there with your date and all of a sudden, one of the brothers would have a few and would get on his skis and come skiing down the stairs and the dates would say, "Oh my God, he doesn't have any clothes on." He was a very good skier. So, you know, completely drunk, he could still come all the way down the stairs, but that's the kind of place it was. Looking back on it, the food was pretty poor, generally, but once every couple of weeks, we had faculty over and we all had to get dressed up and then we got good food and we got ice cream so it was a big deal. But once a semester, the Psi U house had what was called a Gee-Gaw party. And that night we invited all the staff and professors who had been mean to the brothers during the previous semester. And we didn't bother to get dressed up, we just wore raggy tee shirts and old crap clothes. So it would be these professors, you know, there might be seven or eight of them. And when they got into the fraternity, nobody would speak to them. I've always wondered if they got the message. As for the fraternity ritual, I don't think many of the brothers thought much of it. Once a month, we had chapter house meetings and all the brothers would link pinkies And there was a sacred flame that popped up. It was a sacred skull. God knows where they got it. But I had a date up and in those days, the men moved out and women stayed in the chapter room. And the girl somehow had found the skull and said "I'm going to take it." And I said "Why not?" It was a fun weekend. She got a fine souvenir. Of course, the next fraternity meeting the president was running around crying, "Where's the skull?" "Where's the skull?" I never saw the girl again. And to the best of my knowledge, the skull was never seen again north of the Piscataquis River.

Bill Cohen: We had parties that were unprecedented in terms of being barbaric. I recall one time Al stripped off his clothes and climbed on the mantel over the fireplace at Psi U and joined one of our football players. And I have a picture of Al sitting up on the mantel with his pants hanging down below his feet. I had a friend from Bangor called Ziggy. He was a Greek fellow who went into the Navy and came out believing he was black. He came back talking like a black man. And he could dance. He won national dance contests. He had a big ducktail hairdo. His father ran a little sandwich shop down on the "devils half acre" in Bangor. There was a bar near the sandwich shop called the Silver Dollar Café that had a small rock band that I invited to come down and play for one of our Sunday parties. Curtis Johnson, the lead singer, drove down in his Cadillac convertible with a couple of people in it, drummers and whatever. And this was on a Sunday, and you weren't supposed to have any kind of entertainment on a Sunday. Well, they set up inside and we had a batch of milk punch that we kind of mixed up every Sunday on those party weekends. And Ziggy was kind of crazy. He would talk like, "Say, Hey, Baby, what's going on?" "Man, there's some cat over there that keeps screaming on my sky," which meant that he was yelling at Ziggy. "He's a big cat. He wants to know how I got into this place." And I told him, I said, "I'm here because Billy Cohen invited me." He said, who? I pointed you out and he said, 'You know, that's what's happened! That's what's wrong with this place. This is why it's going down around here when a scumbag like you can come in here at the invitation of a scum guy bag like him. This guy was about six foot two, a former swimmer who had graduated probably five years before. I said, "Ziggy, just point him out. And don't say anything. And don't introduce me. Just point him out and step out of the way." So, Ziggy walked over and did exactly the opposite of what I had said. He tapped him on the shoulder and said, "Hey, man, this is Billy Cohen. He's the one who invited me here." There went the element of surprise! Just as the guy turned around, I hit him as hard as I could, and he went down like an ox at that point. Then I got on top of him and I started banging on his head because he was so much bigger and stronger than I was. Then his girlfriend jumped on me, trying to pull me off. Ziggy grabbed her by her hair and pulled her off me. Meanwhile, all hell broke out. It was one of those barroom scenes where people started throwing things. The police came that day and they investigated what the hell had happened there. Dean Kendrick called me over to his office the next day, and while holding his thumb and forefinger just a hair apart, said, "You know, you're this close to leaving!" That was almost the end of it for me. The alum that I punched had looked at Ziggy as being unfit to be in his presence—that Ziggy was a street guy. He was a townie or whatever, but he was not worthy of being at a Bowdoin weekend with gals from the Boston area and the upscale schools, all the way down to Connecticut. I instigated the brawl, but I didn't regret doing it.

Chris Potholm: Bill mentions this milk punch; it literally was a giant milk can, whether it was rum or coke or anything that had been drunk the night before, leftover wine, whiskey, gin, it was put in with ice cream and milk. And people drank it with their breakfast. And I remember that it was right before Ivy's Weekend and we must have been getting ready. So somebody got the bright idea we should put on choir robes and get up on the side of the house roof and pretend we were bats. Eight or 10 guys. And the dean of the college had been to the First Parish Church that Sunday morning. And he's walking by the house. And here are all these bats flapping their wings silently. He pretended he didn't see us, but soon we got a call from him. "Get those bats off the roof or there'll be no Ivy's Weekend." Everybody rolled off the roof. One lad hurt his leg. But we saved Ivy's Weekend. One last story about my mother, my sainted mother: I'm going off to college, and so she bought me a pair of brand new pants for the first football weekend. We used to have huge rallies on the Bowdoin quad with railroad ties and a giant fire. There was this tradition of marching down through the town and through the Cumberland Theater. For some reason, it was really fun to walk down right into the theater without paying and go out the back doors. Well, the townspeople had enough. And so this is the first party weekend and we're all going to march on the Cumberland. And as we came down over the lip of the hill before the railroad tracks, there were police and tear gas and they chased us. Anyway, for some reason, a cop got on my tail and I was running behind the various houses. I came to a fence and I climbed up on the fence and in the process I ripped my brand new pants, just completely ripped them. And he's pounding, pounding on the fence with his billy club. My new pants were ruined. My mother was not happy when she came up for Parents' Weekend.

Bill Cohen: One more story. There was a black fellow named Ed. You probably don't remember him. We had, what, three or four black students at Bowdoin while I was there. Ed was a year or so ahead of me. Ed was a little guy who thought he was Frank Sinatra. He wore a little chapeau hat and used to sing while he played pool. He was a magician with a pool stick. He could make it dance and do all kinds of interesting things. My father earned a little bit of extra money when he would go down to the local pool hall. He was pretty good at it. I said, I've got to have my father meet Ed.

So, we went out to hitchhike out at the edge of Topsham. Normally, it would take me maybe 20 minutes to get a ride to Augusta. Then two hours to get from Augusta to Bangor. We stood out there for three hours. When drivers saw the two of us there, they kept going by. Ed decided to hide behind a tree. Unfortunately, he also had a bottle of Jack Daniels. He's behind the tree and taking a few nips. Three hours went by, and I would then go join him and I would take some as well. Then, I would go out and stand by myself. I got a car to stop. And I said wait, my friend just had to go make a pit stop over here. Can you wait? And then Ed would come out. The driver of the car would see Ed and take off. So that was my first introduction to racism in Bowdoinham and Topsham. By the time we finally got a ride to Augusta, Ed was pretty much out of it in terms of what he'd had to drink. There's a bridge that you go across in Gardiner to get to the other side. I had to carry him on my back. I was exhausted. We had our little bags as well. I had Ed plus our two bags to carry. There's a little hill at the end of the bridge. I climbed up the hill and then just laid back on the grass. The sun was going down. It was all quiet. And then about five minutes later, I could hear a police car coming. Jesus, I thought, they were coming for us. And two officers came out onto the grassy hill where we were just laying down with their guns drawn and shouted, "What are you guys doing here?" I said, "Hey, we're Bowdoin students" (somehow thinking that would grant us protection). They said, "No, no, you're not students. And this one here (pointing to Ed), he's coming with us." And I asked, "Why him?" He said, "Well, because he's under the influence." I said, "Then, you'll have to take us both. You can't just take him. You've got to take me, too." So, I ended up going to the jail with Ed. Around 9:00 p.m. that night, I called my mother. I said, "Mom, I've had a little problem on the way home. Can you come down and get us?" She drove down from Bangor to the station and took us home. End of the story, Ed never got to meet my father as he was too busy working to take time off to shoot pool. We took a bus back to Bowdoin because we knew we couldn't get a ride back by hitchhiking. That was my early introduction to racism.

Jed Lyons: What was your first step outside of Bowdoin after graduation?

Bill Cohen: I went to Connecticut. I went to Niantic to live in a room over a garage. I was living near Chris who got me a job working on some small construction projects for the city of Niantic and I was working nights as a semi-cop at a beach. And so I had two jobs. Diana at that point was working in a restaurant. I was getting ready to go to law school. Chris helped me survive that summer. I was about to become a father in February. So my first job after law school after Bowdoin was in Chris's hometown in Connecticut.

Jed Lyons: Chris, what did you do right after college?

Chris Potholm: When I graduated, I had a couple of weeks off before I became a town constable in Old Lyme, Connecticut. It was the best job in the world. My cousin got it for me. You can't imagine how much fun it was with all the girls and excitement. The first day we went to see the state police trooper who was supervising the summer constables. He just passed us the badge and the gun across his desk, and he said, "try not to shoot anybody." And you know, that was the training we got, and as my cousin and I were driving away, we said "That's silly. I mean, who would take out their gun?" Well, two weeks later, some old guy (who was probably 20 years younger than Bill and I are now) saw some kid blow through a stop sign and the old duffer took out his gun and shot right at the windshield. The state trooper called us all back in and he said "What did I tell you?" So Bill calls up from Maine and says he needs a job. And Bill, I don't think you'd ever held a gun, let alone shoot one. Bill shows up. Duddy Cool. He said, "Now I've got my own gun." I knew he had a .357 Clint Eastwood Magnum, and he's walking around with this huge gun. Pretty soon he got called. There was a rabid skunk under some cottage. Bill climbs under the cottage and shoots it like eight times. And a huge crowd gathers and he comes out. "It's okay" says Bill, "He's dead." You'd think it was a child molester or at least a robber, but no, it was a skunk. And being rabid, of course, he kept shooting. Bill's a legend in so many different arenas but you know in Old Lyme Shores, he's the cop with the .357 magnum that killed the skunk.

Bill Cohen: It was a little more complicated than that. The skunk had sprayed a dog in the eyes and the dog was going crazy. The owner of the dog said, "You've got to get that skunk." The owner saw the skunk and took a pitchfork and drove it into the skunk's tail as it crawled under the steps of the house. The man kept screaming, "You've got to get him! You've got to get him." His dog was yelping the whole time. I said, "No problem. I'll take care of it. BAM! I mean, it was an explosion. It's 10 o'clock at night. Very calm, everybody's asleep. Bam, bam, bam. The skunk is still spinning. Then a final bam. "The skunk's dead," I announced (as if I had just taken out a serial killer). Well, there was a little problem. The residents of that quiet little town were furious. I was called to a town council meeting the next morning. "What the hell were you doing using your gun to shoot at a skunk?"

Jed Lyons: Were you wearing a uniform?

Chris Potholm: Oh, yes, we had uniforms. And that's how I met my wife. She drove by once and the second time I arrested her. But that's a whole different story. You know, the gunplay thing, we got paid on Labor Day, up through midnight. But most people were going back to school and so people would be leaving the beach, three o'clock, four o'clock, and then we would get paid for the rest of the time. Well, that Labor Day that summer, maybe it was a really hot day, and nobody was leaving the beach. And so I got the bright idea that we should have a shark scare. So the chief of police and my cousin and I got in a boat. And we went out with a bullhorn and we said, "There is a shark, a shark, please leave the water, please leave the water." But of course everybody said, "Ah, they're just joking." So I took out the pistol. And I fired three times, boom, boom, boom, yelling, "I think I wounded him." Everybody ran out of the water.

Jed Lyons: Tell us about the time you met your wife when you pulled her over?

Chris Potholm: Well, this was an unbelievable place to be a young, unattached man because the husbands and older men were all down there for the weekend, but then they would go back to Hartford or New Britain or wherever. So it was awash with women, bored women. And young girls, too, wandering around. It was just fabulous. We had this checkpoint where people would come by. The cops checked out each car. And I saw this beautiful face go by, and I turned to the two cops and I said, "Hey, who is that?" And they said, "Oh yeah, that's Sandy. Sandy Quinlin." "How old is she?" I asked. "Oh, she's 19." So I said, "I'm gonna keep an eye out for her." So a couple of nights later, she comes by and I put my hat back and stopped her. "What's the matter?" she asked. I said, "Well, I'm sorry, little lady, you were speeding. Let me see your license." "Here's my license." "Oh, now wait a minute, that doesn't have your telephone number on it." She said, "Oh, it's well, it's PE97468." "Okay. Okay. All right. Good enough." The next time I saw her walking on the beach, I invited her out. That's how I met my wife. Her mother didn't want her to go out with me because I was just an old cop. Luckily her mother relented and the rest, as they say, is history. I like to tell people I arrested my wife, but that's close enough.

Jed Lyons: So you both spent that summer in Old Lyme or Niantic. What happened at the end of the summer?

Bill Cohen: I went to law school at Boston University. The school was up on top of Beacon Hill. And I got a dreadful unit on Myrtle Street. It was 69 Myrtle Street. And it was just a horrible place. There were three stories to the building. And we're on the first floor. It had no bathroom inside. We had to go across a hallway. And then it had a pull chain for the toilet. The window in the bathroom looked out onto an air shaft that stopped just outside the window. The people on the two upper floors dumped all of their junk into it. So, it was pretty grim.

We didn't have any furniture. We waited for people to throw away furniture from nearby apartments when they were moving out. I had a couch that had three legs and I used books for the fourth leg. There wasn't even a bedroom, just a kind of a closet where you could squeeze a bed in. We lived there for a year and a half until the law school moved into a new building on Commonwealth Avenue. We had real economic problems at the time.

Kevin was born in February that year. We had three mouths to feed on $8 a week. And during that time, I developed gingivitis. So, I volunteered to go down to the Tufts Dental School, to have them treat my gums. I did not have a good experience there. I also ended up selling blood every five months or so for $25 to help pay our bills.

I developed eye strain and suffered massive headaches. I asked the school if they had anything that could treat the headaches. They said that I had a "convergence" problem, and that my eyes were breaking away. I needed to strengthen my left eye muscle. The school provided me a little piece of equipment that required me to look at an illuminated screen and place a red dot inside of a green box. It seemed to be working out, but then I was told that since I didn't have any insurance to pay for it that I had to return the equipment. So, the headaches continued. I couldn't go out in broad daylight. When the sunlight hit me, I just couldn't think or focus. I studied at night under a soft light. That first year was really tough. I didn't think I was going to make it. I had too much stress, too many physical ailments between my eyes, the headaches, my gums. I was not doing well and worried that I would not be able to make it.

I took an interview with New England Tel & Tel just in case I failed.

I met with a rather serious, straightlaced man who said, 'Tell me, what were the happiest moments of your life?" And I asked, "happy? You mean Happy, Happy? Just what kind of happy do you mean?" He said, "I want to know when you felt the happiest moments in your life." I said, "Well, I felt happy at Bowdoin behind the fraternity bar. I was happy when I scored thirty points in a basketball game."

I knew what he wanted me to say, but I was put off by his pompous attitude, as he was giving me a Rorschach test. He wanted me to say something like, When I realized that I had responsibilities as a young adult, that I was looking forward to the future. And I had moments of happiness in my faith or when contributing to the well-being of my family and others. . . . I could have said any of the things that I didn't feel just then to make a good impression. He slowly looked through the resume I had submitted, and finally said, "Looking at your record. I don't think you'd be happy working with us." I didn't respond well. "You mean that I was a James Bowdoin scholar and graduated cum laude? I was co-captain of my high school and college basketball teams and was All-State in both? I kept going through the things that I had accomplished and said, "And you've decided I wouldn't be happy with you?" He shook his head no. I said, "Well, you know, you've done me a favor. Seeing a jerk like you tells me that if I joined your company, I would become just like you." Then I walked out. I knew it wasn't the smartest thing to say. But it was just his whole dismissive and condescending attitude—"I don't think you'd be happy with us." But he was right. I mean, he was absolutely right. Given my personality, I wouldn't be happy with his company.

The whole incident was a flashback for me to a meeting I had with Bowdoin's athletic director, Mal Morrell. This was at the end of my junior year. I had been named to the All-State basketball team that year. And Mal called me into his office. I thought I was going to get the, believe it or not, the Paul Nixon Award for sportsmanship. He said, "You had a really great year. We know that. But you're not entitled to this award." I said, "Why not?" He said, "Because you are not acting up to the standards of what is expected of Bowdoin students." I then said, "You mean because I was fighting?" He said, "Yes, that's just part of it. How many games did you get ejected from?" I replied, "I was fighting for the team to win." I was furious. If someone hit me on the court, I hit them back. If someone fouled me hard, then I'd foul them back even harder. Those were the street rules that we had on Hancock Street and the rules that I grew up with.

He said, "No, that's not the Bowdoin way. You're not going to get this award. I just wanted to tell you that." "Mr. Morrell," I said, "if you think I was bad this year, just wait until I come back next year." I walked out of his office, determined to come back and be as bad as I could be on the court. It was an infantile response. Totally immature. He was right to say that the school expected more than a street fighter's mentality from me. But at the time, it struck me as just another unfair rejection, like the one I received at Hebrew school. "We know you're the best student, but we can't give you first prize."

Well, I never got to be the bad boy that I had promised to be during my senior year. During the very first game, I got kicked in the jaw while diving for the ball and suffered a broken jaw. I was eating with a straw for about three or four weeks. It was the second time I had my jaw broken (in addition to three broken ribs and broken collar bone in high school). It took the wind out of me. And it helped change me. When I healed, I started to play by Bowdoin rules and not Hancock Street. I finally got the award for leadership my senior year, still playing hard but not fighting or fouling so much.

Jed Lyons: Bill, when you decided to go to law school, what kind of career did you have in mind?

Bill Cohen: I didn't know what to do. Having majored in Latin, at the behest of Nate Dane, I had few choices. But I could go on to grad school and get a master's or a doctorate in Latin. My father thought he had wasted whatever money he had on me. And I had wasted four years. I had a lawyer friend from Bangor that I was having lunch with. He said, "You should go to law school."

I replied, "Why?" He said, "Because it will sharpen your mind by narrowing it. You've had this broad liberal arts education. But if you go to law school, it'll make you focus on specific things and a specific way of reasoning. It will be good for you. And then you can go on to be a lawyer or whatever you want to be." That's how I ended up going to law school at the last minute. Frankly, I had no idea what I was going to do.

Jed Lyons: At what point did you start writing poetry?

Bill Cohen: In my freshman year. We had Professor Greason.

Jed Lyons: LeRoy Greason

Bill Cohen: LeRoy Greason. He came to the classroom and announced that we were going to write a sonnet. I had never read a poem. I'd never known what a sonnet was. I started to freak out a bit. I went to him and said, "Professor, you know that I'm co-captain on the basketball team. We're going to be traveling for the next couple of weeks throughout New England. On our road trip, I can't possibly write a sonnet." He said," Mr. Cohen, you will write a sonnet, or you will flunk this course." And that really got my attention. I panicked. I didn't know what to do. I ended up going over to the library the rest of the week. One night, I was flipping through magazines trying to figure out, what the hell am I going to write? How do I write it? And I saw an article that compared the mating instinct among animals with the seasons. Click! I wondered if that applied to people. And so, I wrote my first sonnet, "Can Season Be The Reason?" He only gave me a C for which he later came to regret publicly, after I pointed it out at one of our reunions that I could still recite the poem from memory. He said, "I gave a C for that? My mistake." In fact, he wrote me a letter as a follow-up to our conversation. But he helped change me, at least my self-image. I was at Bowdoin to be a jock. I wasn't anything else. He opened my eyes so I could see that there was a whole world out there. He, plus Nate Dane, helping me read Latin poets. So, I started writing a little bit of poetry at that time.

Jed Lyons: Why did you decide to become a Latin major? I know Nate Dane was a big personality who influenced a lot of students. What were you thinking? Why Latin?

Bill Cohen: Actually, it comes down to a memory thing again. I could memorize things very well then. I could memorize the Latin poets. In my mind, I knew what they were writing and saying. And it was an easy course for me to take. And so with no heavy lifting, I devoted myself to playing basketball. I had aspirations about playing, believe it or not, in the pros. In those days, I taught one summer at a basketball camp with Bill Sharman, who was a former Celtic guard with Bob Cousy. I taught basketball at a camp he was running. And he said, "Gee, there's a new league starting out in Chicago, as a matter of fact, a new team, a new league and the ABA. And they have a three-point rule. And so given where you like to shoot from, that would be a possibility for you." So I said, "Mom, I'm gonna go play in the pros." And of course, their team folded that first year. And that's why it left me up in the air as to what I was going to do, because I had planned to try out for a professional team. Now the good news is it would never work. I couldn't shine their shoes or carry their shoes. But with the three-point rule, I thought I was a young Steph Curry. I was up late last night watching Steph Curry play. He put in 49 points last night. It's the 11th game in a row that he scored over 30. He missed one final shot at the end or he would have put up 50 points. He plays for the Golden State Warriors. There was no shooter like him, no one will ever be like him. Because he can shoot from half court with ease, he can go, he handles the ball with either hand. He goes between his legs, behind his back and nobody can stop him. So I thought that if I was in that league, I could shoot three-pointers, it wasn't that far. And so that kind of dashed that. And again, I never would have made it anyway. The closest I came to playing on a professional team is when the Celtics came to Bangor for an exhibition game. Don Nelson was one of the team members and they had a guy named Lou Tsioropoulos, as well. And they had Sam Jones, they had Casey Jones. Bill Russell was not with them at the time. But Nelson saw me. I was the mayor at that time. And he saw me shooting hoops and he said, "How'd you like to play tonight?" I said yes. He said, "Why don't you sub for Casey Jones tonight?" So Don Nelson gave me his uniform. And the pants came down over my knees, and the shirt sleeves were over my elbows. And I had called home and I said to my mother, please bring my sneakers. I went down there and made a complete ass of myself on the court. It was sad. Sam Jones threw me a bullet pass. I mean, it was one of those that took me right into the stands. I went up to catch it and it carried me right into the stands. And it was just a joke out there. These guys were so good. So big, so strong. And I was in the gym taking a shower afterward and this kid came in and said, "You guys were great. But what was that Woody Allen act out there?" And so I got my taste of what it would have been like. The only other time I played at the professional level was with Jim Loscutoff. You wouldn't remember that name but "Jungle Jim" Loscutoff played forward for the Celtics. He was only about six', six", but he weighed 220 to 230. And it was all upper body. And he was missing his four front teeth. And so when he played he took the plate out and just had fangs coming out. When he first came into the pros, he was really a very good ballplayer, but then he had back surgery. Never again did he have the kind of finesse he had when he first came into the league. So they used to bring him in to hurt people. When things got rough, they called him and said, okay, Jim, and he would go in and he would hurt people and calm everybody down. So he came by when I was working at the Barn in Old Orchard Beach my junior year. He came into the Barn, he and Tsioropoulos, for teaching. They had a camp in Old Orchard Beach. And he came into the place where I was working. Diana was the hostess at the door. So he came in one night, and if you could see him, he had a tight T-shirt on that could barely contain his arms and chest. He was just busting out with muscle. Tsioropoulos was about six, five or six. So the two of them really stood out.

Loscutoff got on the floor and wanted everybody off the floor so he could chacha all by himself, daring anyone to say anything to him. I didn't dare to say anything to him. I went up to him after the thing and I said, "Are you in town for your school? "And he said, "Yeah." I said, "Well, I used to play. I played in college." He said, "Do you want to come up?" I said, "Sure." So he said," Come on up, we'll play some four on four." He had two other players. And so I went out onto an outdoor court. And Tsioropoulos threw a full-length pass to him. And as his legs dropped going up to catch it over his head, I got under him and I hit him as hard as I could. He kept his balance and staggered back. He came over to me, took that massive forearm and he hit me across my chest, drove me about 20 feet, ripped all the skin off my knees. He came over to me and said, "Don't you ever f---k with me again" because I was putting his career in danger. I said, "Yeah." I was all apologies. "I didn't really mean to do that." I was trying to show off and see if I could take the big guy down. Wrong thing to do. And I never forgot that. I was bleeding as I stepped off the court. And that was kind of the end of it. Anyway, he retired. He retired from the Celtics, and he became a coach at Boston State College, which is about four blocks away from the law school at that point. And so I would go down and play him one on one twice a week. And I could beat him one on one. As long as I didn't go near the basket. As long as I stayed 30 feet or 20 feet away. He couldn't guard me. The minute I went inside, it was all over. So that was the experience I had playing against a Celtic and probably one of the toughest guys that ever played professional basketball.

Jed Lyons: Chris, tell us about the most influential teachers you had at Bowdoin.

Chris Potholm: The best lecturer I had was Professor Geohegan in religion. Professor Pols in philosophy was probably the smartest. At the end of his life, he had Alzheimer's and he still was writing books and I couldn't really understand the books even then. The classics professor, Nate Dane, taught me an awful lot. But I would have to say the person that changed my life the most was Nat Kendrick, who was the dean of the faculty and the students and everything else. He's the one that got me the first scholarship, and then my sophomore year, my father had a cerebral spasm, and he couldn't work. And I had to tell the dean that I couldn't come back to Bowdoin. And he said, "Well, I'll get you another scholarship." So I had two scholarships. But he also taught a course on European history. And when I was a senior, he let me give a lecture. He asked me if I would like to give a lecture. I gave a lecture on the Battle of Stalingrad. And it was really funny because these guys that were in my fraternity and everything else, they had to write down what I was saying because this is going to be on the exam. And so that was my first time being a professor, seeing these guys that, you know, had to write down my thoughts. I looked at a lot of different career paths. I wanted to go into the State Department, I got into the Foreign Service, the CIA, AID, I thought government, but I didn't think any of them really fit my personality. So I backed into college teaching. But looking back now, that's about the only job I ever really would have enjoyed as much as I have. And so by putting me on that path, even though I didn't go straight there, I would say he had the biggest impact on me. I really owe Dean Shaw and Nate Dane and especially Nate Kendrick so much; without them I'd never have ended up as happy and fulfilled as I did. I just wish they could have lived to see how Billy and I turned out.

Jed Lyons: And why government and initially African studies as a specialty?

Chris Potholm: Well, you know, Bill was talking about what he did out of college. I had been brought up, of course, by these two grandmothers with the stories of Sweden and Denmark. And so when I got out of Bowdoin, I wanted to go and hitchhike around Europe, and go back and find my roots. And, of course, the Scandinavia they had left in 1890 was no longer there. And I was terribly disillusioned. Plus, I was really, truly desperately in love with this Sandy girl that I had met that summer. And so she wrecked my whole European trip. And I came home after a couple of months. I was just miserable. But when I came back, I looked at all of the stuff that I had absorbed about Scandinavia. And it dawned on me that I wanted something completely different. So there I was, in order to avoid the draft, when I got back, I had to teach. I taught second grade. By the way, one of the hardest jobs I've ever had was day in and day out with 30 little kids. But anyway, I got interested in Africa because it was so different from Scandinavia. And it was a whole different world to me. And then when I went to the Fletcher School of Law and Diplomacy at Tufts, I specialized in Africa. So that was really kind of how I got into it. And I don't know if Bill remembers this but I did my PhD on the King of Swaziland, King Sobhuza. The British wanted to get rid of him, but they foolishly let the old King pick the symbols because most of Swaziland's voters were illiterate then. If you wanted the British constitution, the symbol for that was a reindeer, you know. Think of all the beautiful African animals with their horns and a reindeer looks like what was left over when all the beautiful animals were already taken. But if you didn't want the constitution, you had a symbol for that which was the lion, a symbol of the Royal House. Well, in that referendum, the King got 102 percent of the vote. And years later, when Bill and I were going to see Joe Sewall and a couple of big money people, these guys asked what do you possibly know about Maine politics when you studied African politics? I got into tribalism and the Francos and the Irish. And, you know, I could just see this glimmer of disbelief in Bill's eyes. He's beginning to wonder but, I said, "Billy just think of this. If we only do half as good as that old King, you'll never lose." And then we said, "Oh, yeah, 51 percent, that's all we need. We don't have to get 102 percent—51 percent, that's the way it works." The tribalism, we'll get to that, I guess, later on, but the tribalism of Maine, the Irish, the Francos, the English. I mean, that African experience was invaluable, not just in Bill's race, but understanding referenda and everything else that may involve the English, the Irish, and especially the Francos.

Bill Cohen: I just want to say one quick thing about Nat Kendrick. He kept me in school after the fight incident at Psi U and especially after I stayed in Cuba after the spring break was long over. That's another story altogether. And the most influential, of course, was Nate Dane. Do you remember Professor Walter Solmitz? He was a philosophy professor and a Holocaust survivor. I think it was during our senior year when he committed suicide.

Chris Potholm: I never took a course from him. Did you?

Bill Cohen: Yeah, I did. Fritz Koelln, the German professor. They always walked together down the campus. They were very good friends. But I was sorry to learn that Solmitz had committed suicide. But then I've learned a lot about the Holocaust over the years, and he's just one of the sad, tragic examples of what it did to victims.

CHAPTER II

Oral History Discussion with Secretary Bill Cohen and Professor Christian Potholm

Tuesday, May 4, 2021

Jed Lyons: When we ended last time, we were talking about your college years.

Chris Potholm: We did ours. We want to hear a little bit about your beginnings and how the Bowdoin you experienced was either different or similar to what we have been talking about.

Jed Lyons: Bowdoin when I arrived in 1970 was 650 boys in the entire college. The thing about Bowdoin that struck me when I first got there was that it was made up of kids from wealthy alumni families and then a lot of Irish Catholic and Italian kids from around Boston and some rural Mainers. Being a kid from the Midwest, I felt out of place. I wasn't happy there my first year, but I finally decided to join a fraternity, Psi Upsilon, halfway through the year and there I found a great group of friends. A wild place—talk about Animal House. I'll never forget my first big winter weekend. Everyone had their dates and all of a sudden a certain scion from a large shoe company family is crawling around naked on all fours biting the legs of the dates. And this was considered normal for him apparently and no one bothered, no one noticed him, they just said "That's John, don't worry." Another brother was celebrated for his "reverse strip-tease" act. He'd arrive at a party buck naked and then put his clothes back on as guests yelled, "put it on, put it all on!" Even the college's president would join in the fun. Whenever there was a big weekend party at the Psi U house, we'd have a bottle of Ushers Scotch at the ready. It was his favorite.

Chris Potholm: Well, speaking of your early dates, I have a recollection of coming home to my house and having Sandy telling me that she had been invited out to dinner by one of my advisees and I said, "Oh, great," and she said "Well, you're not actually invited. It's Jed Lyons and he's just invited me for my birthday." So somewhere along the line I can't remember if Bill or I ever contemplated asking out a professor's wife, but apparently you came here with more self-confidence than either Bill or I.

Jed Lyons: Well, there weren't any female students on campus my freshman year, Chris, and I mistook your pretty wife, Sandy, for a local, certainly not the wife of my professor! Another memorable night was a Winter's Weekend when there was a snow sculpture contest. The Psi U freshmen decided to make two copulating 20-foot-tall polar bear sculptures on the front lawn of the Psi U house. The project was overseen by Steve Hancock who is now a major league artist. Early that morning, the house got a phone call from the dean of students, Paul Nyhus, saying "take that down right now! There are people driving by and almost crashing their cars." The Brunswick community was upset, as you can imagine. So down they came and the freshmen built one little baby polar bear in their place.

Chris, please talk about how you wound up going from Bowdoin, where you excelled and were valedictorian of your class, to Fletcher School of Law and Diplomacy and choosing to go into academic life, then on to Dartmouth and Vassar.

Chris Potholm: Well, when I got out of Bowdoin I had no idea what I wanted to do. I had this great pilgrimage to Scandinavia; I was going to hitchhike around Scandinavia. But in the meantime, I had met Sandy that summer. I spent a couple of months in Europe, so I came back and to avoid the draft I became a second-grade teacher and that was the hardest job I ever had in my life taking care of those kids. I didn't know what I wanted to be, but I thought, well, maybe I want to go into the Foreign Service, so I ended up at Fletcher. And I got into the Foreign Service and the CIA and AID, but in the process of interviewing I knew I would be terrible in a big bureaucracy with reviews every six months so I kind of backed into college teaching and I remember people at Fletcher said, "A professor? Is that all you want to be in life?" Fletcher wasn't great about placing people in academia. I only had two job interviews—one was at Baypath Junior College in Springfield and one at Dartmouth.

When I was up at Dartmouth at my recruitment dinner the professors all got drunk and the oldest one got up and he went right around the table, saying "Well, let me tell you about this department." He went right around the table saying "So and so is sleeping with so and so's wife, that one professor will never publish again," and you know, like wow I thought, this is like my house growing up. I just acted cool. I guess the other candidate had gotten all flustered when they took the brand-new wine glasses and threw them into the fire and everything else. Today, such a dinner would cost $3,000. Anyway, it was only a two-year position. I got the contract extended for two more years. I did have the advantage of starting out in the Ivy League and I was interested in Africa. That was just when African studies was going strong and then a tenure track position opened up at Vassar. Vassar was just unbelievable. We had self-scheduled oral exams, the girls would come in for the final exam so you'd sit on the quad and—not every one of them, but enough of them—brought dope so you'd start smoking and rapping about Nigeria. I mean, you couldn't make this up. The government department had 15 people, 14 of whom were male and we had a touch football game. We would play the girls on Friday afternoon in front of the administration building, and they would bring lots of grass, but also kegs of beer and there would be you, know, big piles. Can you imagine? Today you would all be arrested. As much as I liked teaching at Dartmouth, and I liked teaching at Vassar, I wanted to get back to Maine. At Dartmouth, I'd worked on Gene McCarthy's campaign and I had big binder books filled with stuff about campaigns and lessons I saw in action. I literally thought I was coming back to

Maine and eventually I would run for governor. And, long story short, I had to take a pay cut to come back to Bowdoin and I was so angry about that, but they did pay moving expenses, and so I had a huge pile—several cords of wood—and I had the movers box up all the wood and bring it to Maine with me. But once I drove across that bridge at Kittery, I just said, God I'm home. I had this life-long strong attraction for Maine.

Jed Lyons: You arrived in 1970, the same year I arrived as a freshman. I remember going over to your little rental house right in town, maybe a block away from campus where you and Sandy were living.

Chris Potholm: That was wonderful. I mean that first year it was great to live on campus, but we wanted to live out in the country so we looked at Brunswick and Bowdoinham and finally Harpswell. Been there ever since!

Jed Lyons: You bought that land and then had students, including me, help you build the house.

Chris Potholm: That's right. Those that wanted to pass courses as, you know, get an apprenticeship. What an opportunity! Just think how fortunate they were. They got to work side by side with a professor, learn a little carpentry. Today it would be called an internship.

Jed Lyons: Okay, so Bill, Chris told us a little bit about the summer after you graduated from Bowdoin and you shot the skunk beneath the porch down in Old Lyme when you were working as a cop. Are there any other good stories?

Bill Cohen: Nothing really. I was working on the city crew, paving roads or filling in potholes or cutting branches off fallen trees. Nothing really too heavy, and then at night I would suit up as a constable on Popham Beach. Not an exciting time, but I was trying to save enough money to pay for the first year of law school. I became an old man very early in my life. I was living up on Beacon Hill and living in a horrible place. It was a rundown three-story tenement building, sort of like the one I was born in. There were two elderly sisters who lived in the front apartment. I was in the back apartment, which consisted of two rooms, a kitchen and "living room." The bathroom was across the hall. The toilet had a pull chain to use for flushing. I turned a closet into our bedroom. It was big enough to allow for a box spring and mattress. Charlie Wing (my college roommate after Dean Kendrick rescued me from the Psi U house) was five blocks away. He was going to MIT at that time. It was really cold during the winters. Diana was pregnant. The temperature in the apartment had dropped to something close to 38-40 degrees in the apartment. Charlie and his wife came up to visit and they were all bundled up because they were freezing, too. So we all got in the bed fully clothed with overcoats and tried to stay warm huddled together. That's how cold it was. Unfortunately, the bed broke, and we all crashed to the floor.

Meanwhile, Kevin came along in February and we were faced with some real stressful issues. I suffered from migraine headaches stemming from an eye convergence problem. The law school provided me with a piece of equipment that consisted of a box with an electronic screen. I had to sit in a very dark room and focus on a green square and place a red ball inside the square.

And it helped until I had to return the device because I didn't have any insurance to cover the monthly charges. I had a situation where I couldn't be exposed to light without getting smashing headaches. I had to stay inside most of the time, except to go to classes. Then I developed gingivitis, an inflammation of my gums. I didn't have any money to go to a dentist so I ended up volunteering for the Tufts Dental School where I was basically being used as a guinea pig for young dental students. I'll never forget the time several students were hovering over me and the student who was cutting my gums said, "Whoops," and pulled back. It was a big cut. At that point I decided to leave the program. We were living on $8 a week for food and I was donating blood in return for $25 every six months or so. About April of that year, I started to panic because in law school you have just one exam for the entire year. The dean told us on the first day of classes to "look to your right and look to your left because one of you won't be here at the end of the year." Statistically, this usually is true. It is really easy to fall behind reading assignments or if you miss a day of classes, it's difficult to catch up. Given the physical problems I was having, the pressure was starting to take a toll. I was worried about how we were going to survive if I was part of the one-third that failed. I decided to take an interview with a representative from the New England Tel & Tel Company as plan B. It did not go well, but it served as an incentive to drive me to study even harder to avoid failing. I did much better than I thought, not only getting a passing grade, but well enough to be named to the Law Review.

Jed Lyons: At this point, Bill, you're how old?

Bill Cohen: I was 22 when I became a father and then, again, two and a half years later with Chris. Very young, lots of responsibility, no money and trying to figure out a way to stay alive.

Jed Lyons: So while you're going to law school, what work were you doing, how were you paying for everything?

Bill Cohen: Diana was working until Kevin was born, and then I signed on to become the "manager" of the building I told you was a real dump.

On the floor there were layers and layers of linoleum, maybe as many as 4 to 5 layers. The panes of glass were so thin that when you wiped off all of the grime coming up from the street, an hour later it was filled in again. Then up on the top floors were a bunch of young people raising hell all the time. They used to roll beer bottles down from the top floor all the way down the back stairs and, because we were on the first floor, they thought that was the exit door. One night, they started tumbling down the stairs and then a fight broke out and two guys crashed through the kitchen door and rolled into the small living room. Diana was close to giving birth and I took that weapon that I had carried in Niantic, and I went out into the kitchen. I said, "Get your asses out of here or I'm going to kill you!" Fortunately, the gun was not loaded, but they finally realized they were in somebody else's apartment and there was a very large gun pointed at their heads. Of course, it was illegal for me to have had a gun in Massachusetts, even though I kept it unloaded. After that incident, I got rid of it because had it been loaded, I might have killed them that night. A good way to go from law school student to prison. As the manager of the building that I was living in, I had no experience, but, basically, I was taking the complaints of everybody, making sure all the holes were painted and whatever, so I did that and I had saved up enough to get through that first year. Then half-way through the second year, we moved out to a place called Brighton and into a basement apartment. I had to take the subway from there to the new law school building on Massachusetts Avenue. The thing that I remember most about it was living next to the furnace room that heated the whole building. I would wake up in the middle of the night and I could not pry my jaws open. It was so suffocating from being next to the furnace. And then there were the roaches that would come out at night. They were very large roaches and when you snapped on a light, they would just scatter. You could hear them click, clicking away as I tried to stomp them out. It was an amazing experience to get through living there while still trying to compete in the classroom. I worked at the law library, to help pay the way through the last two years. I did well and graduated cum laude. But I still didn't know what I wanted to do with my degree.

Jed Lyons: So you went to Washington and Wall Street? You went to look for jobs there?

Bill Cohen: Yes. I was offered a position at the Commerce Department.

Justice was interested at the Civil Rights Division. A Wall Street firm was prepared to offer me a position. On the second interview, I was about to accept, but on the train ride to New York, I was reading a book written about Wall Street law firms that pointed out that if you were not from a wealthy or socially connected family, you were unlikely to ever become a partner. You would toil away and make a decent living, but you were not likely to share in the firm's profits. When one of the senior partners called me down to his office, I must have passed 20 or 30 rooms all jammed with young lawyers and I made the decision right then that that life was not for me. I said, "Sir, thank you for inviting me, but I don't think I can work here." I didn't offer any explanation. I turned around and walked out and never looked back. I still hadn't decided what I was going to do but I had three mouths to feed and another one on the way in September.

On the recommendation of Errol Paine, a friend from Bangor who was a year ahead of me in law school, I went to work for Thomas F. Lambert, Jr., one the most brilliant men I've ever known. He had won the debating and oratorical championship on the West Coast, served as a prosecutor during the Nuremberg War trials, and became the dean of Stetson Law School at the age of twenty-seven. He had a photographic memory and could cite page and paragraph number from thousands of cases. But more than a prodigious memory, he had the ability to speak using words that belonged to a poet. He would blend the words of T. S. Eliot and A. E. Housman with those of preeminent jurists in major legal cases. I had the opportunity to meet some of the very best trial attorneys in the country but not one of them would ever agree to follow Tom to a speaking podium. These were men with very large egos who would stand before juries and persuade them to award millions of dollars to their clients but were embarrassed to reveal that they were mere apprentices unqualified to hold the coat of a true orator. Even though I loved working with Tom at the American Trial Lawyers Association, I decided that it was time for me to begin the practice of law in my hometown where I was well known. Tom counseled me not to practice law because "it would either harden your heart or break it." He was right, of course, but I had to find that out for myself. Chris may remember Lew Vafiades.

Lew had a very good trial practice and maybe about four or five lawyers. It was a small firm, but big for Bangor. And they offered me a pretty good starting salary. I think it was somewhere around $12,000 or $15,000, which was twice the amount I was making with Tom. And, after a few years, Lew promised that I'd be a full partner. I was about to accept the offer but then talked to Errol Paine, my friend from law school days who had returned to Bangor a year earlier. Errol said, "If you come with me, I'll make you a full partner now." I had two children to support and Errol had four. I asked how much he was making and he said $150 a week. I said, "So you and I get $75.00 each? "That's the deal." I took it. I knew that I didn't want to work for someone else. I wanted to be in charge of my life as much as possible. We formed the law firm of Paine & Cohen and six years later we had six or seven attorneys in the firm and eight or nine secretaries.

Jed Lyons: Where was the office? In Bangor?

Bill Cohen: Across from the courthouse. We built a practice basically as junkyard dogs. We took everything—divorces, bankruptcies, rape cases, whatever walked into the office or whatever other firms sent us because they were too messy or unprofitable. But we had to demonstrate that we were good if we were to grow the practice. In those days, it was unethical to advertise (a good rule) so we had to establish our credentials by volunteering for civic functions. I served on Bangor's Zoning Board of Appeals and the Parks and Recreation Committee. Errol ran for county attorney and was elected. There were two assistant county attorney positions open, but no one wanted them because they were too time-consuming and paid only $2,500 a year. So Errol appointed me to both slots. Together we handled all of the criminal charges brought during the course of the year and prosecuted as many as ninety cases every six months. That's how we got our trial experience. But only a third of the cases ever went to trial. We said to defense attorneys they better be prepared to try the case or plead your clients guilty. We were not lenient in recommending stiff sentences if they decided to go to trial and lost.

Jed Lyons: This would have been what year, Bill?

Bill Cohen: This would have been 1967 or 68.

Jed Lyons: Give us a snapshot of what the Maine political scene looked like in 1972.

Bill Cohen: Well, I was a total novice when it came to politics, but there was a man named Howard Foley who had been a county attorney. Smart guy from a well-to-do family and pretty hard-nosed. He didn't have a campaign manager. The local Republicans couldn't find any other warm bodies and asked me to be his manager. I was completely unqualified for the job as I was just starting out with my law practice in 1966, and I knew it was a losing proposition. But that's how I met Joe Sewall and Harry Richardson.

Chris Potholm: Harry Richardson, Ken MacLeod, Dave Huber.

Bill Cohen: That was the basic group that encouraged me along with a friend named Bill Nealy, but that's another long story. I did the best I could, but Howard was taking positions that were not going to fly.

Jed Lyons: Was the Senate and the House of Representatives mostly Republican at that point?

Bill Cohen: The Democrats controlled both the House and the Senate in Congress then. We had Susan Collins's father as a state senator. Her uncle was a state senator. I didn't know much, if anything, about the state legislature. I just knew Joe Sewall, Ken MacLeod, and Harry Richardson. They were really the leaders.

Jed Lyons: Were they what you would call "Rockefeller Republicans" back in those days, liberal Republicans?

Bill Cohen: Yes, I would say so.

Jed Lyons: What do you think, Chris?

Chris Potholm: I think that's a very, very critical point and I'd just like to circle back on Bill and I at Bowdoin and what we took away from it, because listening to Bill last time got me thinking about a couple of things and I just want to share them. We talked a lot about Bowdoin as the animal house and there's all that, and that certainly was true. But there was a sense that it was a liberal arts college, and we were taught that we actually could do anything that we set our minds to. I think there was an openness to it that to blue-collar kids like us was very liberating. We went to Bowdoin, we can do this. And all during the campaign, I never had a feeling that we couldn't do it, that Bill wouldn't be elected, and what Bill said was something that really stuck with me and that was one of the ways Bill handled life was to learn all these things that people from Rome and Greece had said. And I'm not blowing smoke here. I was 40 years in politics and I never saw anyone, not a candidate or a spokesperson for a referendum or causes, that was as good as you are, Bill. When the red light of the camera went on, you never made a major mistake, you just didn't. And you did two things, one of which was when you got going, you would bring in some reference to "Cato said this to Cicero at the marriage of Lucretia." And the reporters, I mean, they knew right away, wow this guy, he's smarter than I am. You would give them an answer they couldn't forget. And if that didn't work, you had this analogy that you used over and over again, which was the glass is half full or half empty. And, by the time you had filled the glass and emptied it three or four times the reporters, they didn't have anything. You know, they're always looking for "gotcha." They want you to make a mistake and you never did. You are famous for your vote to impeach Nixon, but I always thought the most significant socioeconomic, political, military decision you ever made was your deciding vote on the AWACS planes sold to Saudi Arabia. That was so significant. We could not have won or probably even fought the Gulf War had the Saudis not gotten the planes because it was under the umbrella of those planes that we prepositioned equipment and we built all those airfields and everything else and gained the trust of the Saudis that we would be with them. And I remember, for some reason I was down in Washington with you the day you cast the vote and I was over in the Senate chambers and there was Dan Schorr, a nasty reporter for CBS, and he was a "gotcha" guy and he wanted to really nail Bill. Of course, the Israeli lobby was going nuts, because of this AWACS deal, so Daniel Schorr stands up and accuses you of being anti-Semitic for that vote. And, you know, Cool Hand Luke Bill, he starts talking "on the one hand, this, on the other hand that." I don't know if you brought in Cicero or Julius Caesar or something, anyway, it goes on and on. And then Bill says, as if explaining to a not too bright child, "And so, Dan, I have to say that a vote AGAINST the AWACS would have been the height of anti-Semitism!" Schorr's mouth dropped open and he's like a dog hearing a whistle off to the side, he doesn't know what to make of it. A week later the Israeli lobby got everybody all worked up and there's this big problem in Portland. A woman mayor there was Jewish, Linda Abromson, so Bill had to fly up from Washington to explain things to her. I'm with him and Bill had a fever of 102 and on the flight up somehow his ears get all stuffed up and he can't hear at all. But that red light went on, and he talks about this, and about that and within five minutes, you know, these people are clapping and coming up, and saying "Oh, I didn't understand that." I never saw anybody in politics like Bill, who could do that. A few years ago, Colby College had a conference on Maine political figures and there were a whole bunch of political reporters on this panel and somebody asked them, well, how do you close the best and avoid questions. And one was George Mitchell, who did the judge thing. But then Pat Callahan I think said no, we have got to give it to Cohen, and he said, "With Bill, you never got that sound bite he didn't want you to have."

Jed Lyons: Let's ask Bill to respond. How did you acquire that savoir faire and that ability to speak so fluently and confidently?

Bill Cohen: This is a fairly long story. There were students at Bowdoin, you know, the Ted Fullers of the world, who came from fairly well-to-do families. They had prep school backgrounds, they were completely at ease in any social environment. I basically came off Hancock Street, which was a tough little street and spent a lot of time fighting, mostly on the court, but occasionally off the court. I had a great memory at that time, and I think I told you, Chris, that I was so overwhelmed, I spent my evenings anywhere from 12 to three o'clock in the morning, reading the dictionary, to try to increase my vocabulary. During the first six months, that's all I did was study books that helped to improve my vocabulary. And I actually started to lose the vision in my eyes in my freshman year just because I was staying up late, using a small light, and just reading a dictionary. I made up for what I lacked intellectually through pure perseverance. I feel the same way today. I get through things simply because I'm going to make sure that I don't fail. And it was that kind of discipline that has always been there, the determination to do the best I can so I don't fail. I remember playing for Bowdoin I never saw the basket clearly. Sometimes I saw two baskets which gave me I guess a 50 percent chance to get one into a basket. I needed to wear glasses, but I was too vain. I was not going to wear glasses on the basketball court.

I just had a sense I knew where the basket was and in terms of just understanding what it takes to get the ball there. I could shoot that way, without even seeing the basket. And then I brought the same kind of discipline to law school. I wasn't a great student, but I was determined to get through it and I think the reason why Tom Lambert was so important to me is that I was at the feet of an oratorical giant, and for a year I just watched him and listened to how he strung words together to paint powerful images.

When I went back to practice law, there's nothing like standing in front of a jury and you're either defending a case or prosecuting a case. You learn very quickly how you have to relate to a jury. I think those six years doing that, when I was in Bangor practicing law, and when I ran for the city council, then the city council put me on the school board, while I was still serving on the city council to help get control of the school board's budget. This was unprecedented and produced a major controversy. I was teaching at the University of Maine. I was practicing law and also serving as the assistant county attorney. I was getting about three or four hours of sleep a night, which was consistent with what my dad was getting so I kind of grew up in that environment where he could get by on three hours. Just persistence on his part.

I want to come back to the story that Chris told about the vote on the AWACS, which today still haunts me in the sense that of all the things Jewish people remember about me is that vote. Initially, I was opposed to the sale of the AWACS to the Saudis. I was on the Senate floor speaking out against it. I had 100 percent rating with AIPAC. Then I got a call from Christopher Dreyfus, a friend of mine who lived in London. I suspected (but never knew) that he might be an Israeli intelligence agent. He and I and Gary Hart from time to time would end up in London and go to a private night club called Annabele's. Chris called me and said, "I need you to come to London to meet with the Israeli ambassador to

Great Britain." "Why?" "It's important." I flew over to London and met with Ambassador Shlomo Argov. He wanted to warn me that the vote to reject the sale of AWACS to the Saudis was a mistake. He said that the Israelis were not worried about the AWACS. That it was containable. The Jewish supporters in the United States had gotten way out ahead of the issue and believed the Israelis were opposed to the sale, but this was not entirely true. They could handle any threat posed by the aircraft. What they really wanted and needed were . . . then he listed about nine or ten items that would ensure their qualitative advantage over any enemy in the Middle East. He advised me to return to Washington and meet with the Israeli ambassador to the United States, Ephraim Evron, to confirm what he had just told me. I flew back to D.C. immediately and met with Ambassador Evron. I said, "Look, I'm told that you're publicly opposed to AWACS but you want something else." Then I went through a few of the items Ambassador Argov had cited. He said, "Well . . ." and then pulled out a sheet of paper that confirmed what Ambassador Argov had said.

In essence, they were asking me to bite the bullet and go out and vote for the AWACS even though the Israelis were publicly opposed to it as was AIPAC and every other Jewish organization. Howard Baker, the Senate's Republican leader, was trying to round up votes that he didn't have (including mine). So I said to Howard, I want to go down to the White House and meet with President Reagan. I think Jim Baker was there. I said, "Mr President, I've been opposed to the sale, but I think there's a way that perhaps I could support it if you could find your way to do these nine or ten things that would be consistent with your pledge to always ensure that Israel had both a quantitative *and* qualitative military edge.

Jim Baker looked at me and said, "Well, these three things we can't do . . . these seven we can. I said, "Well, Mr. President, do I have your word that you will give them these seven things?" He said, "You do." I still wasn't persuaded what I should do as I went back to my office on the Hill. The intelligence world is a house of mirrors, and I worried about whether I was going to be screwed over by this whole thing. I didn't want to get caught up in all of these different boxes. Israel says this but they really want that. I mean, was it a classic spycraft trap that I was walking into? Saudis get their planes. Israel gets their "great to have" list, Reagan takes the credit, and I get the blame? I called the White House the next day and said I wanted to see President Reagan alone. Just one on one. I didn't want Jim Baker or anybody else. Just the President and me in the room. They granted the request. They were still short one or two votes. I explained to the President that this was a hard vote for me as I had been publicly committed to opposing the sale. On the other hand, I had gathered information that tells me I'm wrong on this. So if you personally promise me you will do the following things that we talked about yesterday, if you give me that guarantee, I will support you. President Reagan said, "Yes. You have my word" and shook my hand. Well, that was good enough for me.

I drove back to the Hill and told Howard Baker that I needed to give a speech and he said, "You've got 10 minutes." I said that I had to have at least thirty minutes to an hour to explain what I was about to do. And then I went on the floor and explained that I was changing my vote without ever mentioning my meetings with the Israelis or the handshake with President Reagan. I took the heat for supporting the sale while helping the Israelis, who were publicly opposed to it, acquire most of the items on their check list. And immediately, members of the Jewish community called me a traitor and threatened to never support me again. That's why I went to the Abromson's house to explain my vote without ever revealing the intrigue of how it all had come about. Anyway, that's the story behind the story.

Jed Lyons: That's a fascinating story, Bill. Thanks for sharing it. Okay, let's go back to where we were on your career. So now it's 1967, you've got several jobs, city jobs, you're running your law firm. At what point did you start thinking about running for Congress? You ran in '72, but when did you start thinking about it? Was it on your mind for a long time?

Bill Cohen: I had never, never had an intent to pursue a life in politics. It seems that instead of running for something, I was running away from something. I did not like the practice of law, partly because the quality of the clients that we had. It was always stressful for me when I represented someone in a divorce.

The husband would say, "Okay, I'll give the bitch $20 a week for the four kids. Not a penny more or she doesn't get the divorce." They didn't have no fault divorce at that point. I watched people bargain away their kids for dollars and cents and witnessed seeing what was once a loving relationship split up at the bargaining table and all of the heartache and the hatreds that had been suppressed start bubbling up. I hated that aspect of it. Those and bankruptcy cases where I helped dismantle someone's dreams. But most impactful for me was the three years I spent prosecuting cases. I had to go to autopsies and that was the most unpleasant experience for me in my life, because I was being taken to the dark side of the moon. Chris Dodd used to say that Tip O'Neill was Irish through and through—without the dark side. And I would say, yes, I'm the dark side.

Going into the autopsy room and seeing beautiful people being cut up and how the pathologists went about it so nonchalantly was a pretty gruesome experience. I remember one autopsy in particular where a young sixteen-year-old girl had pulled out of an auto rest park (where my parents first met) and failed to look both ways. She was crushed by a speeding truck. The pathologist that night happened to be Japanese and approached the steel slab the girl was laying on almost ceremoniously. Before he began the autopsy, he placed a towel over her private parts as if to preserve what was left of the girl's dignity before he started to carve her up. It was a decent thing for him to do as he went about the indecent job of removing and examining what had been her vital organs. All I could think of that night was how thankful I was that the girl's parents were not there to observe what was being done to their beautiful child. And then I saw babies who were killed in car accidents undergo the same process. I forced myself to remain cool while watching a form of clinical butchery, but then, when I came home, I started dipping into the Jack Daniels about ten or eleven at night, just because I couldn't take it. Three years of watching the autopsies and three years defending people who had committed crimes was taking a toll on me. I found that I hated the practice of law, even though I was good at it. Tom Lambert had warned me that the practice of law would harden my heart or break it. It was doing both. I enjoyed being on the city council and the school board, dealing with social issues and trying to be a voice of moderation. So, I gravitated toward public service just to get away from dealing with the dark side of human nature.

When Bill Hathaway announced he was running against Margaret Chase Smith, a number of my friends said I'd be really good at running for Congress. I started thinking that if I run and lose, I'll have almost statewide visibility, which would be good for the law firm. At that point, we were starting to get a higher class of clientele. If I win, I have a new opportunity. When Joe Sewall, Ken MacLeod, and most of all, Bob Monks, came to me and said they wanted me to run and would support me, I said yes. Bob said it would be helpful if the two of us ran the next year. He'd run for the Senate and I would run for the House. It would be great for the party.

Jed Lyons: Tell us what Monks was doing at the time.

Bill Cohen: Bob was running against Margaret Chase Smith in the primary. He came from an old Maine family. His father was a minister, his background goes a long way back into Maine history, but it was really on the theological side, rather than the business side. But, of course, he had a brilliant mind as well, having gone to Harvard, Cambridge University, and elsewhere. I thought he was too smart to be in politics, if I can put it that way. He had too much of everything, you know. He was too tall, he was too smart, he was too well educated, he was too well-spoken. He didn't speak the same language that most ordinary people do in Maine. I'll never forget one of his first campaign stops was in Machiasport or Eastport and Bob showed up at a local event driving a car that had New Hampshire license plates. It was a rental car that he had picked up at an airport, but it added to the notion that he wasn't really from Maine.

Chris Potholm: You know, Monks was really smart and really talented and he did a tremendous job for the Republican Party in Maine, recruiting and supporting good candidates and getting rid of the Big Box on the ballot. Maine Republicans owe him a lot, but he was just too big for the state, metaphorically and physically. If he had run for the Senate in a big state, in Ohio or New York or Pennsylvania, he could have done that, but he was too big and did whatever he wanted and said whatever he wanted. He might have actually done a pretty good job, except he ran against Margaret Chase Smith and Ed Muskie. He saw himself in the U.S. Senate, not in Congress or the Blaine House. He could probably have been either of those pretty easily. I have one Monks story. Hattie Bickmore, the chair of the Republican Party in Maine, invited Henry Kissinger up to get some sort of award. Now Monks was very much against the war in Vietnam, and, for some reason, he insisted on riding in a limo from the airport. Hattie had invited me, too. I guess she knew more about Monks at that point than I did. Anyway, there's a driver and I'm in the front seat and in the back is Hattie, Monks, with Henry Kissinger in the middle. Monks decided that he was going to punish Henry Kissinger for the Vietnam War. We get into the car and Monks lights up a cigar that's about a foot long and he begins to exhale it right at Kissinger. Kissinger is just totally bewildered and trapped, his bodyguards are in the second chase car, he's trapped and Kissinger says, "You should roll down the window" and so Monks rolls down the window about a half inch and continues puffing the smoke at Kissinger. I'm trying to deflect things by asking, "Now when we bombed Cambodia, were most of the B-52s on Guam or in Thailand?"

I don't know if you remember this, Bill, but Kissinger had somehow brought a lot of books to sign at this dinner. You and he and the other celebs were up on a little raised stage, and people at the dinner started to go out and get books and bring them up to Kissinger and so he was being interrupted at this dinner, and he was signing and then, Bill, you signaled me, I was in the back with the other staffers, and you said, "Go over and stop that." And sure, okay, that's what I'm here for. Well, by now the line has seven or eight people in it and they're all excited. I said, "no, no, wait until the Secretary is finished eating" and the second guy in line says, "Get lost." Then Kissinger stands up and says, "Chris, Chris, let them come. Let them come." Like he was a rock star. So, I went back to the staffers for everybody else and they were laughing and saying, "That went well."

Jed Lyons: What was your impression of Kissinger, Chris?

Chris Potholm: Impression? Oh, well, he was obviously very smart and talented and a super self-promoter. I mean why did he need a bodyguard in Portland, Maine, but still, at 99, he's writing important books and world leaders are still checking in.

Bill Cohen: Well, a quick thing on Kissinger. I've known him all of these years. In fact, he's had me and Janet to his country home in Connecticut. They invited us and Lee Kuan Yew, who was the giant of Singapore for so many years, and Lee and his wife came and we spent the weekend together with Kissinger. Henry is the Delphic Oracle. "What will happen if I do this tomorrow?" and Kissinger will give an answer, which is ambiguous. You raise the issue or the problem, and Henry always talks about the need to have a comprehensive solution, but he rarely gives you the details of what the solution should be. But his books are brilliant, I still have all his books and I love reading them just because he's a master of language, and one that's not his first language.

Jed Lyons: When did you decide to make the run for Congress and what was it that helped you to decide? Was it Monks who kind of talked you into it or was it Joe Sewall or did you just know you wanted to do it?

Bill Cohen: No, it was a combination. I got to know Joe Sewall well through the Foley campaign that went bust. I also got to know Ken MacLeod during that campaign. I knew Bob Monks was going to pour a lot of money into the campaign, and that I would not have a problem with raising funds. I was unhappy being a small-town lawyer dealing with small-time stuff.

Jed Lyons: Tell us a little bit about Sewall and Macleod. We know about Monks. What's their background?

Bill Cohen: Well, Joe was the CEO of a big forestry and engineering consulting company. He wore khaki slacks and loafers and looked like Joe lunch bucket, nothing pretentious about him. A good guy, pretty liberal, I think, in terms of his outlook on life.

Just a fun guy to be with, and he practiced the brand of Republicanism that we could identify with. Ken MacLeod was a little more conservative. I think Harry Richardson's a little more liberal, but that troika kind of encouraged me. Bob Monks was a young man, he was 10 years older than me. We both looked like the new Republicans coming in and the old were going out. It gave me a chance to build a higher profile.

Jed Lyons: Why did you decide to hire Chris as your campaign manager?

Bill Cohen: I considered running about the same time I decided to run for the mayorship. I thought being Mayor of Bangor and running for Congress would be a much better profile for me than simply being a city council member running for Congress. Being Mayor would give me more credibility. So it was important that I won that campaign, which is within the council. There were a number of other candidates to contend with, one of them being Bob Baldacci (the father of John Baldacci who years later would become a congressman and Maine's governor) who owned the Baltimore restaurant that later became Mama Baldacci's. As mayor I took on issues that were not routine. For example, when Nixon flew back from the Middle East, it would be in 1971, he landed in Bangor. There was a small group of demonstrators at what used to be the Dow Air Force Base that we had turned into Bangor International Airport. The people demonstrating held up some anti-Nixon signs and the Secret Service just ripped the signs down even before Nixon had arrived. And so I called for an investigation into what had happened at the airport and I wrote a long three-page letter saying why this was wrong. The Secret Service didn't cooperate with the local police and just came in and bulldozed them over.

So that got me into criticizing, not Nixon himself, but the whole process of what I saw was a policy of suppressing political dissent. I thought if I'm going to be dealing with these types of issues, then I need to have someone I can trust and, frankly, there was no one that I knew in Bangor that had the capability I needed and there was no one else I trusted more than Chris.

Chris Potholm: I said, "Hell, I don't know anything about running a campaign, but I'll do it. I can learn on the job."

Bill Cohen: What I remember most about Chris at that time is he internalized everything. There was never a bottle of Maalox that he didn't have in his hand. I don't know how many bottles of Maalox he consumed, but he developed an ulcer during the campaign.

Jed Lyons: It was during the walk.

Chris Potholm: Well, before we go down that road, and I will have a few things to say about that, I do want to return to Harry Richardson and Ken MacLeod because they were really the big honchos and they had reached across the aisle to save the Maine income tax with Ken Curtis. They really cared about the state. Bill and I were up in Augusta for dinner with them and a couple of other reps. Bill was talking to Joe and Ken and I was sitting at the other end of the table with a state rep from down in Hancock or Washington County, call him Ralph, and so they're talking about this bill LD something and I turned to him and I said "Ralph, are you for this" and he said, "Well, I don't know, I haven't talked to Joe. I do pretty much everything 'Snort' tells me." And I said, "well then, you're going to be for Bill," and he said, "Oh yes, if he's for your boy, that's good enough for me." I said "Well, why are you in the legislature, Ralph?" and he said, "Well, you know I'm a lobsterman and it's January, and I could be off Matinicus Rock in the smoke, or I could be sitting here. Then there's that per diem. You can live like a king on the per diem here, and loose women. Okay, there are a lot of loose women in Augusta and they ain't all in the legislature, you know what I mean?" Joe Sewall (also known as "Snort") and Harry and Ken, those guys just loved Bill. I think they saw Bill as a younger version of themselves.

Bill Cohen: Ralph Leonard was Joe Sewall's pal.

Chris Potholm: I remember, at one point he made you write an essay on "why I believe I am a capitalist." He said, "I'm not putting in any more money, Bill, until you sit down to write a paragraph on why I am a capitalist."

Jed Lyons: Chris, were you surprised when Bill asked you and did you have any reservations about taking it on?

Chris Potholm: We were autodidacts from Bowdoin, blue-collar guys used to struggle, and at that point I thought I was going to run for governor. I had all these books, but I remember Bill at that moment and I'm thinking "I'm going to get paid for on-the-job training, you know, and this will be great." And then I said "Oh Bill, we're Democrats, right? "No, no, no, no," he said "We're Republicans. The Democratic Party is all filled with young people, and the Republican Party, the average person is 85 years old. There's no room for us in the Democratic Party. I was for McCarthy and then I was for Bobby Kennedy, but I said OK." I was very excited and I went and looked at all my books and I crossed out "for governor" and put "for Congress." And then I did do a lot of studying about those people who had run against Hathaway in Maine's 2nd District. I was absolutely convinced that if people like Foley or Maynard Connors could get 40 percent of the vote, Bill would certainly run much better. And it was an open seat to boot. I was sure he'd become a great campaigner. I remember one quick little story. Abbott Green, his opponent, was very conservative. He'd been around the track and lived down in Washington County, and so on our first trip down there I was the driver and we stopped to get gas and I said to Bill, "You kind of go in there and start talking." Bill did. There is this old Maine guy and Bill says, "Hi. I'm Bill Cohen" and the guy says "Yeh?" And Bill says "Well, I'm down from Bangor" and the guy says "Yeh?" "Well," says Bill, "I'm just doing a little politicking" and the guys says "Yeh?" and Bill says, "I guess we'll take a couple of cokes with our gas." So I can see there's going to be a learning curve so I take Bill to the next supermarket we saw, I think it was in Calais. So Bill goes in and starts saying hello and I've got this clipboard and I'm anxious to see what the issues are. And Bill goes up to these four or five little old ladies (of course probably 20 years younger then), but he starts talking to them and they start bobbing their heads and smiling. After he leaves, I came over and said, "You seem like you liked him." "Oh yes, we like him!" "Well, what do you like about him?" and they laugh and one of them says, "You know, I like his blue eyes." I got the message. I don't know if you remember that, Bill, on this trip we're in Lubec and I'm the driver and you get a little nervous because we're going to be late and I point to Eastport across the water and say "How long could it take?" and one guy says "Quite a while. You have to drive all the way, around. Take about an hour." So no cell phones, naturally, so I have to call ahead and tell the school we're going to be late. Bill says, "I think I have to get a real driver."

Bill Cohen: One thing I remember is going down to Bar Harbor and I was there to meet the chairman of a big textile company in South Carolina. Roger Milliken was his name. He had this place on the ocean; it's got a saltwater pool right out in the back of this big mansion. There was no small chit chat. He said, "I know you're here to ask me for help." I said, "Yes, sir." "Well, let me ask you how you feel about Social Security." "You mean the cost-of-living increase they're talking about?" "No, I want to know what you think about the Social Security program?" "Well, I'm kind of for it." I was stunned at what he was asking. "Young man, this conversation is over." He had me shown to the front door.

CHAPTER III

Oral History Discussion with Secretary Bill Cohen and Professor Christian Potholm

Tuesday, May 18, 2021

Jed Lyons: Bill, with respect to why you ran, who were the people who influenced your decision?

Chris Potholm: I have actually been thinking a lot about those early days. You had a headquarters in Bangor with a woman who worked there who was pregnant, and her name, I can't remember that exactly, but she was your secretary, and then also a woman who was the wife of one of your law partners.

Bill Cohen: Sharlene Weatherbee?

Chris Potholm: I remember that with my ulcer and her being pregnant there was a steady stream of us going back and forth from the bathroom in the Bangor office. I remember the headquarters. People were wandering in and out, homeless people, people off the streets, and Trish Baldwin would try to get them to stuff envelopes and do things. It was free coffee and donuts and it was really kind of wide open. The campaign headquarters didn't look like anything you'd read about in a book, with structure, things like that.

Bill Cohen: She was living in Winterport, but was actually from the South. Her husband was an architect. Very charming and very pretty.

Chris Potholm: I don't know if you guys knew this, but both my grandfather and my uncle were killed in light plane crashes. So I have no idea why I suggested that we have this fly around where we went from Bangor to Presque Isle where you announced up there, then we came back to Bangor. And that first ride was a terrifying flight because the automatic pilot got stuck halfway and the plane shot up directly. I was terrified and I tried to remember from my science classes how far up do we go before we run out of oxygen? We got to Presque Isle and there was this one TV station there, I think there's still just one. And we went there for a pre-interview, and I was all excited because I had come up with a big issue for Aroostook County. I discovered that McDonalds would not use their potatoes so I thought this was a great issue. But the station manager said don't jump to conclusions. "You know why they don't?" I said no. He said, "The Maine potato people refuse to grade them high enough." He said they do them in crappy little bags with dirt on them. I think you better find another issue. And then, on the way back, the pilot, the same pilot that put us into this great upswing, it was a blizzard and he turned the plane on its side and didn't want to lose visual.

Bill Cohen: I remember that and several others. I remember one of the flights, I can't recall, it would have been later than '72. I was in Joe Sewall's plane and we were coming from Presque Isle and we ran into a tremendous thunderstorm. We dropped a couple of thousand feet straight down and my ears, my watch, I had an Omega watch and the crystal on the watch popped, it was such a dramatic drop. I had a cold and my ears filled up. I still have that problem where I can't hear well, but that was one of the times I don't want to repeat. That was one of the times I thought I was going to buy it. One other time, I was trying to land somewhere Down East and I was flying back from Washington, so it was later than 1972, but anyway, that one came close. Chris is right on the one he's talking about. The plane just dropping straight down for several thousand feet occurred because we got caught in a draft from a lightning storm and the plane just dropped out and lost altitude immediately.

Jed Lyons: The memorable flight I recall is the one during the walk when you landed in a helicopter in Lisbon in a parking lot and threw up this huge cloud of dust. Everyone had to dive for cover to protect themselves from the flying dust and debris. Bill, when did you make the official announcement that you were running in the primary and what was it like when you did so? Do you have any memories of how you felt at the time?

Bill Cohen: I was serving as the mayor of Bangor at the time. I had run for the position against Robert Baldacci. The Baldacci family was very close to my parents and especially to my Dad who used to supply bread and rolls to Baldacci's Italian restaurant. He was older than me and had served on the city council longer than I had, as I recall. He was a respected businessman. At the time I was elected mayor, I hadn't yet decided to run for Congress, but I knew that if I was ever to make the decision to do so, the title of mayor would be more important politically than that of city councilman.

Jed Lyons: Chris, what was the ethnic makeup of Aroostook County in 1972?

Chris Potholm: Well, there was the southern part down near Houlton that was rock-ribbed Republican like Hancock and part of Washington and then there was the St. John Valley that hadn't elected a Republican ever. But in between was Presque Isle and Caribou and Limestone and they were swing districts.

Jed Lyons: What about upper Aroostook County?

Chris Potholm: Solid French Canadian. They were Acadian French.

Jed Lyons: Violette was from where?

Bill Cohen: Van Buren.

Jed Lyons: He was an Acadian French-American?

Chris Potholm: Yes, and Louis Jalbert, Mr. Democrat, he loved Joe Sewall, whose nickname was "Snort," and he got invited to Snort's fishing camp up in Canada and he was so proud of that he talked about it for a decade afterward.

Jed Lyons: Back to the announcement.

Chris Potholm: So I remember the best advice I got from a campaign manager's point of view was from Hoddie Hildreth who was an upscale Brahmin Republican who ran in the 1st District and got slaughtered, but he took me aside and he said, the one thing you gotta remember in the Republican primary is to stress familiar thoughts, don't bring a lot of new stuff because these Republican voters in the primary, they want you to think you're like them, they don't want any new ideas and, of course, we young bucks wandering around the state with a lot of great ideas, this was counterintuitive to us. Whenever we had a choice in that primary I listened to that voice: don't rock the boat. We had very bad intelligence, you know, we were told that Green was way ahead. Everybody knew him. He ran for Senate and he was a conservative, and I remember that first trip we took down there I felt like we were the Roman legions crossing the Rhine River and going into Germany. It was just scary, but it turned out hardly anybody knew him either.

Jed Lyons: Bill, a question for you, a sensitive question. Your last name sounds Jewish and you're running in a state that has never elected anyone with a Jewish surname. What were your thoughts about that when you decided to run District-wide? You're half Irish and half Jewish, but your last name sounds Jewish.

Bill Cohen: Well, actually, I was told that I couldn't get elected with my name being Cohen. I said wait a minute, I'm only half Jewish and people will look at me and see that I'm more Irish than Jewish. It will be a case of cognitive dissonance. I saw it as an asset, because I was different from what they expected to see because of my last name.

Jed Lyons: They said you looked like Robert Redford.

Bill Cohen: As a matter of fact, the movie *The Candidate* came out that summer. Chris may remember.

Chris Potholm: We went to it together.

Bill Cohen: Okay, that was in Bangor.

Chris Potholm: Yes, and you identified with Robert Redford and I identified with the campaign manager that had glasses and there was a fabulous scene in it in which Robert Redford says, as you started to say in the primary "I want to go where I want to go, and say what I want to say" and then the campaign manager writes on the back of a matchbook "You Lose." I show the film to my class every single year. It's the best show ever done on American politics. As the slogan went, "Mackay: the better way."

Bill Cohen: It was such a cynical movie. Here's this idealistic young guy who has all of these great thoughts about saving the planet and by the end of the movie, he's been completely corrupted by the system. "Tell me, what do I do now?" he says.

Chris Potholm: He gets to go to Washington.

Jed Lyons: Bill, did you encounter any overt anti-semitism during the campaign?

Bill Cohen: No, no, I mean, you know, it may have been subtle and covert but openly I can't think of it. I knew it was there when I went down to see Milliken in Bar Harbor.

Jed Lyons: Milliken, the textile guy?

Bill Cohen: Right, Roger Milliken. I sensed it with him. It was almost tangible, especially when he asked me to think about Social Security. While sitting out on the terrace near his large pool behind his mansion, he said, "Tell me what you think of Social Security." I was confused by the ambiguity of the question and said, "you mean as to whether there should be any cost-of-living increases in Social Security payments?" Milliken said, "No, do you believe there should be a Social Security program?" I said, "Yes, I do." He then said, "I'm sorry, son, but this conversation is over." He gestured for me to leave. I didn't know if he was a bigot. Sometimes it's a case of having a sixth sense about someone or that the pheromones emanating around certain individuals give the impression that we don't like Jews—or a half one—that's even worse. But I never encountered anything overt that I can recall. Chris may have gotten something in the mail, but I never saw any of it.

Chris Potholm: We thought that Green was way ahead and we had to catch up, but Bob Monks did a poll in March that showed Cohen at 12 and Green at 10 so that meant that almost eight out of ten people, nobody knew anything. And I remember once we were at a school, I can't remember where it was, I think it was down in Calais or somewhere down there. Anyway, Bill's walking around shaking hands with high school kids and one kid came up and said, "I know who you guys are. You're from that TV show Mission Impossible." "Sometimes it feels like it, kid," I said.

Jed Lyons: I don't recall any anti-semitism on the walk. I was one of the advance men traveling one day ahead of Bill trying to find Republicans for us to visit the next day and a place to spend the night. I never encountered any anti-semitism aimed at Bill in Maine in 1972. Bill, when you first started your campaigns, your first attempts to connect with voters, how did you feel when you met voters face to face? You had done it, of course, as a city councilman. You did it as mayor briefly, but now you're in places that are unfamiliar to you, in rural areas. How did you feel when you first started campaigning against Green in the primary?

Bill Cohen: Well, I worried that I would not appeal to them because I was a "city boy" coming in and trying to establish a relationship with rural or country folks. The one thing I think I had early on, and maybe it came from the practice of law, was how to persuade people that I was credible and that they could trust me. I had the opportunity as a young lawyer to try cases before many juries and had to go up against some of the "old timers" who were in their 60s and 70s wearing baggy pants and spotted ties. I discovered pretty quickly that juries look at you in terms of how you dress or whether you're overdressed; whether you are seen as being "too smart" on a given issue. You have to lock eyes with jurors and try to persuade them they should believe you.

I think six years of doing that helped me relate to people at all different levels. Most of the people on juries were country folk. Penobscot County is not exactly a metropolitan area so they came from rural areas and I think that trying civil and criminal cases before them helped a great deal. In addition, I think teaching at the University of Maine for five years and getting in front of students three times a week, trying to relate to them and sell them on the concept of what the law was in theory and what it was in practice helped. As a result, I never felt uncomfortable in front of people. Also, I came from pretty modest beginnings. Although my Dad ran a small bakery, because of his work ethic, he was viewed as a "blue-collar" kind of guy. I worked in the bakery on weekends and related to people who were not wealthy, just average people eager to buy bread for their families. So I felt comfortable, even though people who had never met me might think I was a "city slicker."

Jed Lyons: You're running in a district that has lots of different ethnicities. You've got the French Canadians, as Chris points out, down in Lewiston, which is in your district. You've got the Acadians in Aroostook County and you have the old Yankee families in many rural parts of the district. What were the other ethnic blocks in the 2nd District that you dealt with? Chris, will you describe that?

Chris Potholm: There weren't any that mattered. I mean there were the Swedes in Aroostook County, there were some Irish Protestants in

Washington County, there were quite a few Irish in Bangor and also Lewiston. A lot of people don't know that before the French came down from Quebec, Lewiston was an Irish city. They built those canals for the shoe factories and the textile factories, and the Irish built a railroad to Quebec. In Lewiston in the 19th century, there were Irish Catholic churches and French Catholic churches, there were Irish unions and French unions. Among the Irish in Lewiston, we referred to him as Bill Cohane.

Jed Lyons: Bill, did you have any trouble relating to any of those ethnic groups or was it all pretty much the same to you?

Bill Cohen: It was pretty much the same. I considered myself as having a workingman's background from my dad's little bakery. Actually I could relate to them more than I could to the "establishment" types.

It goes back to the question of my ethnic background. To the upper-class Protestant majority, I was a Jew. To the Jewish people, I was a "goyim" or non-Jew. I found it difficult to negotiate my way through different levels of bigotry. I just found it easier to relate to the working-class people who comprised most of the constituency of the 2nd Congressional District.

I also discovered that my law practice was helpful to me in preparing to relate to people. It also generated considerable hostility from the legal and business communities. In one case I handled, I sued my best friend's father who had run the Bangor & Aroostook Railroad and was serving as chairman of the board of the Merrill Trust Company (bank) along with the State of Maine's Recreational Authority.

I was told by one of the bank's attorneys that I would never succeed in the practice law again in the city for my arrogance in bringing the lawsuit against such prominent individuals. So I had the challenge to prove to the business establishment that I was "conservative enough" (or in their minds controllable enough) to have their support.

Jed Lyons: Who held the economic reins of the 2nd District in 1972? Was it the Yankees who controlled the big businesses, the paper companies, the shoemaking families like the Bass family, for example? Was it still the case in 1972 that most of the economic power was still in the hands of the Yankee old guard?

Bill Cohen: Yes, the large paper companies owned most of the real estate in Maine. These were the giant paper companies, you know, Georgia Pacific, Great Northern, St. Regis, The Dead River Company, International Paper.

Chris Potholm: The reason it's hard to remember the names is they've all been taken over two or three times by other paper companies. Champion International got taken as chickens to be plucked. I had great suspicion of rich people, and I was there to take the eggs out of their hen house. I never felt that we had trouble with the working-class people, not once in the whole campaign, but these rich people that, to this day, these old rich white males are still whining about the loss of privileges and their loss of income.

Jed Lyons: What else was there besides paper companies? There were, I remember, a lot of factories that Bill had to walk through where new shoes were manufactured. What were the other big businesses in the 2nd District? Agriculture?

Bill Cohen: Basically, there was agriculture, textiles, and tourism.

Jed Lyons: And shoe mills.

Bill Cohen: There also was Bath Iron Works, shipbuilding employees, many of whom were from the Lewiston-Auburn area, that we had to appeal to as an important part of the constituency.

Chris Potholm: But that was easy. Just build ships. More ships. Bigger ships. More expensive ships.

Jed Lyons: What about summer residents? Bill, you mentioned Milliken. He was a Southerner with a summer home in Maine. Were there other summer residents who were influential in the campaign that you got to know?

Bill Cohen: Rockefellers, David and his wife, who was a great environmentalist. She became a supporter. In Northeast Harbor, there was another wealthy summer resident, Brooke Astor. She and her friends were liberal aristocrats from New York. They were very pro-environment and didn't want to see any heavy industry come to that part of the state. They became supporters. It was really interesting to have Roger Milliken on one side of the equation and then you had the Rockefellers and Astors on the other side. I have this great picture of Nelson Rockefeller at the '72 Republican convention and they're booing him. Rockefeller is smiling broadly while making an obscene gesture to the conventioneers. When I was sitting on the Judiciary Committee and he appeared as the nominee for vice president when Gerald Ford became president, I showed him the photo and he signed it "Rocky"!

Attorney General Elliot Richardson came up to support my candidacy. A dinner was being held in Androscoggin or Oxford County. We picked him up in Lewiston and drove him to the dinner. When I introduced him that night I said, "We're sorry we're a little bit late, but I had to stop the car. Elliot saw something on the side of the road on a big billboard that read, 'Is there intelligent life on Earth?'" Elliot got out of the car and wrote on the billboard "Yes, but I'm only visiting." Elliot was amused.

Jed Lyons: I remember the dinner we had with him that night, Bill. I wrote to my parents the next day, I still have the letter, I wrote that I never before heard a person utter a perfectly grammatical sentence that lasted 15 minutes. His elocution, his grammar, he was such an impressive, intelligent man. That was a very long, boozy night.

Bill Cohen: Well, the other thing he loved to do was to doodle. His doodles were famous. Every doodle was intricate and perfectly symmetrical, consisting of interconnected circles. They were frameable, they were so beautiful.

Chris Potholm: Right before and after you announced, didn't you fly down to Washington and have a meeting with Margaret Chase Smith and General Bill Lewis, and I think she said to you "What's a Monks man doing here?"

Bill Cohen: As you know, she had a way of smiling at you that was not at all sincere. She said, "I understand you're supporting Bob Monks in the primary." I said, "No Senator, I'm not supporting him. He's running on his own, just as I am." She refused to accept my declaration of neutrality. "No, you're working with him to undermine my candidacy." I tried to persuade her that my staying neutral did not mean that I was opposing her, but she was not open to persuasion. It turned out to be an exceedingly short meeting. I don't think I ever had a meeting with her afterward on the campaign trail. We tried to latch on to wherever she was going and became part of her whole entourage getting into a town. And they would try to stay ahead of us, so we couldn't feed off her popularity.

Chris Potholm: Oh, this is a key point, Jed. We have to interview Jim Harrington. He was at the University of Maine, poli-sci kid and head of Youth for Margaret Chase Smith. She was having a big rally in Old Town, and we were also there, and he was very loyal, very faithful to us. He was a very important figure. I remember once there was a Margaret Chase Smith fundraiser, and she was up on the stage, and we were there and her eyesight wasn't very good and she looked out at the audience and Harrington had put Cohen buttons on everybody, so there were the Margaret Chase Smith and Bill Cohen buttons on everyone. That was the kind of thing that this kid did, and it was very, very effective, of course. I got a terrible call from Bill Webster and, you know, talk about threading a needle. I mean Monks was our primary fundraiser, he had provided us with all kinds of guidance, he got us a media guy and I remember the budget, I saw it somewhere again, I think the budget for the primary was $55,000 and the general election was $100,000. We had a meeting and, in the words of our consultant, Mike Harkins, "we're in for the whole schmear."

Jed Lyons: Chris, what do you think Bob Monks spent on the campaign for the Senate that year?

Chris Potholm: I'd have to look it up, but, at the time, it was the largest amount of money ever spent per vote in the history of Maine. I do have one funny story. Monks knew he was going to lose, and he knew we were going to win and I was the sacrificial lamb. I had to go to the Topsham Fair Mall and it's the weekend before the primary vote and he had a lot of contacts in the media, so I think it was CBS News, they had a whole film crew up there. And there was Bob Monks, big huge Bob Monks, in a yellow lemon drop suit and he's waving his arms around like that, and there were only about 40 people there. Lil Caron who subsequently became mayor of Lewiston was a big Cohen supporter. One of her children or grandchildren was deaf. She brought the whole deaf school up there. So here's CBS News coverage and Monks is waving wildly around and doing this and that and the person that was signing was signing and then 30 or 40 people are signing back and forth, and it was great agitation in the footage. So I turned to Lil and asked what's going on. She said "Look, they were promised Kentucky Fried Chicken a half an hour ago. You better get that chicken because they're mad." Fun times!

Bill Cohen: There was a major event planned for Senator Smith in her hometown of Skowhegan. For some reason, I was distracted, forgot about it. Then I was told that the event was going to start in 35 minutes! I jumped into my car and drove from Bangor to Skowhegan in 35 minutes, racing along on a secondary road, at times reaching 85–90 mph.

Chris Potholm: I think you put your finger on something when you met with General Lewis, because you came back to me and told that story and I went and spoke to a Professor Hazelton in the Bowdoin education department and he'd been a Muskie supporter, he was in the original group, and I went and told him that. And he shook his head and said "Oh, dirty Margaret, old dirty Margaret, she is going to have General Lewis investigate." And right before the primary, Abbott Green had a huge story. AP, UPI, all the TV stations and it was a whole list of things that Lewis had dug up about what Monks has done and it was just this incredible litany of things that Monks had done to support Cohen, and it was supposed to be the Margaret anti-smear at the end of the campaign. And I remember, Bill, you turned it over to me to answer these charges, and I remember I thought this is just the last-minute smears that unfortunately now have become part of Maine's tradition.

Jed Lyons: Chris, how would you describe Abbott Green's campaign style and his campaign?

Chris Potholm: In 40 years, I never really disliked somebody the way I disliked him. He was a Trumpkanoid before there were Trumpkanoids. There was a nastiness, an edge to him. He supported Neil Bishop. He expected that this Cohen race was going be easy, and, you know, we went in and Bill took the candy away from him. Bill, you probably remember this. WCBB had an open mic call-in show in Lewiston, and Green was there and we had our staff call in. Every call was from a Cohen person. One question was, "Oh Mr. Green, is it true you weren't actually born in Maine?" and he said, "Well, I was born in Massachusetts and moved to Maine when I was one year old." And then the caller said, "So you weren't actually BORN in Maine but moved here from away."

Bill Cohen: That was you who made that call?

Chris Potholm: Moi? Moi?

Bill Cohen: Yes, and then you said that Abbott was not really "a Mainer," and you hung up. It really rattled him for the rest of the campaign.

Chris Potholm: Well, because it was a result of us dominating the whole thing WCBB did not have an open mic forum like this for three or four years. How would you compare him to the other people you ran against?

Bill Cohen: He was the nastiest of any of the others and Elmer was the nicest. He was a wonderful man.

Chris Potholm: Yes.

Bill Cohen: I just found a document. Do you remember one candidate called Cooney?

Chris Potholm: Yes, Leighton Cooney.

Bill Cohen: Leighton was a nice guy. In '78, I went for the Senate.

Jed Lyons: Against Bill Hathaway?

Bill Cohen: Yes.

Jed Lyons: Who was running in 1972 in the 1st District?

Chris Potholm: That was Bob Porteous. Monks recruited him and he got slaughtered by Peter Kyros.

Bill Cohen: Kyros was really slippery. During the very first year I was in office, there was a breakfast meeting our congressional delegation held for Maine constituents who had traveled to Washington. As I walked into the meeting, Kyros said, "Gee, Bill, I see you've recovered from all that heavy drinking last night. Hope you don't have a serious hangover." It really was outrageous for him to toss out a lie like that, but that's the kind of stuff he would do.

Jed Lyons: That reminds me that there was a pretty large Greek American population in Maine back then, wasn't there?

Bill Cohen: Yes, Peter Lupus ran one of the Greek restaurants in town and he hosted the annual Greek dance that was the social highlight of the year in Bangor.

Jed Lyons: In Biddeford, the Droggitis family had a restaurant called the WonderBar. That was in the 1st District.

Bill Cohen: There was the Vomvoris family who owned another Greek restaurant where my dad delivered bread.

Jed Lyons: Let's revisit the staffing of the campaign at the very beginning.

Chris Potholm: Trish Baldwin.

Bill Cohen: Exactly, Trisha Baldwin.

Jed Lyons: Who else was there at the very beginning of the primary campaign?

Chris Potholm: One important guy was a consultant named Mike Harkins. Monks brought him in because Bill and I had so little experience. He helped out with the media, did the TV commercials, and came up every couple of weeks.

Jed Lyons: Mike was from Delaware.

Chris Potholm: We called him "The Littlest Gunslinger." He had some good ideas. One I fought against, but he was right, and that was he insisted that we advertise in these weekly newspapers and, you know, I said, why do we want to do that? Well, you know those newspapers in those days, they sat around in the barbershop and at the fire department and at hairdressers and they sat there all week and so he made us advertise and they were very simple pitches about Bill and his family and some familiar thoughts, but I always thought that was very important. He was like a whirlwind. He had four or five campaigns going, he'd show up in Bangor, open his briefcase and start throwing out all the dirty laundry and underwear and whatnot. "It's in here somewhere, it's in here somewhere, I got some ideas for you."

Bill Cohen: He left the papers for our campaign on the plane.

Chris Potholm: Well, that's what I mean. He had all this stuff and at one point he came up with some ideas for us to do and I looked over his shoulder and it said, "great ideas for Pennsylvania District 7."

Bill Cohen: Our campaign strategy and finances, whatever, they were all packed into his little briefcase and he lost them on the plane.

Jed Lyons: He was on the payroll as a part-time employee, right? Advising as a consultant. When did Tom Daffron get involved?

Chris Potholm: He wasn't involved in the first campaign at all. No, he was working for Senator Chuck Percy.

Bill Cohen: He was the press secretary for Percy.

Jed Lyons: Okay. I knew he was working in Washington for you, Bill, in the summer of '73 so he must have joined you that year?

Bill Cohen: Yes, because Mike was not there to be an administrative assistant, I don't know whether he recruited Tom, but it was unheard of for a Senate staffer to want to come over and work for a freshman congressman.

Jed Lyons: Did Harkins work on other campaigns after '72?

Chris Potholm: Oh yeah, he continued to have a half-life until he became Secretary of State for Delaware.

Jed Lyons: So it was a pretty modest staff and obviously a very modest payroll if you only had $50,000 to spend in the primary. By the time you've won the primary, how many full-time employees were working for the campaign?

Chris Potholm: I think we had a lot of good young field people. Jed, I think you had Somerset, Piscataquis, Franklin, and Androscoggin. I think that's it. I'm trying to think now of when after the primary we had to field people in two or three counties. I think you were a field man for not just Lewiston, but didn't you have Piscataquis, Franklin, and Somerset.

Jed Lyons: Yes, I had four counties.

Bill Cohen: There was Jane Johnson from Houlton. I remember being told that I could not have a woman representing me in Aroostook, that it wouldn't sit well with the farmers. I said either she's going to represent me or no one will. She was terrific.

Jed Lyons: Chris, I remember that you spent a lot of time doing the analytical work of determining what the vote would be not just in every single county, but also in each township. I still have your tabulations of what you estimated the vote count would be in each of those. I remember you predicted the vote outcome almost to the exact percentage in the general election. You developed an ulcer. How did you recover from your ulcer? When did you recover? You were better by the time Bill was elected to Congress.

Chris Potholm: My worst period was right after Bowdoin fall classes began, and this thing, you know, went in cycles, it came back and the doctor said, you have to get off the campaign trail. And I think it was one of the hardest phone calls I ever had to make. I called Bill and I said, "Bill, I had this ulcer flare up again and the doctor said to take some time off from the campaign." Bill was very understanding. "Take as much time as you need." I hid in the Bowdoin library for several weeks. Being a campaign manager is very draining with a lot of responsibility and it got to me for sure.

Jed Lyons: When was the primary election?

Chris Potholm: June

Bill Cohen: And if I can just intervene here, I want to get back to the burdens that a campaign manager has in terms of holding it all together. I had been asked to manage the campaign of Howard Foley back in 1966. I knew nothing about the job. Howard had asked Doug Brown, a successful businessman who owned a chain of grocery stores, to be his finance chairman. He wasn't raising enough money to fund the campaign. Now at the ripe age of 26, I called him and said he wasn't doing his job. He had to dial it up. Well, that misguided comment resulted in Brown telling me that he thought it would be better for me to do the job, and he quit. So then I was campaign manager and finance chairman and didn't know enough about either job. But I found the stresses of trying to hold everything together emotionally draining.

Jed Lyons: So now we're in June and the general is in November. When was the decision made to do the walk?

Chris Potholm: Interesting side note. As campaign manager, I also kept the accounts. I was the guy with the checkbook and the records. The night of the primary, when we won 55-45 percent, we had a great celebration in Bangor. Unlike Muskie in 1954, our supporters didn't run out of liquid refreshment. There was a lot left over so I ended up with a half-gallon of gin that I put in the backseat of the campaign Vega. Imagine my chagrin when I woke up the next morning and went out and in the backseat of the car, on the floor, there were all the financial records and the checkbook and the gin bottle on top of them. It had all leaked out onto the checkbook and notes.

Sometime after that there was a strong financial committee set up with a guy named Tom Needham. The records were kept better after that.

By the way, the doctors didn't do very well with my ulcer. Today you can get some antibiotics, and so on. Then you had to drink Maalox or Mylanta and mess up your lower tract and you were told to drink rich cream to coat your stomach which was the worst thing for it. I did end up throwing my wristwatch away. Never worn one since. Of course, I drove lots of people mad thereafter asking "What time is it?"

CHAPTER IV

Oral History Discussion with Secretary Bill Cohen and Professor Christian Potholm

June 11, 2021

Jed Lyons: I sent both of you some clippings that I hoped might stimulate memories from the walk. I got a kick out of Chris's written instructions to the election watchers at the polls on election day where he says, "Bill Cohen's election hinges on your effectiveness in discouraging voter fraud. The Democrats have consistently toyed with the election results. Look intimidating and identify yourself as a Cohen volunteer."

Bill Cohen: Carry a .357 Magnum with you as you walk around (laughs).

Chris Potholm: God what fun we had in those days. Anything to fire up the troops. Actually, a few years later I was made Republican Statewide Head of Ballot Security by the Republican Chairman Jack Linnell—no doubt due to my law enforcement background—when Ronald Reagan ran for president the first time. No worries about compliance, I went hunting that day. Maine has such a solid record of honest elections, it's amazing.

Jed Lyons: The walk was the brainchild of Bob Loeb who was a student at Bowdoin. He came from Chicago and knew that the Illinois governor had done a similar walk across his state and so we decided to do the same thing in the sprawling 2nd District of Maine.

Bill Cohen: Yes, he was "Walking George Walker." He was the governor of Illinois and he had walked, not the entire state, but a big stretch of it, and there was also Senator Lawton Chiles from Florida. I went down to meet with Lawton Chiles. Of course, I got pushed off to a staffer. I asked how did you guys do it? He did not walk his entire state and didn't stay overnight in someone's home. He just walked. Those were the only two at the time, Illinois Governor Walker and Lawton Chiles, as I remember.

Jed Lyons: How did you get the audacious idea of doing a walk from one end of the state to the other and one that would include consecutive overnights in private homes over the course of many weeks?

Chris Potholm: I thought the whole idea was to cover as much of the state during that period in the summer when there wasn't much campaigning. It made sense in terms of the math and I never realized we would go beyond Houlton. But looking back on it, while it probably made the walk a lot more painful, I was adamant about Bill spending the night in a real person's home each night.

Bill Cohen: Actually, it was really enjoyable, partly because we would stay with families that were pretty modest, on the lower end of the economic spectrum. Not always, but as we got into the Lewiston area and into the Democratic areas, it was fun for me to be able to say, "Look, I come from these roots." If you look at the building where I was born on the top floor of a tenement house that was filled with immigrants, I certainly could relate to these families. They might have as many as six people around a table eating, probably pasta, or something comparable. And then, after the meal, they would invite their neighbors and expand from six to maybe 12 or 15 in the living room where I could sit, either in the middle, or on a sofa and just ask them what they thought about politics. What were they looking for, how can I help if I got there? It was really connecting to them in a way that was unique, that a politician would spend the night with them, eat with their family. I knew that they would tell at least 15 more of their friends the next day, and their friends would tell 15 more. I never felt exhausted, even though some of these meetings went on till 10 or 11 o'clock. They had to go to work and I had to be up and ready by 6:30 to get out there and start from the spot that we marked where we had stopped the night before. And we always made sure there was no cheating. The media would basically know where we stopped, and they would come out to see if we were starting from there. I never felt exhausted. I was energized by the whole experience and it wasn't quite the "Second Coming," but it felt like that on many occasions where people, especially in the rural areas, would sit out on their porches and wait for me to walk by. We had a rule that I would never go up and try to knock on the doors of homes. Along the walk, if people were outside, I would walk up to their driveway or on their porch but I wouldn't be knocking on doors and disturbing their privacy. The local newspaper would say, Cohen is scheduled to walk here tomorrow morning, and so people would actually be out there, some for hours, waiting for me to walk by and talk with them. So, it took on a messianic feeling for me. One, they couldn't believe that I would make that effort, and two, that I would spend time with them. So that was energizing in and of itself and I never felt tired. My feet were hurting because of the big footwear mistakes I made at the beginning of the campaign and even that turned out to be a political plus when I went to the hospital to have my blisters cut and then my feet taped so that I could go back out on the walk. A photo was taken of me soaking my feet in a steel tub that appeared in the local papers. I think there were two occasions when I had to seek medical treatment.

Jed Lyons: I remember that you went into many shoe factories and were handed a new pair of boots. It was the last thing you wanted to see, but you gamely put them on and walked out and your feet were killing you.

Bill Cohen: We gave them all away at the next stop.

Jed Lyons: Yes.

Bill Cohen: Every time we stopped in a small town they were doing a fundraiser for a charitable cause, and would ask me to donate something. I said, "Yes, my shoes." I could afford to do that because at the time there were a number of shoe factories in Oxford county where we had started out. We were almost the shoemaking center of the country before the massive transfer of those jobs to Asia. I always looked forward on the walk to see if there were any kids playing basketball. I would ask if I could shoot baskets with them and they would be impressed that this old guy could still shoot. And so that was part of the fun of it as well, showing off a little bit in the pickup games. Beyond that, I just recall looking ahead, watching out for cars. You may recall, Chris, that was the route where the Canadian cars came flying down 70-75 miles an hour on a two-lane highway. I kept looking to make sure they weren't getting too close. I think a couple of times people tossed bottles out of their car windows. They didn't come close to hitting me, but it was a warning sign that not everybody was honking and waving and shouting hallelujah. I remember that walking in the rain was really dangerous because visibility is down, wipers were clicking away, and the people were still traveling pretty fast. Those were the moments I worried about the most during the walk.

I believe that it was Jane Johnson of Houlton who arranged for me to take part in a race at the Spud Speedway near Presque Isle. I'm not sure at this time whether it was on The Walk or a year later. I had no knowledge that she had done that so I was surprised when I arrived at the Saturday night event. They would get these old banged-up cars, remove the interior padding, and weld the car door shut, so you had to climb through the windows to get into the car. This was not something that I was eager to do, but the organizers of the race handed me a helmet and gave me little choice. I might get injured if I entered the race or be wounded politically if I rejected their offer. They had a picture of me with a guy called the "Flying Frenchman of Madawaska" who looked at me as if I was going to be his meal on the dinner table that night. The cars had no mufflers, they were stripped down to the metal bones of the car. No dashboard, and just two gears where you go from low to high very quickly. I said "Well okay, I guess I can do this." There were about six or seven cars in the race, and I thought I would go to the very end of the starting line and let all of the cars pull out ahead of me and let them get ahead of me and just hang in last place. That's not what they had in mind. They insisted that I be the lead so that the other drivers could bang me all over and ultimately push me off the track.

Every time I tried to slow down, Bam! Someone smacked me from behind. Then another car hit me from the side. Bam! Two cars had me pinned on the inside and were trying to push me off the track. The fans in the stands were cheering and it wasn't for me! I made it around the track, I think, a couple of times and then I pulled off. They were disappointed that I wasn't having as much fun as they were and said, "Well, you got to stay here. We want you to flag the next race." They had kind of a plank-like structure built over the speedway and they had me walk out on the platform and wave the flag to start the race. Unfortunately, I had to stay on the platform until the race finished. The problem was while I was up there, one of the tires came off the cars on the last curve and was bouncing toward me on the structure. I managed to retreat just in time.

I didn't get hit by the tire, I didn't get turned over into a ditch on the racetrack, but this wasn't a great idea even though the local press played up my being a good sport.

Jed Lyons: I remember we entered you into a fundraiser "swimathon" at the YMCA in Lewiston and you were not happy about that, either.

Bill Cohen: I had the flu or something and I was feeling really ill, but you said, "You gotta swim."

Jed Lyons: And you did. You got in a bathing suit and you swam up and down the pool and you earned money that you contributed for each lap. Being competitive, you continued to swim and swim and swim to make money for the YMCA. This was right in the middle of the walk. You were exhausted before you even got in the pool.

Bill Cohen: Right.

Jed Lyons: You weren't happy with us that day.

Bill Cohen: No, well, probably many other days, too. I remember that one well.

Chris Potholm: How about the time you two decided it was a good idea to do some politicking in the drive-in theater?

Jed Lyons: That was in Houlton near the Canadian line.

Bill Cohen: The movie playing that night was *BoxCar Bertha*. The goal was to get there by 6 o'clock or 6:30 as the cars were coming in and shake the hands of the drivers. Unfortunately, we didn't get there until about nine and it had already become dark and we said well okay, what do we do now, folks? And Jed said, "Well, we're here so we might as well give it a shot." And so I went around knocking on the steamed-up windows of the cars.

Jed Lyons: I remember that night. We had nothing planned, no dinner at a private home or an event. And so I suggested that we go to the drive-in and meet some voters and you said, "Are you crazy?" But, because we wanted to meet voters, we went and when we got there, there were no voters to be seen. So I suggested that you go over to a nearby car and knock on the window. You knocked on the driver side window and there was no response. Then, all of a sudden, the backseat window comes down and the guy says, "What the hell are you doing?" and you said, "Well, I'm Bill Cohen and I'm running for Congress" and the rear window went right back up. We stopped by a few more cars and the same thing happened. Do you remember that?

Bill Cohen: Oh, I do, I do and I've got you to blame. That's one of the more memorable events, *Boxcar Bertha*. There was also the time, I think I mentioned before, when I went into a bar. And there were two rules I talked about: don't go into a beauty shop where women are having their hair done. That's a no, no, because they would scream for me to get out.

That was their time and their place to become beautiful. Men are not wanted! The other rule was to never go into a bar. I had violated both rules of no beauty shops and no bars. I was in a small town, I think it was near Lincoln, and decided to meet some of the local folks in the bar. I started walking around shaking hands and one fellow refused to shake hands. I ordered a Coke and asked him if we had ever met. He said, yeah, without volunteering more. "Did I represent you on a legal matter?" "Yeah. You're the son of a bitch that put me in jail!" The man was mean-looking and I decided to finish my Coke and get the hell out before my attempt at pleasantries turned really ugly. I decided that I wouldn't go into a bar again looking for votes. People who are drinking, usually they're either happy or very angry, one or the other. They're almost never happy to see a politician. Those are two experiences that remain vivid. Also, having to watch out for farm dogs. They don't like strangers. I managed to get nipped a couple of times, but nothing serious.

Jed Lyons: We had a car in front of you and a car behind and a hand-painted sign that said, "Bill Cohen ahead, Honk and Wave." I recall that when we were in a slow area, a quiet area, I'd go forward a day ahead to try and find the local Republican committeemen or committeewomen to help organize an event the following day when you'd be walking into town. I remember how excited people were because they knew you were coming and they were vying to be the host or hostess and have you stay overnight at their home. One family I remember very well was the St. Cyrs in Lewiston. A lovely couple. We stayed there that night during the walk and they were very helpful in the primary and the general campaign in the French-American community in Lewiston. After the St. Cyrs, I remember, we really got into some rural areas and you were walking sometimes without seeing a single car for hours at a time.

Bill Cohen: The Haynesville Woods, you may recall. That was about a 19-mile stretch where you'd see nothing but pulp trucks and black flies. And we had to make a decision to walk that 19 miles or skip it. We decided that since I had said I was going to walk the entire district, we weren't going to take any shortcuts. It was an unpleasant experience but it turned out that all the guys driving those pulp trucks talked to other people at rest stops and restaurants down the line, saying that they saw some crazy SOB in the woods slapping flies on his neck and face. He must really want the job.

Jed Lyons: I remember when Elliot Richardson, who was then Nixon's Secretary of Health, Education and Welfare, joined us for a couple of days on the walk. One of the cars that he was riding in blew a water pump on that visit.

We had dinner with him that night and I'll never forget how eloquent he was. He was incredibly eloquent and articulate. I still have a letter that he wrote after that trip saying, "You may be interested to know that later in the same weekend during my visit to Maine, a second car in which I was riding also blew a water pump. Fortunately, these were not omens of electoral disaster."

Bill Cohen: Well, he was one of the most brilliant people to have served in public office. The problem was he was such a Brahmin. If you look at him and see all the photographs of him, I mean, he was Clark Kent. He was as handsome as Superman. He spoke in an aristocratic manner with every sentence perfectly formed. I think I told you about his drawings, he was an artist and he also drew doodles. I would be sitting in his huge office talking to him while he was doodling on a pad of paper. The doodle was just as symmetrical as his language. It was just an example of how his mind worked. He had served as Secretary of Health, Education and Welfare, Secretary of Defense, Secretary of Commerce, and Attorney General, and had been elected Massachusetts lieutenant governor and attorney general. I went to campaign for him in Boston when he was running for the governorship or the Senate and I thought he was never going to make it, but the minute he started talking, it reminded me of what Tip O'Neill said when he took Sarge Shriver out to campaign for the presidency. He took him to a local Irish bar (Tip could get away with that in Boston) and ordered a round for everyone. Everybody ordered either whiskey or beer. Sarge ordered a Courvoisier. Tip said he knew, at that moment, Sarge's campaign wasn't going anywhere, although he did become the Democratic Party's nominee for vice president in 1972.

When Elliot spoke, his language was so perfect, so measured that when he finished his thoughts, his audience was not quite sure what they had just heard.

Elliot became a good friend and after he resigned from the Justice Department, he went to his law firm, Milbank, Tweed, Hadley & McCoy. I drove him to his office every day, and it was during that time that he counseled me on the issue of impeachment. Ironically enough, he was never critical of Nixon. He never said a critical word about Nixon, but talked about events and kept it at a very nonpolitical level. I remember the time General Al Haig did a number on him when Elliot was really upset by what Nixon was saying. Eliott tried to get a call through to Nixon and Haig blocked it. Elliot went home from the office and I think Haig called him around eight o'clock that evening.

Elliot said, "I've had a couple of drinks and have calmed down. Everything's okay." Haig later used that call to suggest the reason that Elliot had to resign was because he had a drinking problem, and that was all during the impeachment investigation. Elliot was the only one who came from the administration. There may have been one other person, Nixon's brother, Edward.

Jed Lyons: Well, Nixon's son-in-law, Cox, came to campaign for you. I still have a photo of you and him one day in Maine during the campaign.

Bill Cohen: The year before I ran, I was serving as the mayor of Bangor. Nixon stopped in Bangor for a rally. He had flown back from the Middle East, I think. He stopped and landed at Loring Air Force Base to refuel. And then he came to Bangor and there was a crowd gathering at the airport. There were about three hundred people and they had signs protesting Nixon and the war. The crowd was orderly and there were plenty of police on hand, but the Secret Service took over and immediately tore up every anti-Nixon sign and anti-war sign. I was there to help facilitate the president's arrival. I asked what the hell was going on and they said, the signs were obstructive and posed a national security issue. Following that,

I wrote a letter to Merle Goff, who was the city manager, and gave him all the reasons the Secret Service's actions were unacceptable. I wanted to have the city conduct a full investigation into what was wrong with the way the city simply folded.

Jed Lyons: Bill and Chris, I have before me a copy of the *Valley Times* newspaper dated Thursday, August 10, 1972, and it's reporting on your walk the day before in Canaan en route to east of Skowhegan where you were joined by Bob Monks and a couple of other local politicians. There are photos of you with five other people walking on the campaign trail and a picture of the sign "Bill Cohen Ahead, Honk and Wave." And also Roosevelt Souci, incumbent state representative from Pittsfield, Elmira, Canaan, and Detroit. "The trio set off at a fast pace talking among themselves and were relaxed and seemed to find a way to go about the serious business of getting elected." Do you remember that?

Bill Cohen: I do. He was a great looking guy. And a pretty popular figure, as I recall, in the state legislature.

Jed Lyons: The article was published by the newspaper, but the photos were taken by my Psi Upsilon fraternity brother and close friend, Gridley Tarbell, who unfortunately was killed by a drunk driver the following year. Do you remember Gridley? He took some of the best photos of the walk and we used them in our campaign literature.

Bill Cohen: I do. His father was an architect, a very somber fellow, about six foot three, dark hair, kind of a foreboding presence and I remember his son.

Jed Lyons: He was a remarkably talented guy. It's sad that he died at the young age of 20.

Bill Cohen: You sent me something from a paper in Aroostook County. Dewey DeWitt was the name of a popular radio host who used to call the games between Bangor and Houlton and Presque Isle. He wrote a nice column about my travels up there.

Chris Potholm: And Roosevelt Souci, the guy looked like he was a senator or president and he had a really great presence and I think he was a huge authority figure up there, and when he was supporting you it made a big difference. I got quite a few calls from reporters before they went out on the walk and they were very cynical, but after they walked with you for an hour or half a day, universally, if they called back, they were tremendously impressed with not only you walking but the way that people reacted. Over time these impressions really added up. I remember having a very strong feeling that we were going to win because there was a poll done, I think it was in August, and among people who had heard about the walk, you were ahead of Elmer Violette something like 2-1, and if they hadn't heard about the walk you are basically tied so that's why, after the walk, it became pretty simple to make sure that you told the story, your backstory, of who you were but then focus on the walk because there was something extremely authentic. Today you've been describing where that authenticity came from. It was real because you were real—your background was real and you weren't a normal Republican of the time. I think it was that authenticity you brought day by day, hour by hour, that ultimately won that election for you.

Bill Cohen: I think there was quite a contrast. I mean Elmer Violette was looked upon with affection and admiration in the sense he'd been in politics 30 years. There was no hint of scandal, there was no corruption, he was a very decent and honest human being that people felt good about. He had a Franco-American accent, which was a plus in Lewiston and in the St. John Valley, but less so in other areas of the state. I think the difference was the age factor and the image factor. He seemed not old, but older. I obviously was younger and had more vitality to campaign with the walk. Symbolically, it was important. As you pointed out, he was kind of the old-fashioned politician doing things the conventional way and we were doing something quite different.

Chris Potholm: Yeah, and the other campaign mistake they made, and I remarked about it at the time, was that he was extremely diffident when he was around Hathaway and especially Muskie. And while you were out there meeting people on the ground, I remember he went to the Democratic Convention in I think it was Miami and flew over to the Bahamas for a weekend.

Bill Cohen: I think that's right.

Jed Lyons: Let's recall the night when Chris, having recovered from his ulcer, came up and joined the walk. You came back and joined us at the end of the walk. That was the night, I believe, when we stayed at Susan Collins's parents' camp and there was a party that night at Susan Collins's parents' house.

Chris Potholm: I remember before that I came up because I had promised I would do the first day, the last day, and one in between. And you were there and we stayed in the family's hunting camp, and I think there was a turkey dinner that night. I mean it was like the perfect overnight. But then we had to leave early in the morning and somewhere there's a picture of the three of us leaving and going through the woods and heading north. I do remember, we were walking in the St. John Valley and I still, to this day, have a tendency to overdo certain things. A man came up and he was a real estate agent and I told him how much you liked the St. John Valley and that you are going to retire there and he was so excited and he ran and he told everybody in Frenchville. Two hours later I'm walking beside you and he comes running up with sheets of property for your retirement!

Bill Cohen: I think we were overlooking a gravesite up in the St. John Valley when that happened.

Chris Potholm: I was trying to distract Senator Collins and the other local politicians. I wanted the shot of Bill crossing the finish line alone, but I couldn't hold them back. They wanted to cross the line with the rock star Bill Cohen had become. People were cheering and waving. It was quite magical. I hope we have a picture of that, maybe in the Cohen Library or the Ft. Kent paper.

Jed Lyons: Explain which Senator Collins you're referring to. It's not the current Senator Susan Collins. It was her father who was a state senator, maybe her uncle? We went to a party at the Collins's home that night and I believe that was the first time Bill met Susan Collins who was a student at St. Lawrence University. She and I are the same age so she would have been a sophomore at St. Lawrence at the time. Bill, do you remember meeting her that night?

Bill Cohen: Yes, that is true.

Jed Lyons: There was another night that you and I wound up sleeping on the same bed. I think that was the only night that happened, but often we'd be on couches. In this case, we were staying at this farmer's house and I remember his daughter was about my size, six foot three. I wouldn't want to arm wrestle her, I remember thinking.

Bill Cohen: Well, there was a number of nice families up there. Carl and Lena Savage, they were a wonderful couple from Fort Kent, in addition to Rose Nadeau.

Jed Lyons: I remember Rose.

Bill Cohen: A more wonderful couple I have not met on the planet and it turned out about, I don't know, 25 years ago at least, they won some kind of a lottery with a million plus dollars and ended up moving out West somewhere. I stayed with them on several occasions since the walk. On any occasion when I went back to the Valley, I always stayed with them, really wonderful. And then there was Robert Michaud, he was married to Mira who was Nepalese and they had four beautiful daughters.

Jed Lyons: Bill, where were we when you jumped over the barbed wire fence and ripped your pants?

Bill Cohen: We were in Oxford County. We were out in a field.

Jed Lyons: What were we doing out in a field?

Bill Cohen: Well, the helicopter landed out there. They looked for a place to land it and they unfortunately landed in a field filled with cow patties. I had my best and only suit on and was sidestepping all the cow shit and then had to climb over the barbed wire fence, ripping my pants in the process. I think I was headed for the Freyburg County Fairgrounds at that point.

Jed Lyons: I remember that day. We kept it secret, though.

Bill Cohen: I changed clothes.

Jed Lyons: Yes, after the event.

Chris Potholm: Well, the one story that just came to mind was after Bill crossed the finish line and the walk was officially over and you guys went somewhere else and I was driving Dick Morgan back to Harpswell in the campaign's Vega that Joe Sewall had provided and somewhere between Mattawamkeg and Patten it died, the engine block just froze up completely. So there we were, the campaign had moved on. Of course, we didn't have cell phones in those days.

And you'll get a kick out of this. I don't think either of you know this. We called frantically around to get a ride, started to hitchhike. We weren't getting any rides for some reason, so Mike Harkins, our media consultant, was in Augusta. I don't know whether it was for you, Bill, or for another candidate, but we finally located him. And he rented a car and came and picked us up and brought us back. So the high point of the end of the walk really did end when you crossed the finish line.

Jed Lyons: Chris, it's worth repeating that story about the evening after the Collins party when you and Dick Morgan, your fellow professor of government at Bowdoin, and I wound our way out into the wilderness to that little hunting cabin that Senator Collins owned where we stayed that night. Bill was back at the main house staying with Susan Collins and her family. Dick Morgan, who at that time would have been only 34 years old, was an old fogey at 34.

He was wearing a smoking robe, like a long dressing robe he had brought along, and drinking this very expensive single malt Scotch. He had a pipe going and he was walking around, pronouncing on this and that in this little lakefront cabin. He was not happy about the modest accommodations that night. Do you remember that evening?

Chris Potholm: I do. That night I drank the water in the camp and got sick. The next day I complained to Senator Collins and he said, "Oh Chris, nobody drinks the water at the camp." I guess the water was better at the big house. But yes, Dick Morgan did look quite spiffy in a 17th century way with his dressing gown. And his ten-year-old single malt Scotch probably killed the beaver shit bacteria that got me.

Jed Lyons: He was very amusing.

Bill Cohen: Is he still living?

Chris Potholm: No, he was teaching and fell over a couple of times and by the time they took him to the doctor and diagnosed him he had 14 different tumors in his brain and he died within a very short period of time after that. He was really a professor's professor. Amazing guy and well loved by his students. Great sense of humor.

Jed Lyons: That's a shame. That was maybe 10 years ago. Are there any other stories that we remember about the walk.

Chris Potholm: How about you in the water tower?

Jed Lyons: Well, that was not during the walk. That was in September, the September before the November election of 1972. I was horsing around on Cape Cod that weekend, bar hopping with a couple of friends.

We spotted a water tower around 2 a.m. and decided to climb up and go for a swim. We were soon discovered by two Barnstable County cops who yelled down into the tank, "What are you doing skinny dipping in the town water supply? Get the hell out now!" I still have a letter from the Barnstable County office dated September 29,1972, which included a final billing from the water commissioners. It said, "Please make your check for $299 payable to Barnstable County First District Court. Payment must be made by certified check." The night this happened, they locked us up in the local jail. The next morning, they said you can make one phone call each. I called you, Bill, and I told you what happened. The election was about six weeks away. You were not amused.

Bill Cohen: Dumb. Chris, tell us about when you had Abbott Green's "Green Machine" locked down at the crossroads at the railroad crossing in Brunswick. The boom would come down and somehow you had secured a lock so that the "Green Machine," a van, could not cross.

Chris Potholm: My recollection is that Jed did it in a place like Brewer. I don't think the Green Machine would have been in Brunswick, but I know, Jed, there was some girl you were trying to impress in the Abbott Green mystery machine and you did chain it to something which I thought was a fire hydrant.

Jed Lyons: Yes, we got some chain and padlocked it to a fire hydrant.

Chris Potholm: You just walked off and left it and there was a big flap, but they couldn't trace it to you.

Bill Cohen: The reason I'm probably way out on this, Chris, may have been because during our Bowdoin days we locked down the crossing when we were marching on the city and they called the police out. We had torches and we were all celebrating something or other, and it may have been the police who locked the crossing down, I don't know.

Chris Potholm: I think they did. That reminds me of my ripped pants story. My mother had bought me one good pair of pants and, for some reason, I was on the march on the Cumberland. We got teargassed by the police and chased by the police and I ran and climbed over a fence and ripped my pants from the top to the bottom. That was in Brunswick and I think they put down the railroad gates.

Jed Lyons: I have a question for both of you. The walk made its way through mostly rural parts of the state and never veered over to the oceanside of the 2nd District of Maine Why did we avoid that? Why did we choose the route we chose?

Chris Potholm: Well, Hancock County was the one county that was going to go Republican even if we had put up the proverbial yellow dog. It was based on that. I remember that I had picked all the swing towns, and so the walk made some funny curlicues based on whether the voters in those towns could be swayed one way or the other and how many Independents there were. I remember distinctly, we said we can't go Down East. It's not worth it, we need these other towns. It ended up in Houlton and then we decided to go all the way to Fort Kent in Aroostook County.

Jed Lyons: And so the direction that the walk took was based on your analysis of what mattered in terms of the vote?

Chris Potholm: Yeah, and I think that's why some of it was through extremely rural areas because those were the places where Republicans said no candidate had ever been. We wanted to target the places where there were swing voters; that's why the walk took the path it did.

Bill Cohen: And we did go Down East the next year after the election.

Chris Potholm: Because they all complained. That next summer, wasn't that where you were filmed by helicopter or there was someone staying down in that stretch of woods, the Haynesville Woods. We were filming a commercial in some out of the way place and it was because they complained we had left them out the first time around.

Bill Cohen: Haynesville was on the first walk going north, the other walk was the Airline Road.

Chris Potholm: Airline Road, right.

Bill Cohen: That was during my first walk from Gilead to Fort Kent. I had gained 18 pounds. The irony was that on the second walk I lost almost as much weight as I had gained the previous summer. I had come back from a trip to Taiwan and I went up in a bus to the top of this mountain in Taiwan, Taroko Gorge, and crossed a bridge that appeared to be made out of marble. There was a little restaurant at the top, not a restaurant, but a store, and we all were warned not to drink the water. So I got there and I said okay I'll have a Pepsi. They poured the Pepsi over ice and I came down with Montezuma's Revenge in a major way. So during the 2nd District walk, I barely made it. I lost almost 18 pounds.

Chris Potholm: The 1972 primary is over and we have survived. We owed a lot of money, and I remember being in a little plane of Joe Sewall's and we're flying somewhere and the subject of your campaign debt and raising money came up and he focused like a laser right on me and he said, "Everybody's got to pull together. We're going to divide up the debt and just pay it off" and he's looking at me and I'm like, "Where am I going to get any money?" I didn't sleep well that night. Somehow, I would be on the hook for $10,000 for the "Littlest Gunslinger's" bills. I was scared. But Bob Monks came through and I never got a bill. He was great that way.

Bill Cohen: And I remember during that time in the walk I was not getting any salary from the law firm and I had my mother and father bringing groceries over to our house to feed Diana and the kids. So that was not a happy occasion.

Jed Lyons: I remember a party at Olympia and Peter Snowe's house in Auburn that we attended and where I met Olympia for the first time. You probably knew her before that, Bill.

Bill Cohen: I didn't.

Jed Lyons: You met her for the first time that night, too?

Bill Cohen: Yeah, I didn't know Olympia.

Jed Lyons: Her husband, Peter Snowe, was the president of the Maine State Senate and he ran a family concrete business. He died in a snow-storm driving home from Augusta in 1973.

Chris Potholm: I remember his death was so tragic. Poor Olympia. When he died that weekend, she was at such loose ends and she came and spent that weekend at our house. And, as you can imagine, it was a terrible, terrible time and the Republican Party executive director, Alex Ray, was constantly calling her to say they wanted her to run for Peter's seat. She was agonizing over what she should do, and she said, "I could either run the concrete business or I could do this." And the more she talked to Sandy, the more we got the impression that she did not want to run for office and that running the concrete business was going to be a good way for her going forward. And when she left our house that weekend, she pretty much decided to do the concrete business. We, of course, supported her in that and looking back on it, it is a good thing she didn't take our advice. She got back there and then the Republicans said, "You've got to run for his open seat."

Bill Cohen: Chris, you mentioned a name I had not forgotten, but passed over: Alex Ray. What was his role during that time? Alex will pop out every other year or so and send me a note. As I recall, he was not a fan of ours at that time.

Chris Potholm: He wasn't, but looking back on it, we could have easily co-opted him, but he perceived rightly that we didn't like him, we wanted to get rid of him, and we eventually did get rid of him. But get Amazon to send you his book, which Jed published, called *Hired Gun*. He ended up being a very good friend to me and we shared many political stories, often about when we are on opposite sides of state committee fights when he was executive director. Great fun. His book *Hired Gun* is a classic. Amazing stuff.

Jed Lyons: Is he still alive?

Chris Potholm: No, he died a few years back Please, please glance through that because it is a funny book and you'll recognize the cast of characters. It's just a marvelous read.

Bill Cohen: The driver of our van was named George Smith. What was George's brother's name? He was even more conservative than George. Is he still around?

Chris Potholm: You're thinking of Gordon Smith. He ended up being the head of the Maine Doctor's Association and of course his sister Edi turned out be a superb political operative in her own right. Helped win a ton of referenda. George ended up a very, very liberal Republican. Either that or the party swung so far beyond him but when he died, he was on the outs with a lot of the conservative wing of the Republican Party in the state of Maine. He was the campaign manager for Dave Emery. He went to Washington with Emery and eventually came back to be the head of the Sportsman's Alliance of Maine.

Jed Lyons: We did a book for him, too, on the great hunting and fishing camps of Maine. That was about five years ago.

Chris Potholm: He died during COVID.

Bill Cohen: One other thing about Republicans, the name Jack Linnell. He was a big supporter and I remember that when I was going through the impeachment business, he still supported me. And there weren't many who were during that time, but Jack was a friend over the years.

Jed Lyons: Then there was Harry Richardson.

Bill Cohen: I remember Harry. When he got sick, he called me and said he was in a nursing home and he just started crying over the phone. "Look what's happened to me." Harry was this robust, physical brute of a guy, a Marine, I think. A good lawyer and part of the Joe Sewall team. They were just fun to be with, Ken MacLeod, Harry, and Joe.

Jed Lyons: Did he get elected to any office?

Chris Potholm: He was a State Senator.

Jed Lyons: He ran for governor.

Chris Potholm: Yes, he lost by 500 votes to Jim Erwin in the Republican primary. I think that was really a very important election. If Harry had won, I don't think Longley would have won. I think George Mitchell would have won that and history would have been very, very different. But I don't think Harry could have beaten Mitchell in a three-way race, but one on one, definitely. He would have taken a lot of votes away from Longley as he hated Longley. He wanted to go after him right away. He thought he was a fraud and phoney. You can just imagine Harry banging swords with this guy. It would have been something to watch him against Longley and vice versa. I'd have paid real money to watch that.

The current governor is Janet Mills. "Tough as any man and twice as smart" was her nickname.

Bill Cohen: Her dad was from what county? Oxford County or Somerset County?

Chris Potholm: He was from Farmington.

Bill Cohen: He became a pretty big supporter even though he was a little to the right of where I was.

Chris Potholm: You had a great personal following, a lot of Democratic people and Independents. You weren't a typical Republican and there was a whole Cohen group that didn't care what your party affiliation was, they bought you, they were Cohen people, it didn't matter what party you were in.

Bill Cohen: Sort of a Trump-like culture?

Jed Lyons: More like Rockefeller Republican.

Bill Cohen: For sure or John Lindsay-type Republican or a Richardson-type Republican or an Eisenhower Republican.

Chris Potholm: Bill has always been the opposite of a Trumpkanoid, that's for sure. Damn sure.

Chapter V

Oral History Discussion
with Jim Harrington

June 24, 2021

Jed Lyons: Jim Harrington, please take a moment to remind us of your background and how you came to be involved in the 1972 campaign.

Jim Harrington: Well, I was born in Vermont in Montpelier in 1950, lived there all of a month. Then we moved to Skowhegan, Maine, until I was four years old. We moved to Winthrop, Maine, and stayed through my sixth grade, moving to Amherst, Massachusetts.

Jed Lyons: Why did you move to Amherst?

Jim Harrington: My father at that time bought a construction company he was working for in the winter. He got the majority shares. The Massachusetts offices are still there in a town called Ware.

Jed Lyons: What kind of construction work did they do?

Jim Harrington: They built mostly colleges and medical facilities, including Eastern Maine Medical.

Jed Lyons: Is it still in business?

Jim Harrington: Yeah, it's about 145 years old. We no longer own it. It was sold after my father's passing. My brother finally bought out the two brothers' shares and then my brother saw the light and he sold it to some existing partners.

Jed Lyons: What was it called?

Jim Harrington: HP Cummings Construction Company.

Jed Lyons: All right, so you chose not to go into the family business, obviously.

Jim Harrington: I wanted to be a lawyer since I was in fourth grade. And I did the Perry Mason bit. I had some incentive to go to law school because I was one of the few people in my family that had an advanced degree. I was a fairly motivated student.

Jed Lyons: You went to college and law school where?

Jim Harrington: I went to the University of Maine and then I went to Suffolk University Law School in Boston, which was the second largest law school in the country.

Jed Lyons: The first place you practiced law was where?

Jim Harrington: In Winthrop, Maine, where I grew up. The office is still in existence.

Jed Lyons: So you hung out a shingle, so to speak.

Jim Harrington: Yes.

Jed Lyons: When did you first meet Chris and Bill?

Jim Harrington: It was my college senior year and somehow, I got invited to Bill's house for a talk and we sat down and got into the interview process. I was fairly active in the Republican Party statewide. I was the Republican vice chairperson. I was also head of the Distinguished Lecturer Series at Maine. I brought Vice President Spiro Agnew there. I believe the purpose of the meeting was to find out my availability for a summer job. I could have worked for the construction company, but my interest was politics. I was a correspondent for the Ripon Forum, a liberal Republican organization. In the summer of 1969, I interned for Senator Edward W. Brooke in Washington, DC. Obviously, my parents encouraged me to do what I wanted to do. I first met Chris Potholm at Bill Cohen's house. It is clear that I found the right team.

Jed Lyons: Chris, do you remember the first time you met Jim?

Chris Potholm: Yes, I do remember that. I'm pretty sure that we were at some function, and I do remember Dale Gerry and he was very impressed with Jim early on, because he was very articulate but he wasn't an overbearing college student, and the things that Jim said about the Republican Party, about why they liked Margaret Chase Smith, seemed to be very incisive and I was very impressed with him from the very beginning.

Jed Lyons: What was it that you had in mind for Jim once you'd gotten to know him well enough to figure out what role you'd want him to play?

Chris Potholm: Well, I thought he was a godsend because at that time we had ties to Monks and Monks's money from the 1st District. Abbott Green professed to be Margaret's heir apparent. So there were these two titans fighting for the Senate race and I perceived that Jim could be very helpful in all matters with Margaret Chase Smith. Jim proved to be very adroit at telling us what we should do to make sure that Margaret didn't become an active enemy.

At the fundraiser for Margaret Chase Smith, Jim made sure that all the people that were there, including me, had to wear Cohen buttons, those little red buttons, and I do remember Margaret Chase Smith got up on the stage and I don't know whether she asked you or General Bill Lewis, she looked out and she said, "What are all those red buttons?" And you said, "Those are all Cohen people," and she was very impressed.

Jim Harrington: Yeah, Margaret Chase Smith in her own way was a fundraiser, but she didn't want fundraisers. That was, you know, a party and she'd always pay for everything and the money raised, like, I think was $1,500.

Jed Lyons: Jim, how did you first get involved in the Cohen campaign and why?

Jim Harrington: Well, I've always been what I would call a liberal Republican and, although Abbott Green was a fine gentleman, I think he worked for the airlines as a pilot, I didn't like the data coming from some of the supporters saying, well, even Cohen's bumper stickers are red and yellow. That intrigued me a little bit, kind of like the Spectra guys. I was a correspondent with the Ripon Society in Maine and contributed to them in a non-paid capacity. I certainly felt that we needed Bill, that type of person, in Washington DC.

Jed Lyons: How close were you to Senator Margaret Chase Smith at that point?

Jim Harrington: We were close to the extent that I've been to her house, and I think I met her when I was eight or nine years of age when she visited my town in Winthrop, Maine. It must have been something in the water. George Smith was involved in the campaign and Gordon Smith, his younger brother, we all grew up in Winthrop and we had an interest in politics early on.

Jed Lyons: I remember the late George Smith very well because while I was one of the advance men on that 1972 walk, George was the driver of the van that followed Bill. Did you bring George into the campaign or did George bring you in?

Jim Harrington: I don't think so. Dale Gerry and I were hired at the same time. At our initial meeting at Bill Cohen's house, I suggested the idea of a walk without any details. Not my original idea. Dan Walker (former governor, now deceased) of Illinois had done it. A way to meet people, stay in their homes, remove perceived aloofness of a Republican candidate. Bill reminded me it was payback time and I was going to join the walk at the end of Aroostook County as he was getting close to the end of the walk.

Jed Lyons: When did you intersect with the walk that summer?

Jim Harrington: I think I was more of an event person.

Jed Lyons: Do you remember any other events or evenings during the walk when you were participating?

Jim Harrington: I was on the walk in Aroostook County and making arrangements for where he was staying, and so on.

Jed Lyons: Do you remember going to Skowhegan? What do you remember about that stop?

Jim Harrington: Well, just a lot of good optimistic Republicans that wanted to win. One of the secrets to his success was that he had so many prominent Republicans on board, whether it be Dave Benson, Ken MacLeod, Dave Huber, or Joe Sewall. They were good and I thought the cream of the crop of the Maine Republican Party at that time. We had to get through the primary, but Chris had a plan. It was going to be pretty easy to get through that primary, but we still had to reach the average Maine voter for the general election in order to win. The walk was a way for him to branch out and not just be with the so-called "entitled and college educated." We needed to get some union endorsements. Stan Tupper was the most liberal Republican in the state of Maine when he was in Congress.

Jed Lyons: So what do you think Senator Smith thought about the Cohen campaign? Do you have any insights into that?

Jim Harrington: I think that she really thought he was the up and coming guy. That he could be a superstar that would do what she thought was right, maintain independence when necessary, and not just be what would be called a hack today. You know, not to be always 100 percent right, to do what's right for the country and the district. I think, Margaret Chase Smith believed that she would object when she thought the Republican Party was wrong. Bill would maintain what the people wanted. I think Senator Smith and General Lewis thought Bill Cohen would remain independent from the party's leaders when they were wrong. The Margaret Chase Smith philosophy would continue. "Country over party."

Chris Potholm: Well, I was wondering if General Lewis or anybody like that ever asked you "was Cohen a Monks man?" because that's the phrase when Bill went down to meet with her and Lewis—that was her first question "What's a Monks man doing down here talking to me?" I just wondered if it had filtered down with you and your activities.

Jim Harrington: I recall assuring Senator Smith and General Lewis that, in my opinion, Bill Cohen was a person that would continue in Margaret Chase Smith's tradition, to do what was right, regardless of the consequences, country over party's best interests.

Chris Potholm: Did you ever meet Abbott Green?

Jim Harrington: Yes, I did.

Chris Potholm: What was your overall impression of him? He had run against Neil Bishop, I believe, for the Senate during the previous cycle and then became Bishop's campaign manager, so we always assumed he thought he was next in line. Did you ever get any sense from the other Republicans where they thought he fit in?

Jim Harrington: I think Abbott Green, from my vantage point, both from the Maine Republican and state committees, should have been given another chance. He was a decent guy. I worked for Danny Shute when he ran for Congress, and he was saying there was nothing bad about Abbott Green. He was very conservative and he was from a tiny village, Columbia Falls. I think he moved to a small place a few years ago in Alaska.

Chris Potholm: I would be very interested to see whether he thought he should have naturally gotten the nomination, that it was his turn. There were a lot of people in the party in those days who believed that, too. You know, you serve a time and did this, and then it was your turn and I always thought he must have been very frustrated to know that we had Monks people supporting us and Monks people donating a lot of money and all that and at the same time, we were trying to be independent and it must have been frustrating not to be able to pin Cohen to the Monks operation, but that's just conjecture on my part. I don't know, I think it would be very, very useful to get an unvarnished set of opinions from him.

Jed Lyons: We'll follow up with him and try tracking him down. Jim, what do you consider your major contribution to the '72 campaign? Someone described you as "invaluable." Why were you invaluable?

Jim Harrington: I think everybody likes to have some responsibilities, and whatever they were back then I seemed to accomplish them and they were pleased with my results.

Jed Lyons: Could you be a little less modest?

Jim Harrington: My biggest contribution was introducing Dale Gerry to Bill Cohen and Chris Potholm. While I elected to attend law school,

Dale worked for Bill Cohen in various capacities for many decades. A great guy who died several years ago of a brain tumor. He was too young. Without my introduction, Dale would not have been able to enjoy a great career with Bill Cohen.

Jed Lyons: Did you work in the Bangor office?

Jim Harrington: Yes.

Jed Lyons: With Jackie McDermott, right?

Jim Harrington: Yes, with Jackie.

Jed Lyons: Please name those people with whom you shared the office.

Jim Harrington: There was Trish Baldwin, the wife of Alan Baldwin, an architect, and Trish Weatherbee whose husband, Peter, was an attorney. There was also Charlene Weatherbee and Trish Forward, they were the secretaries that kept everything running.

Jed Lyons: What was her job and the two Trishas?

Chris Potholm: I think Charlene was in charge of the volunteers in Bangor, and Trish was more the personal secretary for Bill and the campaign and I also think she was a scheduler.

Jim Harrington: I think you're right.

Jed Lyons: Jim, we've been talking about some of the funny things that happened on the walk, such as Bill jumping over a fence and ripping his pants on his way to greet voters. We thought it was funny; he probably didn't. Do you recall any humorous stories from the office or during the campaign?

Jim Harrington: It was hard to get him out of a suit at one time and get him into a working man's attire. He wouldn't wear the L. L. Bean boots or dungarees or a working man's shirt. He wasn't walking on a beach in a white shirt and tie, either.

Chris Potholm: I think it was his second term in college before the jeans became pre-washed and the shirt was a double knit. Jim, do you remember one of the volunteers in the Bangor office was a homeless person? And he and his dog would show up early in the morning, eat the donuts and drink the coffee and the little dog stayed right inside his shirt. So about 3 o'clock in the afternoon, he would drift off somewhere else but he'd be coming back the next morning to lick stamps or whatever else they had him doing and I just wonder if you remember this guy and the inseparable dog.

Jim Harrington: I guess I do, but I wasn't in the office that much as I recall. And we didn't have cell phones back then. I don't recall seeing the dog with him there. I remember meeting Bill's father, Ruben, at the bakery. It was a wonderful experience for me. Bill encouraged me to go to law school. That's what I wanted to do. He told me I should take Tom Lambert's course, a tort professor—world renowned. *Tom on Torts—American Trial Lawyers Publication.* I followed Bill's advice, took the course and did well. One of my favorites. Dale died that horrible brain tumor death. It was tough on me. He made the *Bangor Daily News*, the front page.

Jed Lyons: Jim, did you ever get down to the Lewiston office? Do you remember any visits there?

Jim Harrington: I do not. We lived in Old Town during the campaign, and I don't remember going to Lewiston.

Jed Lyons: Do you remember the last day of the walk? Were you present when Bill finished the walk in Fort Kent?

Jim Harrington: I was.

Jed Lyons: Do you recall a split among young Republicans around 1972 and can you shed any light on it? Young Republicans, meaning college age. I recall a split between liberal and conservative Republicans around 1972.

Jim Harrington: There were Maine college Republicans, of which I was vice chair. We would challenge the far right or traditional right run by Bowdoin's Neal Corson. When I was elected vice-chair, I was a student at the University of Maine. I paired with Field Reichardt, a Colby College student. We were both considered moderates to liberal. Our friendly opposition came from students at Bowdoin College. Neal Corson became an attorney in Skowhegan, Maine, and died in January of 2022.

There was a big election field and I won. It was pretty close. There was a lot of rivalry between the schools, some of which remains to this day. We went to some conventions. We went to Rhode Island. That may have been where the election was held. We had a good time. After graduating, Field went back to his home state of Michigan and I stayed in Maine. I have not spoken with Field since my early years practicing law in Winthrop. He still resides in Michigan.

There were differences of opinion, of course, about what was the right course for the Republican party. I never thought a conservative Republican could get elected. He could win the primary, perhaps, but not the general in the state of Maine.

Jed Lyons: Was there a divide between the old WASP aristocracy of Maine and the young up-and-coming Republicans at that time?

Jim Harrington: I think there was. The Republican Party was the one that brought the income tax to Maine. The log drives on Maine's lakes and rivers became extinct due to the efforts of State Senator Howard Trotsky of Bangor. All my friends were up here in the party, I was just the mere person, but the elected officials in Maine, whether it be Joe Sewall or Ken MacLeod, they took a look at the bigger picture and tried to do what was right, especially at the time the job passed over to Bill. We definitely thought we were on the right path to have more equity. The more traditional Republicans, Republican State Committee folks, favored conservative candidates even though they seldom won in congressional, senatorial, and gubernatorial general elections. Some of us thought we should nominate a candidate that could win in November. Enter Bill Cohen. Like Margaret Chase Smith, he built his own election team, not relying on the traditional GOP state, county, and local committees. Maine voters have a long history of electing candidates who demonstrate independence from party, when necessary. Senator Smith voted against two Supreme Court nominees of President Nixon, Carswell and Haynesworth, and differed with some of his defense policies. Obviously, her speech, Declaration of Conscience, opened the door for candidates renouncing fear and intimidation. Mainers simply wanted elected officials to do what is right, not my party, right or wrong. I was confident Bill Cohen would continue that policy.

I am friendly with Congressman Jared Golden and his family. I knew that serving in the Marine infantry, with three tours of duty in Afghanistan and Iraq, would give him the backbone to withstand pressure from Nancy Pelosi and other Democratic leaders.

Jed Lyons: Chris, do you have any other questions for Jim.

Chris Potholm: This really has been very, very helpful and very interesting and I'm so happy we had a chance to talk.

Jed Lyons: Thank you so much, Jim. We really appreciate your time.

Jim Harrington: If you have a hard time finding Abbott Green, let me know—I might be able to help.

Jed Lyons: Thank you so much.

Chris Potholm: I think the average political junkie today is not going to understand how tremendously different politics is today from what it was in 1972. I just came up with four or five things that I wanted to mention. The first of these is the context of The Walk. The Walk really made sense, because in those days you didn't campaign a lot. Campaigns began on Labor Day. People were supposedly at the beach; it was common wisdom that you didn't do a lot in the summer because nobody was paying attention to politics. And I think we were one of the first to break that mold by making the walk a centerpiece of a summer-long emphasis. And

I think Elmer Violette went to the Democratic National Convention in Miami that summer, he went to the Bahamas. I think he was in a more traditional mode of "you don't really start till you get to the Labor Day period." I think in that context the walk had much more prominence than it would have today.

The second thing that is very noticeable is that campaigns did not have money for constant TV. Now somebody today who is subjected to two years of TV nonstop in the 2020 U.S. Senate race, they wouldn't believe it, but neither we nor Elmer did much advertising until the last month of the campaign.

The third thing is, we made fun of the campaign laws of the time, but they were pretty open and they allowed for cash to come in envelopes and stuff and, of course, today that's under a little more supervision, but the most important thing I want readers to get out of this was as campaign manager in those days I had control over most of the advertising that you and your supporters did. In the Senate Race of 2020, I'll bet Tom Daffron, the chief strategist and Senator Collins, I'll bet they didn't have control over more than 15-20 percent of the total spent on TV. All the PACs and dark money and third-party expenditures, no control at all.

Jed Lyons: You're saying that you had control of 100 percent and Collins might today have control of 15 percent. By that you mean the 15 percent of the money spent is what she spends herself and the other 85 percent is being spent by parties that she does not control?

Chris Potholm: Correct. She can't cheat. Let's say you're the PAC for a Free America and you're going to spend $50 or $60 million in support of her. By law they can't show the commercial to her and then have them say no, we don't like that, that's too negative or I don't like the atmospherics of it.

Jed Lyons: So the 85 percent of the money that Susan doesn't control is spent on ads where you're not going to see her or someone else at the end say "this ad was approved by Susan Collins," is that right?

Chris Potholm: Correct. These super PACs have unlimited money to push outside the control of the campaign.

Jed Lyons: That's an important point.

Chris Potholm: It is an important point in the difference between then and now, but, as you can see in the politics of a particular state those interest groups don't care about who represents Maine. All they care about is that their single issue will be supported by the person that wins in May.

Jed Lyons: One other question. If you were to estimate what the percentage of total spending on the '72 campaign was in terms of advertising, what would the difference be in what Collins spent on her last campaign? I'm guessing the expenditure for advertising would be a much higher percentage for Collins today than it was for Bill in '72.

Chris Potholm: Oh, absolutely, and that's where I was going with my fourth point, and that is Bill and I were extremely lucky to get the quality of field people, paid and unpaid, that went out and worked for him. Field people 10 years after that campaign—you don't have them anymore if you want signs. But by the time Angus King was running against Brennan, well we'd just pick up the phone, call the firm in Massachusetts and say "two weeks from today, the weekend, we want 1,000 signs in Joe Brennan's senate district, where he lives, put up those signs." They would come up like mushrooms, do the job, and go away. We had dedicated people, as you know, you were one of them, that were out in the field, and I could trust that if we gave you 50 signs, you would put 50 signs up. Well, increasingly, you know those you send out 10 years later you'd send out 50 signs, and lucky if five of them got up. They'd throw them in the town dump sometimes. Back in 1972, the control that you had over the campaign, including the field people, was much greater. And the quality of our field people, you know, they were supervised a little bit, but I didn't check in with you every day or Dale Gerry, what's going on, what's happening here? The reliance that our campaign put on a few people, it's very important. The strategic decision that we talked about last time but didn't flesh out: Even when we're running against Abbott Green, we made no effort to organize Hancock or Washington counties because it was too far away and, this has always been my bedrock assumption in politics, and I think I was successful in my ballot measures for this reason as well. I always like to play for the whole field. And to me if we could get one Democratic vote in Androscoggin or Oxford County, well two votes of Republicans because you subtracted it from your opponents' potential. Absolutely key in my mind. Not like today at all.

Jed Lyons: That was a very important part of your strategy, I remember that well. You said to me when I was running the office in Lewiston that the votes in Androscoggin County are essential for that very reason, because getting some Republicans to vote and not stay home is more important than adding to the vote count than it is to get the expected votes up in more rural and more conservative counties.

Chris Potholm: Today it's all about getting out your basest base vote and tearing down your opponent. Terrible. In our era we tried to convert votes on issues and substance and yes style. We had control over most of our campaign, and if the Republican state committee wanted to do something we didn't like, we told them. Now politics is the lowest possible common denominator. Everybody wants to get out their base so that's what's so pernicious about today's politics, because by playing to the fringe elements in your own party and trying to get more people to join the fringe by scaring them and coming up with weird things, and totally made-up stuff that's not changing voters' minds on issues. Maybe we had 30 percent of the electorate to actually fool around with and try to convert. I bet you between Collins and Gideon, if we had the polling there, I bet they spent like $100 million for 6 percent of the vote. Ghastly. Just terrible for our democracy—or what's left of it. Demonize your opponent and get out your base vote. That's a terrible recipe for democracy.

Jed Lyons: Going back to the field workers, one of the things I remember from the '72 campaign is the huge army of college and high school students that we recruited to work all over those counties. It was literally in the hundreds, and it was all about knocking on doors, delivering literature, engaging, talking to the homeowner, many of whom had never seen anyone, Republican or Democrat, at their front door. You and Bill made a big point of emphasizing how vital it was for us to get in front of the voters by going door to door and knocking on the doors. I'll never forget the book *The Advance Man*, which came out right around the same time. The author was the advance man for Robert F. Kennedy. And that was a Bible for me. It was all about the importance of knocking on doors, going door to door, and we really had a terrific army of young people doing that for Bill.

Chris Potholm: It was very important because other campaigns did not do that in rural Maine or in the Democratic strongholds. If you were a Republican, it became a self-fulfilling prophecy in those days. Republicans never went to Lewiston and other Franco-American communities. They did poorly there. They didn't expect to do well, and they didn't go there and then they didn't do well. Today, with all the emphasis on big data and getting out your base, you don't bother to try to convert your opponents, you just try to arouse your base in voting NO or against whatever it is you are running against. These "imaginary horribles" drive so much of our politics today. It's hard to imagine what we did in 1972; our central goal was to convert, not turn out. Margaret Chase Smith could have won in the fall of 1972. She should have won and would easily have won if she had put anything significant on TV. She assumed, as she always had assumed, that if you win the Republican primary, which she did actually, she did not have to do anything in the general election. Look at Patrick Lahey in Vermont. He was just as old and out of touch as she but he mounted a modern campaign with slick advertising and he won reelection very easily, so the great irony in 1972 is Monks wounded her but it wasn't a fatal wound in and of itself. What was fatal was that her campaign strategy was the same as she had employed for 40 years, but times had changed and her campaigning emphasis did not.

First day of "The Walk" on the New Hampshire—Maine border.

First day of "The Walk" in Gilead, Maine, with Oxford County field rep, Charlie Peterson, Chris Potholm, and Bill Cohen.

Bill Cohen and Chris Potholm in Millinocket, Maine during "The Walk."

Bill visiting with a farmer during "The Walk."
Photo by Gridley Tarbell.

A typical backyard barbeque dinner at a host's home during "The Walk." Bill Cohen and Jed Lyons in rear of photo.

Bill (center) greeting voters.

Mike Harkins, "The Littlest Gunslinger," gestures to the camera.

Bill and a local resident.

One of the two hand-made wooden signs that were attached to the cars that accompanied Bill on "The Walk."

Bill Cohen landing in Lisbon, Maine, to campaign in early November 1972.

Bill visiting with a local hardware store owner. Photo by Gridley Tarbell.

Bill talking to farmers during "The Walk." Photo by Gridley Tarbell.

Advance man Jed Lyons, Bill Cohen, driver George Smith, and Deputy Campaign Manager Bob Loeb during "The Walk."

On the road, summer 1972.

Surprise Lewiston Vote Keyed Rep. Cohen's Win

By JIM BRUNELLE
Staff Writer

LEWISTON — William S. Cohen, the man who brought the Second Congressional District back into the GOP column for the first time in eight years, said Thursday he has the voters of traditionally Democratic Androscoggin County to thank for it all.

"Basically, it was a rejection on my part of the conventional wisdom which said a Republican should write off the Lewiston-Auburn area," Cohen said.

"I've never believed that to be true. I've always felt that people all over the state will judge you on your merits if you take the time to meet with them and talk to them. I think that was proven to be true in this particular case."

Although Democrat Elmer Violette outpointed Cohen in Lewiston Tuesday by better than a 3-to-1 margin, Cohen counted a victory for himself in this defeat. Normally, he said, any Democrat could expect to carry Lewiston by a 7 or 8-to-1 margin.

"I think that made quite a significant difference in my election," he said, pointing out that he carried the city of Auburn as well as all of Oxford County in the balloting.

Cohen said he felt that Violette lost the election in part because he "took some areas for granted," Androscoggin and Oxford Counties, concentrating his campaign efforts chiefly in Penobscot County where Cohen's support was strongest.

The 32-year-old congressman-elect, whose term as mayor of Bangor expired only last week, held a series of news conferences at various locations in the sprawling Second District Thursday to discuss the election results. He was accompanied by his wife, Diane, and sons, Kevin, 9, and Christopher, 7.

With the defeat of Sen. Margaret Chase Smith by William D. Hathaway, Cohen becomes the only Republican member of the Maine congressional delegation. He was asked by reporters here whether he now considered himself the titular head of the GOP in Maine.

"Well, that would be a little hard to accept I guess," he replied. "But I do consider myself one of the leaders at this point, and I hope I can play a role in helping to rebuild the strength of the party."

Cohen announced that he is one of four newly elected congressmen to be named a John F. Kennedy Institute fellow at Harvard. Beginning next week he will undertake a month-long program involving studies of the congressional system and political organization materials. He said that among his first priorities in Washington will be to inform himself about the inner workings of Congress as quickly as possible.

"I want to establish myself as a hardworking and dedicated individual and gain the respect of my colleagues. I think that's very important before you can look forward to introducing legislation."

Turn to Back Page
of this section

Portland Press Herald

VOL. 110—NO. 122   Second Class Postage Paid At Portland, Maine   PORTLAND, MAINE, FRIDAY MORNING, NOVEMBER 10, 1972   PRICE FIFTEEN CENTS   ★ ★ ★ ★ 44 Pages

Lewiston's vote for Cohen was higher than the Democrats expected.

Approaching the end of "The Walk" in Fort Kent.

Chapter VI

Oral History Discussion
with Peter B. Webster

June 28, 2021

Jed Lyons: Peter, please share with us your background, where you grew up, where you went to high school, college, and law school.

Peter Webster: I was born and raised in Wakefield, Massachusetts, and I went to Wakefield High School. Bowdoin admission director Hubert Shaw came to my high school in October 1957 and I had an interview with him and he told me that if I wanted to go to Bowdoin College, there would be a place for me there. I applied to Bowdoin and Harvard. I was accepted at both. Most of my teachers were aghast, but choosing Bowdoin was the best decision that I ever made in my life. I spent four years at Bowdoin as a classmate of Bill and Chris. I was a government major and then, during my senior year, Athern Daggett called me into his office and he said, "Peter, I think you should go to law school." I hadn't thought about going to law school; I was an education minor and a government major. Professor Paul Hazleton put me in touch with a fellow in the Virgin Islands who was a headmaster of a school and who had graduated from Bowdoin. So I had a teaching job in the Virgin Islands after I graduated.

But after Professor Daggett told me that I should go to law school, and I had such respect for Mr. Daggett, he put me in touch with the folks at Cornell Law School, whom he knew very well, and it was a much simpler system then. And so I was accepted at Cornell and I spent three years there and then came to Portland in 1965 to practice law. I retired on January 11, 2021, my 80th birthday, after 56 years at Verrill Dana, the firm which I joined in 1965, so I absolutely loved the practice of law. I couldn't get enough of it. I loved to go to work in the morning. It was an extraordinarily successful relationship and so for that I'm very grateful. In 1972, which is what you're most interested in, I was certainly aware of Bill Cohen's run for Congress and, as with most Bowdoin students and particularly classmates, I was really thrilled about the prospects of his becoming a congressman. And when he won it was fabulous, and he just kept winning for the next decades, so it was just great fun for me to know Bill and to see his successes from a bit of a distance.

Jed Lyons: Was Verrill Dana where Louis Bernstein practiced law?

Peter Webster: No, he was at another Portland firm.

Jed Lyons: He was a longtime member of the Bowdoin Board of Trustees.

Peter Webster: Louis Bernstein, a singularly wonderful man. In 1969 I ran for Bowdoin overseer and I lost to Dick Downes who was an Episcopal minister.

Jed Lyons: I knew Dick Downes. He found a place for me to live in DC the summer of '73 when I was working for Bill in Washington.

Peter Webster: Louie Bernstein was kind enough to call me and he said it had nothing to do with you, it's just that Bowdoin needed a minister, not another lawyer.

Jed Lyons: Dick was a nice guy. He wound up marrying the late Bowdoin Professor Jim Bland's widow.

Peter Webster: Absolutely, and took over the St Paul's Church when the fellow took a leave of absence some years ago. He spent some years in Brunswick, being minister to the Episcopal Church in Brunswick.

Jed Lyons: Yes, and he helped raise the Blands' three wonderful sons.

Peter Webster: Right. Well, I owe my life to Dick Downes, because if I had won that election, I could never have served as Bowdoin's lawyer. So, because he beat me, I was chosen by the prior college lawyer to succeed him as the lawyer for the college.

Jed Lyons: What was the reaction in the Portland legal community to Bill Cohen running for Congress?

Peter Webster: I think people were extraordinarily impressed and enthusiastic. He was a lawyer and, of course, lawyers like lawyers, because we are in a minority, and there were a lot of jokes about us and things like that. Bill was a good lawyer, an honorable lawyer and served his community. He had been the mayor of Bangor and served on various boards, so everybody was very enthusiastic about his running for Congress. I hope some of that enthusiasm translated itself into contributions being made to Bill for his run for Congress.

Jed Lyons: What was your role in the 1972 primary and general campaigns?

Peter Webster: I really didn't have any role, Jed. I was a distant admirer and a supporter. I suspect I sent a check to that campaign. But I didn't have any real role in that campaign. In 1972, Roger Putnam, who was a senior lawyer at the time, was the chairman of the Republican Party in Maine so he and I were very enthusiastic. I think when I joined the firm in 1965, all of the people there were Republicans. We subsequently allowed a couple of Democrats to sneak in but, at the time in '72, it was primarily a Republican firm, and we did a lot of lobbying in Augusta, so that was helpful when Bill Cohen ran for Congress.

Jed Lyons: Let's pause here and ask Bill and Chris their recollection of Peter's role.

Chris Potholm: Well, Peter has put his finger on what to me is the most interesting dimension. The campaign answered the question of was it just a young lawyer from Bangor who was running and didn't have the backing of the Portland establishment. And I think he indicated the opposite was true, but I have been curious as to what role Roger Putnam played in the ascendancy of Bob Monks, because it was the Verrill Dana lawyers who would show up at our fundraisers and leave behind, of course, in those days, perfectly legal envelopes filled with cash. And so I've always assumed that somewhere in the Verrill Dana world there were people who wanted Monks to beat Margaret Chase Smith and, of course, Bill Cohen to beat this guy from Washington County.

Peter Webster: Well, in response to your comments, Chris, we did have representational relationships with Monks and the Sprague family that were important relationships. Monks challenged Margaret Chase Smith and it was looked upon as heresy by many Maine Republicans, but, because of our representational relationship and the friendships that some of our people had with Bob Monks, I think we were enthusiastic about the primary contest between Bob and Margaret. I'm not sure that we were particularly hopeful that he was going to be able to beat her, based upon the fact that she'd been a four-term senator. Bob waged a campaign and I think he may have been assisting Bill, because he wanted Bill to run in the primary, because it would provide maybe a more youthful balance for Republican voters in the 1972 primary and therefore in the election.

Chris Potholm: Oh, that's an excellent point. I'd always focused on the general election, where he wanted to have strong Republicans running in the 1st and 2nd Districts, but you're right, there had been an antecedent to what is going on now. I think he also, in addition to not only recruiting Bill, but financing a big part of our operation and backstopping me with all kinds of advice and ad media support. I think Bob Porteous was also recruited by Monks to run in the 1st District, because, again he wanted somebody that was a little younger. I've always assumed that after General Lewis had his heart attack, Monks figured that Margaret wouldn't run and was surprised when she did. I never saw any polling that showed Monks within even striking distance of Smith. Maybe he was hoping that lightning would strike.

Peter Webster: Absolutely, and you know I think there were some people who were tired of Margaret Chase Smith and that eventually showed in the general election. It didn't show in the primary, but that was the year that she lost to Bill Hathaway in the general election and ended her Senate term.

Chris Potholm: Yeah, although I do think that if she had run any TV commercials and if she'd taken the general election seriously, as she did the primary, I don't think Hathaway would have won. She had a career of winning the Republican primary and then the general election. She also had the strategy if you wait until the last minute and have some eleventh hour radio or, in this case she did go on TV, but by then the election was all decided.

Peter Webster: Absolutely.

Jed Lyons: And what about Mert Henry? Was he a partner of yours?

Peter Webster: No, he was not. He was at Jensen Baird, Jed, and he was not a partner, but he was also a significant factor in the Republican Party.

Jed Lyons: He had been very involved at Bowdoin College, too.

Peter Webster: Absolutely, he eventually became chairman of the Board of Trustees. At the time, Mert was on the Republican National Committee for a while. I don't know if he was in '72 but he was a very important Republican in the state of Maine and, I assume, because of the Bowdoin connection, he was quite enthusiastic about Bill's run in 1972.

Jed Lyons: I wonder what credibility that brought to the ticket?

Peter Webster: It brought a lot of credibility, Jed, because, particularly in the southern part of the state, Billy was not very well known. He was certainly known in Bangor and environs, but in the southern part of the state, he was not as well known, and I think that kind of support helped him.

Jed Lyons: How about Lew Vafiades?

Peter Webster: Well, yes, I'm sure Lew was very helpful to Bill. He was another important Republican in Bangor and a well-respected attorney.

Bill Cohen: I want to go back to the comment made by Chris who said that if Smith got through the primary then the general was kind of a slam dunk. I don't think she ever had a primary, prior to Bob Monks. I don't know that that was a factor in her mind; I think she was stunned that anyone would dare to run. I think, Chris, you're right. She was probably giving serious thought to not running. Her eyesight was so much worse than people had any idea of until you looked at her and talked to her.

They were pretty glazed over and so she may have been thinking at that point when the General had his heart attack of hanging it up, but I think Monks actually stimulated her to say she was not going to be beaten by this upstart from Massachusetts. Mert was devoted to Margaret, I mean he worshipped her. I was in a position of having to negotiate being friendly with Mert and asking him for support while not aligning myself with Bob visibly so that was always a difficult challenge in terms of getting Mert's support even though he was very much in favor of me. And I think you're right, Chris, that Monks came and said, "Well, we're going to run two young people." I can't recall, did he get the Big Box voting eliminated in 1970?

Chris Potholm: Yes, he did, I think that was an absolute key to our success. He got rid of the Big Box and, interestingly enough, it was George Mitchell who headed up this committee that investigated the history of the Big Box. The Democrats were the ones that thought the Big Box helped the Republicans because all the little towns automatically voted Republican. But in fact Mitchell did a big study and showed just the reverse, that there was a big plus to Democrats by having the Big Box, especially in the Franco-American areas. So, then all the leaders like Muskie and Violette and everybody else had to do a backflip. When Monks accomplished that, our strategy of dealing with the Franco Democrats and independent-minded Democrats, that's what made that whole strategy viable. Today, Monks doesn't get a lot of credit with Republicans, but I think he deserves a lot of credit for making the Republican Party viable statewide in the 1970s and 1980s. Certainly, Emery would never have come close to beating Kyros in the next cycle.

Bill Cohen: I don't think I would have won, frankly. I think just by forcing the elimination of that Big Box ballot made it much easier for me.

Chris Potholm: Well, normally the Republican candidate for Congress came out of the Androscoggin Valley down 23,000 votes. And with the elimination of the Big Box and our strategy of having you go up there and Jed and the field people and being able to tap all the Bowdoin students who would go up there. You know, in the end, we eventually lost the Androscoggin Valley that first time, but only by 6,000 votes, so in a sense all that came together, the strategy, in that time and place.

Peter Webster: You know, a resource for access to Bob Monks would be a guy named Bill Webster who came up here from Massachusetts to run his campaign for Senate. He subsequently became president of J. B. Brown & Sons and is still living in the Portland area. He was Monks campaign manager for the '72 primary run for the Senate. He'd be a helpful resource on that score.

Chris Potholm: Not only do I know the name, but he was a tremendous help to me whenever I had a question. I learned a lot from him, and he was always willing to share advice and help me out during the campaign and afterward. I was also the recipient of some of his phone calls when he thought we were trying to get too close to Margaret Chase Smith. I remember once we attended a Margaret Chase Smith fundraiser in Bangor at Millers and he was none too happy. I never blamed him, he was just doing his job and the hardest thing in politics is putting a good face on a campaign you know is probably not going to succeed. Webster always wanted Bill to win in the primary, and even after Monks lost the primary, he was a big supporter of Bill in the fall. Bill Webster was also a very smart political operative, and he knew why we weren't jumping on the bandwagon of a guy who probably had 30 percent of the vote at the time. He was really terrific and understanding when all was said and done. Bill also helped us hire Mike Harkins, the "Littlest Gunslinger," of which so much has been written. I always felt Bill Webster was a class act.

Jed Lyons: Okay, what about Abbott Green? Peter, speaking from the vantage point of a member of the Portland community, the legal community, what was your view of Abbott Green?

Peter Webster: Abbott Green was a commercial pilot from some place in Washington County and was a very conservative Republican.

I didn't think he made any sense from the standpoint of the future of the Republican Party to get behind. By contrast, Bill made all the sense in the world—he was young, he was obviously fit, I think the walk through the congressional district was absolute genius. I don't know if that was Chris's idea or Bill's idea, it was certainly Lawton Chiles's idea, but I think that ability to be seen as a young, vibrant, athletic person was very helpful to Bill and I don't think Abbott Green did much operating in the southern area. I mean it was the 2nd District, obviously, so they didn't include Portland, but I don't think he did much except rely upon his conservative voting people in the primary to get through the primary and it was a huge mistake.

Chris Potholm: You know that's a very good point. I remember in those days going in to the Cumberland Club in Portland; as I remember, it was the place where Republicans went to plot and plan, and I think maybe it was Roger Putnam, I don't know, but I was at the Cumberland Club and the name Abbott Green came up and nobody in that world knew anything about him, other than that he had been Neil Bishop's campaign manager. So yeah, I think that his lack of viability, or even visibility in the Portland area, certainly must have hurt his fundraising. Yes, he ran and lost ignominiously to Neil Bishop, but then in a mode of unity and looking to the future, he became the campaign manager for Bishop, so I think rightly he thought, well, I'm next in line and then all of a sudden, he wasn't.

Bill Cohen: And may now be living in Alaska as a huntsman and guide.

Peter Webster: Wow.

Chris Potholm: It was almost as far away as he possibly could get from the scene of that early defeat.

Jed Lyons: So, Peter, when you think back to 1972 and you think of Republican movers and shakers in the state, of course, there was Margaret Chase Smith. Bob Monks wanted to succeed her. Who else do you think of when you think about Republicans around 1972, those that would have formed a nucleus of the not necessarily elected Republican officials, but the Republican movers and shakers, powerbrokers, so to speak?

Peter Webster: Well, I think Horace Hildreth Jr. was significant in the southern Maine Republican Party. He ran for Congress against David Emery and I think that year was 1970.

Chris Potholm: No, I don't think he ran against Emery. I think he had run in the cycle earlier sometime before 1972. Because I do remember going to him as the campaign manager and I went there with all kinds of ideas and position papers and a whole bunch of bullshit. And he just calmly and carefully sat me down and he said, "You know I'm only going to give you one piece of advice and that's in the Republican primary stress familiar thoughts. Republican primary voters do not want to hear anything new. Stress Familiar Thoughts." I never forgot that. What great advice for primary voters.

Peter Webster: I think another person was Harry Richardson from Cumberland, who was a significant factor in the Maine legislature, and I think he was an important figure in the southern Maine Republican community.

Jed Lyons: Yes. How about Joe Sewall, the State Senator?

Peter Webster: Yes, he was from Bangor. And I think he was a very well-respected, honorable man of integrity and I think people had great respect for him. I don't think he made much headway in southern Maine, but obviously was well respected as a member of the Bangor community and as an important person in the Republican Party.

Jed Lyons: Peter, do you think that Bill being a Bowdoin grad was a plus or minus? Let's say he had graduated from the University of Maine rather than Bowdoin. Was there any impact on the vote insofar as his being a Bowdoin guy as opposed to a Maine graduate?

Peter Webster: Oh, I think Bill can certainly address that question better than I, but I think you know, based upon the support, I think Mert Henry was happy to support Bill because they both graduated from the same college. I think you know Bowdoin has a wonderful reputation throughout the state of Maine, and I think Bill really benefited from that reputation of being a Bowdoin graduate.

Bill Cohen: I think it helped enormously from my perspective. You know Colby's a good college. Bates is a good college where you can get a good education, but Bowdoin stands as unique in the state and is seen as an elite college. It's not quite the same as saying that I went to Yale or Harvard or Stanford, but you cannot mention Bowdoin without people saying yeah it's a great school. The fact that I was able to play basketball for Bowdoin and be known as a student athlete, that kind of helped in selling the whole notion of this guy walking 600 miles. How is he able to do that? And they said "Oh well, he played basketball and was All-State in high school and college." I think Bowdoin has still to this day a unique status and was a major selling point politically.

Jed Lyons: Chris, do you have a perspective on that question?

Chris Potholm: I think that's exactly right. For the era, I think it was even truer; 60 years later, I think Bowdoin still has an extremely high reputation, but I think both Colby and Bates as institutions have improved not only their actual but their proportional sense of where they belong. I think both of them have made pretty considerable strides from where they were in 1972.

Peter Webster: I think also, Jed, that in some respects Bill was a bit of an underdog, you know, he was from Bangor, and the background, nobody was quite sure of the background, and I think, being an underdog, Bill placed a greater effort and attention on his being a Bowdoin graduate and I think as Bill suggested it helped enormously. It went a long way in overcoming some of the underdog status that his background provided him.

Bill Cohen: There was also my law school background. Even though I only practiced for six plus years, I took on and argued two important cases in the State Supreme Judicial Court and won. One had to do with landowners' liabilities and the other pertained to state banking laws.

Chris Potholm: There is an adage in politics, "all the big mistakes are made early" and Bob Porteous I think served in the legislature and sponsored the bill that would allow the skin-diving recreational harvest of lobsters. And I think that's the best example I can think of, at least in the state of Maine, of shooting yourself in the foot, the leg, and the head. He managed to do that. I did talk to him and after the fact, he said, "You know, if I had to do that over again, I wouldn't have introduced that bill in the legislature."

Peter Webster: Did he run in the '72 election, along with Bill in the 2nd District?

Chris Potholm: Yes, but Bob Porteous ran against Peter Kyros.

Chapter VII

Oral History Discussion
with Robert Loeb

July 6, 2021

Jed Lyons: So great to see you after 40 years. Let's take a moment to ask you to summarize where you were born and raised, how you wound up going to Bowdoin College, lead us up to 1972.

Robert Loeb: I was born and raised in Chicago and its suburbs. I was applying to colleges in New England when they told me to check out Bowdoin. I did so and had the best experience when visiting there so I went to Bowdoin. During the summer after my freshman year, I joined the staff of the U.S. Senate campaign of Adlai Stevenson in Illinois, and stayed through the fall, so I had some campaign experience. Fast forward to junior year. I had gotten to know Chris, and he knew of that experience, so he asked me about coming on to the campaign. I asked him to let me think about it while I went home for spring vacation in March. Dan Walker had just walked the state of Illinois to win the Democratic primary for governor. So his nomination was fresh in my mind when I returned to Brunswick about a week later. Chris asked again about my joining Bill's campaign and suggested that I ride with Bill for a day and see how we got along, then make my decision. I did just that. We drove around for a day, and I was very, very impressed with Bill as a person and as a candidate. We went to a paper mill in Rumford and were there for the first shift change. One of the workers asked Bill, "What do you think of everybody on welfare? I think they should all be shot." Bill kind of paused for a minute and then gave an evasive answer, because there is no good answer to that question. And I realized that if Bill were to walk across the 2nd District (which was certainly physically large enough to be a very impressive achievement), he could avoid answering difficult questions like that, look down at his shoes to remind everybody how hard he was working by walking across half the state, and establish an image as a man of the people. I told Chris I would like to join the campaign, and asked, "What do you think about him walking across the district and meeting people in every town?" Chris responded that it's a great way to get name recognition, as well. The rest is history. After Bill won the election and I graduated from Bowdoin, I went to law school, I became a prosecutor for ten years in Chicago. Since then, I've been in private practice doing state and federal criminal defense. And in the tradition of Bowdoin, I've taught a class at a law school for over 30 years.

Jed Lyons: Thank you, Bob. Bill, do you remember that Rumford story?

Bill Cohen: I remember obviously meeting Bob and I remember him talking about the walk which I thought was insane in terms of marking where we'd stop for the evening and pick it up the next day and crisscross the whole state. There was Dan Walker and Senator Lawton Chiles in Florida who walked, as well. Not the entire state, only a part of it. So I thought Bob's suggestion was a touch insane and that someone would send out a butterfly net to rescue me.

Robert Loeb: Dan Walker did walk the entire state, which was 1,000 miles. Bill's walk was initially going to be like 400 miles within the 2nd District, and then we added on Aroostook County and that was another 250 miles.

Jed Lyons: Bob, what are the memorable moments of the campaign that you recall or some of the memorable individuals on the campaign?

Robert Loeb: I certainly remember Jim Harrington, Dale Gerry, George Smith, and of course, Mike Harkins, our media consultant. I remember a funny incident with George, who was driving the car on the shoulder of the road with the sign "Bill Cohen Ahead." He was supposed to remain in front of Bill so that people passing in cars would see and recognize Bill walking. Bill repeatedly caught up to George because George was sitting in the car, not moving, and loudly singing what was then a current hit, Chuck Berry's "My Ding-a-Ling." It was a bizarre little scene, and Bill was justifiably not amused. Chris got sick at one point during the summer, and I was dealing with day-to-day operations. We wanted to get more press coverage, because we had an awful lot of positions on political issues that we wanted to communicate to the electorate. We weren't getting the coverage that we necessarily wanted, so I remember that every week I would call the U.S. House Minority Leader's Office to learn what bills would be voted upon in Congress during the coming week. Gerald Ford was Minority Leader at the time. I talked to him once. The other weeks I ended up being put in touch with Bob Hartman, who was his speech writer and was his main legislative aide at the time. I would ask Hartman what was coming up for a vote next week in Congress, so that we could issue the release of our positions to coincide with what might be making the news in terms of national bills in Congress. Hartman would always be able to tell me the House bill number, he was usually able to tell me the title of the bill, and he was always able to tell me the administration position on the bill. But only rarely was he able to tell me what the bill actually did. So that was my baptism to learning how party politics worked in Washington then. It goes without saying, obviously, party influence has increased in recent years.

Jed Lyons: Bob, did you participate in the walk?

Robert Loeb: I would join at times. I spent the majority of time back in Bangor coordinating contacts in the various towns. I did a little bit of arranging places for Bill to stay, a little bit with fundraising and campaign finance, a bit with press and issues—just kind of filling in all the things that Chris had been doing. But then, from time to time, I would join the walk. One of my favorite events, and I'm sure you'll remember this, was in one of the last three cities of the walk. It was in Elmer Violette's hometown, Van Buren, if memory serves. We had a three-on-three basketball game against three of the members of their high school team. And of course, Bill was the star because he still had that two-hand set shot.

Jed Lyons: I remember, Bob, that we were losing until Bill got focused. He wasn't about to lose and all of a sudden we surged into the lead. Were you there the night of a party toward the end of the walk that was hosted by Susan Collins's parents?

Robert Loeb: No, I don't think that I was there that night. I do remember that Susan was involved. I do remember that her family members were leaders in Republican politics, and it was definitely amazing how many future Republican leaders worked on the campaign as volunteers.

Jed Lyons: Bill, any questions for Bob?

Bill Cohen: Question on the mechanics, Bob. Did Dan Walker stay in different homes along the way as you had recommended that I do?

Robert Loeb: Absolutely. He was the outsider from the point of view of the Democratic Party, and so the homes that he stayed in became his local coordinators for the most part, because he didn't otherwise have an organization. They ended up working harder than the official Democratic Party workers. He stayed in local homes, as you did.

Bill Cohen: Did he stay with Republicans?

Robert Loeb: I don't think he stayed with active Republicans much. He did his walk to win the primary election, so he stayed with a lot of independents who might still vote in the Democratic primary.

Bill Cohen: Okay, I was just curious as to whether there was a difference between what we did in reaching across the aisle in places like Lewiston and the St. John Valley, where we went out of our way to try to attract votes from the Democratic side. I'm just wondering if Walker had done that or if Lawton Chiles had. I thought it was unique for our effort.

Robert Loeb: The difference, I think, was he ran for purposes of the primary so he stayed with Democrats and independents for the most part, whereas for us it was the general election, and we were clearly reaching out across party lines.

Bill Cohen: And did the walk during the general.

Robert Loeb: He also did it to cultivate a certain image. He kept the same image, the same blue work shirt, and the same red bandana while campaigning in the general election. The image was effective. He was a very staid corporate lawyer before and this helped him loosen up. I think Chris would say that your image also developed, and you became more casual, and it was good for your image, as well.

Bill Cohen: Bob, I'll just say it was a brilliant idea and I think it's the single most important thing that turned the election for me, along with having you, Chris, and Jed and the whole team together. But the very concept of the walk, I think, was the most important thing for the campaign. Again, I defer to Chris and the whole team, but the idea itself certainly generated more press than I might have gotten otherwise, and certainly set me apart from Elmer Violette.

Chris Potholm: Oh, I agree with Bill a hundred percent. I think the moment I heard that idea, I thought it was pure genius. And I've always given Bob a lot of credit for not only coming up with the idea but also getting into the nuts and bolts of how we would do it. And I've always thought for Bill it was a pretty big leap of faith to go out and put his future on the line for something that was at that time quite unusual to be doing and his campaign manager was so enthusiastic for. And then later on when I had my ulcer problems, I was very, very appreciative of the fact that Bob could and would step in and do an awful lot of the day-to-day stuff that not only did I not like to do, but at that point, I was unable to do. I owe Bob a great deal of gratitude from beginning to end, and it really was a great team effort but among people that stand out, Bob is right at the top.

Robert Loeb: Well, I appreciate that very much. I appreciated the opportunity and how it came out as planned. I remember, there was a memo early on from Chris, in which you had a plan for the campaign and predicted a victory by a 55-45 margin, and I think we were within half a point of that at the end. I know I'm very thankful for the opportunity. I don't think the idea was genius because I got overwhelmed with the news of Walker's primary victory when I went back to Illinois just a few days after Chris and I talked. I couldn't avoid thinking about the fact that a walk by Bill was consistent with the campaign that was already in progress. It blended in very well with "the man the people found" so it was a great experience for all of us.

Jed Lyons: Bob, did you continue to work in politics after that?

Robert Loeb: I got involved in a few independent Democratic campaigns in Illinois, but I realized that when you run for office in a political campaign, your life isn't your own. It's the same thing for legislators who have to give up their life when you are in a legislative session for part of the year, then you go back home and you go spend all your evenings or weekends on a campaign.

I needed to learn how to practice as a lawyer and focus there so I never ran for office or got as involved in a big way with a campaign since then. I also have to say that I had the attitude, accurate or not, that I contributed to Bill and Bill contributed hugely to the country by being a leader in the constitutional crisis that was Watergate. It gave me a good feeling that Bill's election and leadership in Watergate might be the pinnacle of what I might achieve being involved in the periphery of politics.

I think that everybody who has contributed to this oral history can be very proud of their contribution to Bill's election, and even more proud of the role he has played (and continues to play to this day) in American politics and government for the past 50 years. He is one of the few statesmen we have had, putting the country ahead of party and personal power, ignoring the aisle that separates the parties, and putting integrity and the interests of the country above all else.

Jed Lyons: Where are you living now? I think you said you had a daughter who went to Bowdoin?

Robert Loeb: Yes, I've got to say that was a real highlight to return to campus with my daughter, Sarah. She is now 31, and I am very thankful for the education, growth, and friendships she had at Bowdoin. And when I returned to campus with her I felt like a helicopter dropped me off blindfolded. I could close my eyes and walk around campus and get anywhere; it just felt like home again. In one of the years when I was visiting Sarah, I went to see Chris. He was wearing his professor hat and he asked that I wear my parent hat. He asked what I thought of the education that Sarah was getting at Bowdoin. My answer was short, with the obligatory praise. I've got a little bit more perspective now, and I have to say that the professors were great, and her peers were great and together, they form the culture of the college. Bowdoin really lives up to the Offer of the College, that it molds students with the Common Good in mind. My daughter arrived there as a recently graduated high school kid. She emerged from Bowdoin as a great young lady and I'm really grateful for that. She worked in Boston and Cambridge for tech companies, then went to the University of Michigan Business School. She is now living in Chicago and working for Google.

Chris Potholm: Bob, I think as we get different accounts there seems to be a consistent theme about Bowdoin and the opportunity Bowdoin gave each of us. First, admitting us and then exposing us to all kinds of different things that, in the sense that we could do whatever we put our mind to, I think that that's unusual and Bowdoin always had this tradition of being the best school in Maine and the one that was such an incubator for political leadership. I think that that attitude is still prevalent and it's a very positive dimension of the Bowdoin experience in terms of involvement. Students are encouraged to get involved in politics and the Common Good, the greater good. The whole notion of the college being established for the Common Good, I think that's certainly served the college, its students, the state, and the country well throughout its history. Bowdoin has been such an incubator for leadership in all walks of life.

Robert Loeb: Some of Bowdoin's peer schools in New England have been described at times as more ambitious or Wall Street oriented. The word that I use to describe Bowdoin is nurturing, that it was a very supportive community and continues to be.

Chris Potholm: We're trying to track Abbott Green down in Alaska. Green moved to Alaska to get as far away from the 2nd District as possible. Jed mentioned Mark Harroff. I don't I don't think Mark Harroff was involved in the '72 campaign, but he eventually came on board for the Senate race and he was part of that, and he did start working with Mike Harkins before he went off and formed his own firm Smith and Harroff.

Jed Lyons: Bob just asked if your son, Eric, is still doing politics.

Chris Potholm: Well, he is. He is flapping his wings and flown so much higher and farther than I ever could have. He has a media firm in Washington that does Republicans, and he has a couple of pretty big clients, the governor of Ohio and the governor of Texas. And we've been able to work together on a dozen or so campaigns in the ballot measure and bond areas. I've always been so grateful that Erik and I got to do so many Maine referenda campaigns together—Widening the Maine Turnpike, Casinos, NO!, Assisted Suicide, Bear Hunting, school consolidation, and the big $50 million research and development bond. It was one of the great joys of my life. I'm so glad we were able to work together so many times. I always knew when Erik was doing the media for our referenda that I wouldn't have to worry about it and we would have the best commercials. The very best. I always wished we had been able to play soccer together on the pitch but doing politics together was the next best thing.

CHAPTER VIII

Oral History Discussion with Bill Webster

July 21

Chris Potholm: So glad you can participate in this project. It's been so much fun to walk down memory lane to '72 when we were all young pups.

Bill Webster: You certainly were. I don't know if I was.

Jed Lyons: When did you first connect with Bob Monks and come up to Maine?

Bill Webster: I was involved in Massachusetts where I knew a lot of people working with the governor and then I ran a campaign for a guy who wanted to be mayor of Boston. Monks was a guy that I had met at meetings, and he was the big backer of Elliot Richardson. He and I both lived in Cambridge. Richardson was running for lieutenant governor so we became friends, and then we were involved in and out of some minor commercial things. Monks approached me and said, "I want to run in Maine. Would you go to Maine and set up a campaign organization," so I came up in the fall of '71.

Jed Lyons: Give us a quick summary of your background, please.

Bill Webster: I went to Amherst College and I went to Harvard Law. Through an unusual set of circumstances, I ended up working for John Volpe running for governor. He had been governor in '64, which was the Goldwater year and nobody gave him a chance. My senior year of law school the governor called me. He was elected by a few votes, but he overcame the Goldwater defeat, which was substantial in Massachusetts. So he called me and said I'd like you to come work with me on my staff, and so I did when I left law school. I went to work with him. We knew we're going to be running again. So I got my National Guard service out of the way and came back and worked on that campaign fairly high in that organization. We beat Eddie McCormack. I then was campaign manager for John W. Sears's attempt to be mayor of Boston. When that was over, I went into the survey research business and had a company and we bought Becker Research. We did a lot of the polling research and everything else, and from that Monks contacted me just through the fact that we were dealing with each other, and I agreed to come to Maine to set up a '72 campaign to run.

Jed Lyons: You stayed in Maine?

Bill Webster: I've never left.

Jed Lyons: Where do you live?

Bill Webster: Portland.

Jed Lyons: What year did you graduate from Amherst?

Bill Webster: '62.

Jed Lyons: Same as Chris and Bill at Bowdoin.

Bill Webster: We were running in a primary against Margaret Chase Smith. We didn't spend a lot of money on polling because we started with zero, you know, and so I think we did some polling, but I didn't count, it wasn't a marginal thing.

Jed Lyons: What did you think about the Republican primary prospects, both for your candidate Monks and for Bill Cohen in the primary?

Bill Webster: In terms of Monks, we were working as hard as we could to see if we could find ways to overcome a senator who had been in office a long time that had a lot of fans. We knew we were doing fairly well. We made some inroads but I don't think that anybody knew for sure that we would win. We might. I mean everybody was enthusiastic, but you know we also live in this world, and we thought that the age question might be a problem, but I think we were realistic.

Jed Lyons: Was it difficult to get press for Bob Monks in the primary?

Bill Webster: Not particularly, because it was a story. And you know, he was labeled the Cape Elizabeth millionaire, so we had to live with that press label. They always started, there's a millionaire, Robert Monks, running against Margaret Chase Smith.

Jed Lyons: One of the things that everyone so far has pointed out is the importance of eliminating the so-called Big Box. Tell us how that happened.

Bill Webster: My job was to set up a campaign and give us a chance, and when I traveled the state and listened, I said, getting rid of the Big Box can help because basically that locked in voting patterns in the cities. So, we said we have to get rid of the Big Box. We organized the campaign, and we got the signatures and we got in the legislature, we got it passed, and then there was the famous lawsuit of *Kelly v. Curtis* that was really the key. *Kelly v. Curtis* and Curtis was the governor. Kelly was our lawyer, and the issue was we had gotten through all the hoops that you have to do to get this on the ballot. And we wanted the ballot in the primary.

The Democrats, Curtis, Hathaway, they wanted it in the general election. Okay, and the question was could they pull it off and delay it until the general election because then it wouldn't affect the general election. So, *Kelly V. Curtis* forced the governor to put it on the primary ballot.

Jed Lyons: That's a very important piece of information which we didn't have. Thank you. How involved was Joe Sewall in that process? When you think back to the 1972 Republicans in Maine, there was sort of a division between the old-school Joe Sewalls of the world, for example, and some of the more ethnic areas. There was the French-Canadian community, of course. There was rural Maine and more urban parts of Maine. Can you describe?

Bill Webster: When you're running in the Republican primary, you're dealing with an older demographic.

Jed Lyons: My question was about the ethnic make-up of the Republican Party in 1972.

Bill Webster: I would say the Republican Party was as it is today, basically it was older with older people in the towns. And there were more Democrats in the cities, but basically there wasn't any great ethnic element to the primary.

Jed Lyons: Chris said that you had some really great field people working on your campaign in '72 including a brother and a sister combo. Does that ring a bell? Can you talk about how your team interacted with the Cohen people?

Bill Webster: A brother and a sister in the primary campaign? Up in the Bangor area. I can't remember their names. They were in the bus business. That's the only brother and sister I can remember.

Bill Cohen: I would ask what were your expectations when you undertook to represent Bob? If you were looking at the poll numbers in the beginning, what did you think was possible? Was he, as a candidate, one whom you thought could connect with voters?

Bill Webster: When, as I said, he was a big backer of Elliot Richardson, and I was a big backer of Volpe we met from time to time. We scheduled him to do all the things that you would do running in a primary, the types of organizations you'd go to—it's not like running in the general election, particularly back then, so against Margaret, we were working with anybody we could find, and the themes were basically age and time for new blood from our viewpoint. We thought it was worth a shot and you never know.

Bill Cohen: How did you feel Bob was relating to the average Maine person?

Bill Webster: As you know, Bill, he was basically always labeled the Cape Elizabeth millionaire, the capitalist millionaire, Robert Monks, and that's the way that every single sentence began. The people that we were putting him in front of were mostly Republican primary type voters, as opposed to general election types and so some of those people were not too happy to see him running. But it was not the same thing as the general election; we had different strategies trying to find different things.

Bill Cohen: Did you find that Bob was optimistic throughout?

Bill Webster: I think he was optimistic. You're in the field, people telling you that you are doing well. I mean I've never met a candidate yet that was not an optimist. It rightfully seems to be a common trait.

Bill Cohen: Do you know if he felt that at any point along the way he had made a mistake or would have to do better? Did you have a sense he knew he wasn't connecting?

Bill Webster: I mean basically, sometimes you've got people telling you not to run, people working hard against you, but she wasn't running a big campaign so we didn't run into her and she didn't spend any money at all and basically ran on her record and her presence in the primary crowd so it wasn't as if it was a pitched battle or anything like that. It was an effort against a popular person who beat us in the primaries.

Chris Potholm: So it's really like two parallel campaigns. You were doing yours. She was doing hers, and there wasn't a lot of interfacing. Is that right?

Bill Webster: She didn't campaign, didn't raise any money, right. So if you raise no money, you don't campaign, not much to punch at.

Jed Lyons: Bill, do you have any questions for Chris or Bill that you'd like to ask them about the campaign.

Bill Webster: That primary was over, so we were not actively engaged in the general election.

The campaign the senator put together was very, very effective. He had a lot of things going for him, not the least of which is getting rid of the Big Box, so we helped them there and it helped that Nixon was going to be president.

Jed Lyons: Elliot Richardson came up and helped during the campaign. Were you with him at the time?

Bill Webster: I wasn't involved in his relationship with the senator. When I was working with both, he was running for lieutenant governor, and John Volpe was the gubernatorial candidate, so sometimes the three of us traveled around together.

Bill Cohen: Is it unfair of me to say that he was not a great candidate?

Bill Webster: Elliot? That's a really, really interesting question. You know, he wasn't a bad candidate, he really wasn't, and he was such a bright guy. Massachusetts is a different kettle of fish, but he was elected governor and attorney general.

Bill Cohen: He was brilliant. He became a very good friend. He was Clark Kent/Superman. One of the most handsome men I think I've ever seen. He talked in sentences that were perfectly balanced, almost as symmetrical as the doodles he used to create. I used to sit in his office, and he wouldn't even look at me. He listened while I spoke, and he'd be drawing beautifully crafted doodles. I kept thinking he would be much better off if he didn't speak as a candidate because his language was so sophisticated and above the average voter. I used to think a perfect candidate would have Elliot's brain and Gerry Ford's persona.

Bill Webster: Bill, out of curiosity, one question, did you get to know Marty Linsky?

Bill Cohen: Not really.

Chris Potholm: Marty Linsky was my roommate when I went to Fletcher.

Bill Webster: I'll be damned. Well, he was a law school grad and he was a very big help back in the old days.

Chris Potholm: He was a very, very talented guy.

Bill Webster: Very talented. Very loyal to Richardson.

Bill Cohen: So, are you still with the Republican Party?

Bill Webster: Yes, candidate specific.

Bill Cohen: I just finished a long interview with some young students at the university.

Bill Webster: Trump's a phenomenon. He is going to be there for a little while longer and then see what happens next. He may run for president.

Bill Cohen: I think that, also.

Jed Lyons: How many miles was the walk, Chris?

Bill Cohen: 650.

Chris Potholm: Oh, that's right, yes.

Bill Cohen: Well, the point was to stop at any establishment, be it a fruit stand, a corner store, or a factory, whatever side of the road it was on. I just kept crisscrossing the road to make sure I spoke to and shook hands with as many people as possible.

Jed Lyons: How many pairs of new shoes did you have to put on in the shoe factories?

Bill Cohen: I gave away practically every pair of boots I wore during the walk, maybe six or seven pairs.

Jed Lyons: I remember you putting shoes on your blistered feet and smiling, even though it hurt like crazy, and walking out of the factory waving and smiling. As soon as we got out of sight, those boots came right off.

Bill Cohen: Never let them see you sweat.

Jed Lyons: Did Bob Monks ever think about walking across the state of Maine?

Bill Webster: I am laughing to myself because I don't think that was ever contemplated.

Chris Potholm: I wanted to give you a lot of congratulations for helping me when I was starting out as Bill's campaign manager. You were somebody I could always turn to and I always trusted your judgment. On the Monks front, I did have a meeting, I think it was at Bowdoin, it may have been at Bob's house, but it was Bob and his father. And this was when he was thinking of running against Muskie. Bob said he wanted to go on a walk across the state and I said, well, it's been done, you know. Dave Emery did it. Bill Cohen did it. And his father, I don't know whether he was a minister, but he was a person of style, he was used to speaking with great authority, and he said, "Well, Chris, we won't call it a walk. It won't be a walk. It'll be a trek. That magically could change the nature of it from a walk to a trek."

Bill Webster: I was not involved after the primary campaign. I was not involved in Monks's organization versus Muskie. You know we're friends, but I haven't been involved politically. So I wouldn't know about that, but you're right. Reverend Monks was a heck of a guy.

Chris Potholm: The walk was turned into a trek.

Bill Webster: No, but again it's hard to explain what it's like to run against Margaret Chase Smith in a Republican primary.

Bill Cohen: Well, I always felt that Bob wanted me to run. For the optics of it as well.

We had two young guys representing the future of the Republican Party running together.

And at the same time, I was trying to separate myself as much as possible, because Margaret accused me of supporting Bob against her. There were times when we would catch up with her small entourage as she entered a small town to look as if we were campaigning together. She would do her best to outrun our car. I had a lot of good advisors, and we could feed off you, Bill, as well. Chris was my guru.

Bill Webster: As I said, I thought that the effort against Elmer Violette was well run. When the moon and the stars are just right, you know, you end up as a Secretary of Defense.

Bill Cohen: Elmer was the nicest man in politics. He was a kind and unassuming individual.

Jed Lyons: Bill, where did Bob Monks wind up on primary night election in Maine?

Bill Webster: That's a good question. Let me think about it. We would have been down in Portland somewhere, but I honestly don't know where we were. We had a suite at the Hotel Eastland, might have been, but I'm not positive. If I were to guess, we had a party at the Eastland. That would be my guess, but I wouldn't swear by that.

Jed Lyons: Was your opponent friendly immediately after the end of the primary campaign or a little frosty?

Bill Webster: I don't think they spent a lot of time chatting. I don't think either had any interest in talking.

Jed Lyons: If you don't mind, please briefly repeat the great story you told us about the *Curtis v. Kelly* lawsuit.

Bill Webster: So what happened was we started the campaign to get rid of the Big Box. We gathered the signatures, we got it to the legislature, there are certain strictures about when it has to be voted on. Hathaway and Curtis and the Democrats did not want it voted on in the primary because they thought it would affect them and the general election. And by the way, I'll give you a hint after I'm done with this. So we had to sue them. The lawsuit was *Kelly v. Curtis*. John Kelly, our attorney went to Colby to force Governor Curtis to put that issue on the primary ballot which he did. At that time, the Hathaway people were very discouraged because they felt that by eliminating the Big Box it would hurt them during the general election. I won't make any comment. He won the general election, so draw your own conclusions. And if you want to draw your own conclusions, talk to his aide, who everybody knows: Angus King.

Jed Lyons: Oh, interesting. Angus King, did you hear that, Chris?

Chris Potholm: Yes, I did. I did not know that.

Bill Webster: Angus King came here with Hathaway.

Jed Lyons: You probably know that Susan Collins volunteered in the Cohen campaign and during the walk we had an event at her parents' home upstate.

Bill Webster: Good place to have it. I think, everything was aligned. I had an occasion a little while ago to talk about Senator Cohen with a friend of mine. I referred to Bangor Billy and that was our greatest asset; the guy can still jump shoot. Those little towns love to play.

Jed Lyons: Bill, you live in Portland now. You moved there in 1971. What are your thoughts about the future of the Republican Party in Maine today?

Bill Webster: Well, the city of Portland, became quite liberal. If you look at the results of LePage's election, he basically took every place in Maine except a little bit up in Mount Dessert (the college radicals) and Portland, but after that, if you look at the colored map, he won everywhere. One aspect is that a reasonable candidate can still win statewide in Maine as a Republican, like a LePage.

Chapter IX

Oral History Discussion
with Rob Witsil

July 21, 2021

Jed Lyons: Rob Witsil, thank you for joining us. Remind us of your background, where you grew up, high school, college, law school, and so on.

Rob Witsil: I was born August 29, 1951, to Bob and Jean Witsil and grew up in Wilmington, Delaware. I attended Tower Hill School in Wilmington before attending Bowdoin. I was a ski bum in Stowe, Vermont, for three years before matriculation at Delaware Law School. After graduation from Delaware Law School in 1980, I served three years as a Delaware state prosecutor in Sussex County and then worked as the Sussex County Attorney. I opened my own practice in 1980. I've been 40 years in the law practice. I sold my law office location in May 2020 and am practicing part-time now, splitting my time between assisting clients and working art for the Mt. Mansfield Ski Patrol in Stowe, Vermont. My memories of the campaign are mainly from having been out on the road during Bill's walk across Maine. After the election, I spent one summer interning in Bill's Washington office.

Jed Lyons: Tell us your memories of the campaign, about working in Lewiston and the office there, tell us about the walk.

Rob Witsil: Holy smokes, well, I helped set up the Lewiston office with Jed. We didn't have a lot of staff, but we took in volunteers. We were downtown near the redlight district.

Jed Lyons: I think we were on Main Street.

Rob Witsil: Yes, you and I set that office up together.

Jed Lyons: We did. That was in '72. What I would love to hear from you is some of the color of what it was like campaigning in a city like Lewiston which was a Democratic stronghold. I recall that we got a lot of volunteers to go door to door for Bill. We ran into some real characters. Do you remember any of that?

Rob Witsil: I remember going door to door and talking to people, which was generally a good experience. We didn't have too many doors slammed in our face. We generally walked up to the front doors and rang their bell and handed them the brochures and talked about Bill and often stuff other than politics, trying to get a word in about the campaign and just being accommodating to whoever came to the door. I do remember walking down the street and having a police officer come up to me and ask for 10 minutes of my time right in front of the office. And I said "Okay, what can I do," and he asked me to walk up to the police headquarters with him for a minute, and I did. The next thing I knew I was in a police lineup for a suspected sexual assault on the street behind our office. I stood there in line with the four other thugs and the son of a bitch picked me out as the guy who had done the crime. Luckily, I was able to walk out of there without further hassle. I remember seeing the Lewiston office fax machine for the first time and thinking that it was the most marvelous, crazy device I had ever seen.

Jed Lyons: We had an important relationship with a friendly French-Canadian family named St. Cyr. We slept in their home on the walk and then we kept going back there because they were so welcoming. Was it St. Cyr or just Cyr.

Bill Cohen: I think it was St. Cyr.

Jed Lyons: Rob, do you remember what it was like working for that slave driver Potholm during the campaign (laughs)?

Chris Potholm: I've been listening with baited breath to you. Being in a lineup! I had not heard that story before. That's priceless.

Rob Witsil: Yeah, once only in my life, thankfully.

Chris Potholm: And that's the biggest surprise of all.

Rob Witsil: I can remember Bill and Chris coming in, but more often, it was on the phone.

Chris Potholm: Was I always calm and reasonable?

Rob Witsil: Well, he always showed up with his sidekick from Delaware, Mike Harkins. I haven't heard anything for a long time about Mike. He came back and worked in the political scene here in Delaware and then he got a cherry political job with the Delaware Bay and River Pilots Association, which is a very well-founded and well-respected group of river pilots. It oversees all the operations for the ferry between Cape May and Lewes and all of the professional pilots on the Delaware Bay and Delaware River.

Jed Lyons: Do you remember Bob Loeb? He was the one who came up with the idea for the walk.

Rob Witsil: Yes. My best memories were on the walk and meeting people with Bill. In preparation for this I thought about all the hours that I spent out on the road with the "Honk / Wave" and "Bill Cohen for Congress" signs. That was the summer before I was going to play football at Bowdoin. No one knew this, but I was trying to get in shape for football, so I put the signs up on the roadside and I'd run two miles up the road hoping I could get back to the sign before Bill got there. So I wasn't often standing by the road waving at people and telling them that Bill was up the road . . . but that's how I tried to get in shape and held down the fort.

Bill Cohen: But which stretches of the state did you work?

Rob Witsil: Mainly, I remember a fair amount of walking that we did north of Bangor.

Jed Lyons: Do you remember Bill reciting poetry on the walk?

Rob Witsil: Not to me, he didn't! I knew that he had quite a repertoire of poems, but Bill and I just talked about the weather, where we were headed and how his feet hurt!

Jed Lyons: I remember him reciting quite a few poems while hoofing it on the road, including one about a man with a question mark wrapped around his heart. Bill, can you recite it for the record? I think I still have a version of it somewhere. Chris, you were the one who recruited Rob and me and many other students to work on the campaign. We got hundreds of students involved in that first campaign in 1972 canvassing up in Lewiston and other towns. Chris, talk a little bit about how you did that.

Chris Potholm: Threats, bribery.

Rob Witsil: He almost promised a grade better than I would be able to get.

Jed Lyons: He gave you a B plus? The son of a gun did that to me, as well.

Chris Potholm: It was a B plus. Rob, you've heard this many, many times but Jed is obsessed with the B plus that he got on a paper. I gave him a B plus, but he's never forgotten that it should have been an A.

Jed Lyons: Haha well, it was about the campaign.

Chris Potholm: That's right, I think it was a major part of it. If I remember, it was Jed who organized the ladies of the night in Lewiston, on behalf of Bill Cohen.

Jed Lyons: Rob, do you remember that Chris got an ulcer during the campaign and was sidelined?

Rob Witsil: I do remember him out of commission for a while, but I didn't know what it was.

Chris Potholm: Well, I never had reports of you running away from the sign. I didn't know you ran ahead and then back again.

Rob Witsil: I also remember being a terrible inconvenience to Bill one night on some lake in northern Maine when we went waterskiing and I broke my finger. Someone at the lake house was nice enough to take me to the hospital. I'm sorry for that time.

Bill Cohen: The poem you mentioned came back to me:

> Here lies a man
> who died in youth
> for no apparent cause.
>
> A post mortem chart
> said a question mark
> was wrapped around
> his heart.

Jed Lyons: That's it! You did a lot of poetry reciting on the road, to no one in particular.

Bill Cohen: Over the objections of Mike Harkins or somebody else who said that it didn't fit "the man of the people" image.

Jed Lyons: You did it when there was no one else around.

Bill Cohen: I wrote most of it on the walk.

Rob Witsil: One last point: I specifically remember being instructed by Harkins and Chris not to engage in conversation regarding the Nixon re-election campaign issues. I think it may be interesting to address our "hidden reluctance" to endorse or even become associated with the Nixon presidential campaign. I clearly recall now the preliminary instructions given to Jed and me, as advance men, and to door-to-door volunteers to avoid talking about the national campaign and to specifically not align Bill's politics and issues with those of the CREEP. We of course didn't know that Bill would be appointed to the JC, but we were constantly aware that he would be walking a tightrope to acquire Republican financial support and loyal Republican votes while distancing himself from Nixon, his politics, and Vietnam war issues during the campaign and that he would most likely not be in step with Nixon politics when elected. The fact that we were in a clearly Democratic state also played into our hidden reluctance, but it was the avoidance of alignment with Nixon that carried more import. Only Bill and Chris can opine as to how and when the real distancing occurred after the election and during Bill's first term, as I was out of the picture until I came to DC to intern in 1973.

Additionally, and with significant humor, I now recall phoning in from remote areas of the walk to Bill's radio call-in interviews and, particularly on a radio debate with Bill and Green in the primary. With very poor faked Maine accents, Jed and I would pitch Bill homerun questions about local issues and then call back in and ask Green very tough international political questions, with which, of course he struggled immensely! I think that he might have even mumbled that Bill had some "darned college callers" phoning in! Chris, of course, loved this plot and further encouraged it in the ensuing campaign.

I am grateful to Bill and Chris for the political and government experience you afforded me both on the campaign trail and as an intern with the DC staff. I am sure that having those credentials on my CV may have helped me get accepted into law school. I know that the experience provided me, as a young lawyer, with sufficient confidence and some wisdom to not only succeed as a deputy attorney general for the state of Delaware in the prosecution of many serious crimes, but also to represent government entities and political boards throughout my years of private practice. I am fraternally grateful to Jed for his friendship over these many years.

Chapter X

Oral History Discussion
with Cindy Watson-Welch

July 26, 2021

Jed Lyons: Remind us where you were in 1972 and where you grew up, where you went to high school, where you went to college.

Cindy Watson-Welch: I grew up in Portland, Maine. I went to the Wainfleet School then to Wheaton College. I was one of the exchange students at Bowdoin in 1972. I am now living in the beautiful Berkshires of Massachusetts and working as a broker for a luxury real estate company.

Jed Lyons: You married a college classmate of ours, Tucker Welch.

Cindy Watson-Welch: He is still around, sitting on boards and playing lots of golf.

Jed Lyons: Tell us how you got involved in the 1972 campaign.

Cindy Watson-Welch: Oh, that's a good story. I was friends with Bob Loeb and I was looking for something to do for the summer. Bob said, "Well, why don't you come and work on Bill Cohen's campaign? That would be a good job, you will learn a lot and you'd get very little pay!"

So I said "It sounds great." Bob suggested that in order for me to be hired, I would need to be interviewed by Chris and approved by him, so he arranged our meeting. Bob and I went to the meeting together, and I think Bob answered every question from Chris for me. I basically sat there and listened. One of the questions that came up was, "Can you type?" and Bob said, "Yeah, of course she can type." Well, I got the job as the secretary of the Lewiston, Maine, campaign office. I was on the job maybe three days before they discovered that, in fact, I could not type! So, I was removed/fired from that position, and I got to work on the walk which was really a wonderful experience for me. I mean not only was it fun to be on the road in the outskirts of Maine for the summer, it was also educational. It was challenging at times, and just a really good way for me to understand the politics of an election campaign.

Jed Lyons: There weren't many of us who were actually on the walk. There were lots of people in the campaign, of course, but Chris, for example, really didn't spend much time on the walk at all, nor did Bob Loeb. He wasn't on the walk very much either. When Chris became sick, Bob stepped in, and he was in the main office up in Bangor. Tell us about your memories of the walk.

Cindy Watson-Welch: The walk had been in progress and I am not sure at what town I joined in. I know that they were pretty far north in the 2nd District. We were in very rural areas. Rob Witsil was one of my teammates on the walk. I was the only girl, which was fine and did not seem unusual, because Bowdoin had only recently gone co-ed and it was a predominately male environment. We had co-ed fraternities, co-ed dorms, etc. I never felt outnumbered or out of place. My role most of the time was to be a front person. I would travel a day or maybe two ahead of Bill's destinations. I would put up signs announcing that Bill was on his way and then explain to the locals who Bill was. I would also scope out the town and the townspeople to see what was important to them for feedback for Bill. I remember one town, for example, they had a little local newspaper and on the cover of it was a big picture of this damaged telephone booth. Everyone in the town was outraged that their only telephone booth had been vandalized. So I told Bill about that and when he arrived in the town he started talking about crime and vandalism and, boy, that town was united behind him immediately!

Jed Lyons: You remember the town?

Cindy Watson-Welch: Sorry, I do not. All of the small Maine towns started blending together.

Jed Lyons: Where did you stay while you were doing this work?

Cindy Watson-Welch: We were on a very tight budget so basically we stayed in small motels. We sometimes had three to five of us in a room. Being the only girl, I would often get the bed (out of chivalry) and the others would share the second bed or sleep on the floor. I did do my turns on the floor, to be fair.

Jed Lyons: How would you eat on the campaign? On the run, I guess?

Cindy Watson-Welch: We would stop at some local outpost and pick up sandwiches. No time for dining! It was really roughing it in many ways. One evening really sticks out for me. On the walk, it was arranged for Bill to stay with a local family. And that local family would usually invite their friends and neighbors to come by and Bill would make a little speech and introduce himself to all of the group in that particular town. We all went to those and sometimes the host family would feed us. At this one particular town, everybody was invited into the living room to hear Bill speak, and so I went along with Rob and everybody else from our team. I was standing in the room to listen to Bill speak and the owner of the house and host turned to me, and he said, "I think you would be better off in the kitchen with the lady folk." I've never forgotten that one and it reminded me how far women have come in my generation. The guys on the team, who got to stay for the talk, got a laugh out of me being "kicked out."

Jed Lyons: Do you remember what the "lady folk" had to say?

Cindy Watson-Welch: The women weren't talking politics, most likely talking about cooking, so I had little to offer. I was stewing. I do want to share an incident that shows how magnanimous Bill was despite being tired and having sore feet. For some reason I was in the trailing car, which is the one that would follow slowly behind Bill. This car had a sign announcing that Bill was walking ahead. We were moving very slowly and had a good distance to go to get to the next host family home. I had mentioned that at this speed I was going to miss the show at the Bowdoin theater. Someone mentioned that to Bill, and you know what he did? He started running so we could finish early. I still feel guilty about that. I didn't end up making the show anyway.

Jed Lyons: That is great. The man who voted Nixon out of office was running so you could get to the Bowdoin theater on time. Chris, do you have questions for Cindy?

Chris Potholm: Well, first I think she has put her finger on something that we have talked very much about, but it was very, very important and that was crime in the streets. That was a major pillar of Nixon's election efforts. Even though Maine had such little crime, the crime rate was perceived to be very high nationwide. I think it was the number two or three issue in Maine at that time. I remember going to a meeting of Republicans with Bill up in Old Town. And Abbott Green, his opponent, was there and was talking, and I got a sense that they wanted to hear about law and order. And so I highlighted Bill Cohen's tremendously successful crime fighting effort as a policeman in Old Lyme. I must have spoken for 10 minutes about all of the wonderful things he had done to fight crime and they really responded extremely well. When you think of the crime rate in Maine, it's never been significant but to these people, it was certainly high in their mind. The other question I have, as you're driving that car, did you get a sense that people were stopping to talk to him or turning around and following him or was it just strictly point to point.

Cindy Watson-Welch: Our destination was from one point to the next point but people would slow down, they would wave or they would look at me or sometimes when I was in the back car, they would say, "Who's Bill Cohen?" So yeah, I mean, he got a lot of attention that way, passersby, of course, most of the time. Sometimes people would stop and offer him a beer or a sandwich or something like that. He actually gained 20 pounds on the walk, which is really amazing when you think he was making 20 miles a day, but every family made a feast for him. They were really happy to be hosting him and having friends come in and speak to everybody. How many pairs of sneakers did you go through?

Chris Potholm: I don't think he wore sneakers. I think that was the problem. He wore work boots and every place he went they gave him a new pair. They were always having to be broken in. He went to the hospital three or four times to have his feet taken care of.

Jed Lyons: But he would always gamely put on the new shoes or the new boots in the shoe factories and walk out with them on. Then, of course, he took them right off and gave them away to people.

Cindy Watson-Welch: There were many factories in Maine, that's for sure.

Jed Lyons: Back then.

Cindy Watson-Welch: Bass and everybody.

Jed Lyons: I remember when we were going through Rumford and the paper factory smells. You remember that?

Cindy Watson-Welch: I do!

Chris Potholm: They used to say, "That's the smell of money."

Jed Lyons: Cindy, were you there the night that we were at a party hosted by Susan Collins's parents? Do you remember meeting Susan Collins during the campaign?

Cindy Watson-Welch: Yes, briefly.

Jed Lyons: She was working on the campaign. Toward the end of the walk we were at her parents' place somewhere between Houlton and Caribou. It was very rural. Bill got to stay in the main residence with the Collins family. Chris and Dick Morgan and I were directed to their camp on some remote lake and Chris drank the water and got sick as a dog.

Chris Potholm: That was the night before the end of the walk so that was a terrible time to be sick.

Cindy Watson-Welch: Terrible timing.

Jed Lyons: Dick Morgan didn't get sick because he was drinking from his bottle of Scotch.

Cindy Watson-Welch: There were some other fellows on the walk besides Rob. I think there was a couple of other Bowdoin guys that would come and go.

Jed Lyons: Harvey Lippmann?

Cindy Watson-Welch: Yes, I remember his name.

Jed Lyons: Chris, does that ring a bell?

Chris Potholm: Yeah and Holly Rafkin. I remember she drove a car, at some point, but it may have been the next summer.

Jed Lyons: So you had no budget. Did you spend your own money on your motel rooms or were you reimbursed?

Cindy Watson-Welch: The campaign paid for the hotel rooms. We pretty much were on our own for picking up meals, but the host families and others involved with the campaign would stop by with donuts or other treats.

Jed Lyons: So our esteemed campaign chairman Professor Potholm gave you no budget other than for a fleabag hotel room shared by three people?

Chris Potholm: Live off the land, that was our model, live off the land. and the other example I gave them, which seems wildly inappropriate, was Joseph Stalin, who as a revolutionary, to finance the revolution, he robbed banks. I wrote several memos that I sent out: "Remember Joe Stalin, you know he kept his campaign going by robbing banks." When you write some of these things down and then you look at them in print years later, you say, "Why, I could be thrown in jail for that." Compared to today's overbought, wildly expensive campaigns, I mean, we really did it on a shoestring. You know, as you remembered it, three people in a motel room and no food! You guys were real troopers doing everything on a shoestring. Today you'd be eating sushi and staying in suites with all the money washing around. Thank you, Cindy, for what you did way back then. You made the Cohen campaign what it was.

Cindy Watson-Welch: I know, but it was always interesting. I mean from one town to the next it was always something new. There were some really long afternoons in which there were very few cars going by. I think it was tempting to just have Bill hop in a car and move on to the next town, but he was determined to walk each mile. Slow days could get a little tedious but, for the most part, it was really fun.

Chris Potholm: Did you get to eat with Bill and the families?

Cindy Watson-Welch: No, we usually did not. Bill was with the group the host had assembled and we would be offered meals, but we sat separately.

Jed Lyons: Cindy, I remember many evenings in the backyards of rural homes, where, as you said earlier, the families would gather their friends and there might be 20 to 25 people standing around and there would be a home-cooked meal served or there'd be barbecued hot dogs and hamburgers. Then Bill would speak and the family and the neighbors would ask questions. I think that is where Bill cemented a relationship with voters. That was really important, because all of those 25 people would go tell all their friends the next day and word spread pretty quickly. "What an authentic, nice young man."

Cindy Watson-Welch: He was only 32 and absolutely a new and fresh face. That's why everybody gravitated to him, it's why they talked to their friends about him. I mean that's really grassroots. He went right for the heart of the people who are going to vote.

Jed Lyons: As a native Mainer, how did it look to you, having this young guy who had been mayor of Bangor? Did he seem to have potential? What got you interested in working on the race in the first place?

Cindy Watson-Welch: Probably because he was a young guy with a lot of enthusiasm and he was not your typical candidate. He had a vision and a really good message that resonated with everybody. It was an incredible ride for me to participate in this innovative campaign.

Jed Lyons: Cindy, one of the things Rob Witsil said after he was interviewed is "I've been thinking about this, and I was remembering how much we in the campaign opposed Nixon's reelection in '72." Do you have a memory of that?

Cindy Watson-Welch: No, not really.

Chris Potholm: I think the cognitive dissonance was that actually Nixon ran quite well in Maine overall but for us the key to winning was cutting the Democratic margins in Androscoggin and Oxford, so we didn't accent Nixon at all. We were trying to get more Democratic votes out of Lewiston than the average, so it made no sense to highlight a connection with Nixon and then, of course, the irony is that Bill ended up voting to impeach him. So we really, without articulating too much, had a couple of different campaigns going on: we had the one in rural Maine to get out Republican voters and the other one making us seem to be semi-Democratic on the issues of jobs and security and the kinds of things that people cared about in Lewiston-Auburn.

Jed Lyons: That was really helpful. Thank you, Cindy.

Chapter XI

Oral History Discussion with Bob Monks

August 4, 2021

Jed Lyons: Thank you so much for joining us, Bob. I want to begin by reading something that Chris Potholm wrote in a book that our company published in 1998 called *An Insider's Guide to Maine Politics*. "It would be too bad if all that people remember were Bob Monks' losses, instead of what he did to make modern Republican politics better. Monks was a major force behind the elimination of the straight ticket voting Big Box and his early support, financial and otherwise, of Bill Cohen, Olympia Snowe and Jock McKernan helped make them all viable candidates. It is difficult to see how the post-1972 Republican Party would have had the winners it did and succeeding for two decades without Bob's involvement. He deserves a more positive position in the history of Maine politics." So let's stop right there. Just about everybody we've spoken to has made the same point Bob, so we wanted to share that with you.

Bob Monks: Thank you.

Bill Cohen: I agree with that.

Bob Monks: I am glad to be accorded credit, but the reality is that Bill Cohen made the Republican Party and the party lasted about as long as Bill held elective office.

Jed Lyons: Bob, how did you get involved? Can you take us back and walk us through, first of all, how you wound up in Maine? You're from Massachusetts originally. How did you get involved in Maine politics?

Bob Monks: My family has always had homes in Maine and Massachusetts, so when Milly and I moved full time to her family's home in Cape Elizabeth in 1969, we were just making a change of year-round residencies. There is no question but that the absence of a birthplace in Maine, to say nothing of either school or college, was a political liability. I had a vast interest in politics, but, as my beloved sister would continually remind me, I had little aptitude for it. What I really wanted to do was to get to know the people in a community. My background of extreme privilege was one of houses at the end of a locked drive and private schools. I needed to have the opportunity to get to know people. That wasn't possible in the urban environment of Massachusetts. I had early been exposed to the small towns in eastern Maine and it seemed to me that this would be the kind of place I would like to represent. My wife's grandfather had assembled a lovely piece of property in Cape Elizabeth as a summer home. Milly and I moved there in 1969 as a permanent residence.

Jed Lyons: Was there ever any doubt that you'd be running as a Republican?

Bob Monks: My mother was always a Republican and my father inclined from Socialist to a modern Rockefeller Republican. Alas, party membership was largely a matter of religion in those days in Massachusetts. If you were a Catholic, you were a Democrat. If you were Protestant, you were Republican.

Jed Lyons: What was it that you saw in Bill Cohen that made you decide you wanted to support him in 1972 when he was the mayor of Bangor?

Bob Monks: I had been told that Bill Cohen had been appointed by the court as investigator of a transaction in land in the Moosehead Lake area that involved the most important citizens of Bangor. Bill did what most lawyers do not do, particularly when they are just starting a practice. He evaluated the facts and came to the conclusion that was contrary to the interests of the principal banks. There was one leader in Bangor named Curtis Hutchins who was generally recognized as the leader. He told me that Cohen's decision was very difficult but he had nothing but respect for him. So I immediately concluded that I wanted to meet this guy!

Bill Cohen: We first met in a radio station.

Bob Monks: I looked across the room and there was this guy who had a real sense or presence, a sense of integrity, a sense of being "good within his own skin." And I said, boy, this is the kind of guy I really want to work with in politics. So, whatever I could do to be helpful to Bill, I wanted to do it. I just felt that he was the answer to our need for character and integrity in politics. I have always felt that helping Bill is the single best thing I did in politics.

Jed Lyons: Bill, do you remember that meeting, and what your impressions were of Bob, not just from the meeting, but from having known about him.

Bill Cohen: I do remember the meeting. I can't recall the radio host's name, but it was something like Emié Gauvin. He was a Hemingway-looking character, had a great voice and a very liberal following. I was surprised to meet Bob there. I asked him what he was doing there.

It was the first time I had met him. My first reaction was that he has too much. He's too tall, too wealthy, too educated. And how is he ever going to relate to the people Down East, in Machias or Calais, or wherever? I think we met up one time after that, Bob, somewhere down the coast, and I felt that he suffered from an embarrassment of riches. He had so much in the way of a physical and intellectual presence. I didn't know how he could relate to people like me or those living on the coast or in the rural areas. So that was my first impression, that he had such a big presence. And then, when he said he was thinking of running for the Senate against Margaret Chase Smith, I wondered if he realized what he was getting into. In addition to the embarrassment of riches, he exuded enormous self-confidence. He had been responsible for eliminating the Big Box, so I thought if I ran, I was going to have a shot, based on what he had done.

Jed Lyons: Bob, when you decided to run against Margaret Chase Smith you knew that you were up against an icon. What was your game plan? What was your strategy? Who was helping you and your campaign? We've heard a lot about those who were helping Bill, including you.

Bob Monks: In politics, you never know who's going to win until it's over, and there are all kinds of strange things that happen on the road and it's hard to predict who is going to win. Who was going to win the Maine Senate race last year? When I first ran for the Senate, I felt that I would have at least the experience of meeting people all over the state and gotten decently well-known and to be in a position to go further if I wanted. So, I thought it was a no loser when I think of my objectives.

Jed Lyons: To whom did you look for support and advice in your campaign?

Bob Monks: Well, Bill Webster, my manager, came from Massachusetts and that probably didn't do either of us any good. The failure to have someone from Maine compounded the problem of being perceived as "being from away."

Jed Lyons: It's been said that you did not use TV in your campaign, TV advertising.

Bob Monks: No, that's wrong, we did use TV.

Jed Lyons: Where do you think that impression came from? Are you hearing it for the first time? Chris, you were the one who mentioned that. Where did you get that impression?

Chris Potholm: I was talking really about the level of television. I've always been struck by the fact that Bob's Senate campaign seemed to take away the advantages that he was talking about as disadvantages, and I think that may have been because it was the beginning of the age of the use of TV. But my sense was I can't ever remember seeing an ad about Monks in that time period. So he may have had some ads, I just never saw them.

Bob Monks: If my ads did not make an impact on Chris Potholm, they probably weren't effective generally.

Jed Lyons: Chris, you were running Bill's campaign in 1972. Bill has shared with us his perceptions of Bob's campaign, why don't you share yours?

Chris Potholm: Well, I distinctly remember going to Portland to meet with Bob and Bill Webster. I remember meeting in an office in Portland and, like Bill, I had a sense that Bob was just this huge figure and the dominating force. So I thought it was great that he was supporting us and I thought he had access to all these different resources that we didn't know about. We certainly didn't know Mike Harkins or the agency. I don't know where they found Mike or why he was there; do you remember that?

Bob Monks: I do. I basically delegated all of that to Bill Webster, and I came to the meeting with the same attitude you did. I was glad to meet Mike Harkins and know who he was.

Jed Lyons: So when you were running in '72 and you looked around at the Republican landscape in the state of Maine, did you see it in terms of ethnic groups in different parts of the state—Protestants, Catholics, you had the French Catholics down in Lewiston and some of the old guard WASPs up in other parts of the state. How did you perceive the race and how did you think about how you would go about parsing those different ethnic groups around the state in order to secure their votes?

Bob Monks: Fortunately, I spent a year being educated in France, and so I attacked the French vote in French and walked around Lewiston and Biddeford and in the county. Alas, I didn't appreciate the difference between Parisian French and French Canadian. I started with a blank slate because people knew very little about me. I went in with the attitude that, if I met someone, they were a presumptive supporter. I took this attitude in contrast with the politics I'd been involved with in Massachusetts where I actually was the chairman of the State Committee before I came to Maine. There the divisions were so sharp it would have been silly to go after an Irish Catholic, which, of course, is an ultimate irony in that my great-grandfather, John Patrick Monks, was an immigrant from County Meath. In the main I tried to be as open as possible with everyone. Bill Cohen did us all one better when he walked around the state, ending up twice in the hospital. Even though I wasn't walking, I nearly did get to every town in Maine in the course of a year and it's a lot of ground to cover. What was beginning at that time was what I would call "Movement Republicans." In the Goldwater campaign, they emerged as a powerful force in the party, but they were just emerging in 1972. People would ask me questions that I didn't really think were political issues. I didn't think, for example, that whether or not you were for abortion was a political issue. Whether I thought it was or not was actually irrelevant. The people I talked to thought it was very important and if I wasn't on the right side of it, they weren't going to vote for me. I think that as conservative energy matured in later years, after Bill was elected to the Senate, he asked me to be the State Chairman. I was glad to do this primarily because of my belief in him but also knowing that Movement Republicans were a continuing force that had to be dealt with and their party was not what Bill Cohen or I had in mind.

Jed Lyons: Bill, do you want to comment on that?

Bill Cohen: I was going to make a comment about coming from Massachusetts and Maine politics. I know John Kerry reasonably well. I always thought he took advantage of the name Kerry in Massachusetts politics.

I once asked him if he was Irish. After all, he has an Irish name, has Irish hair, and hails from Boston. I was stunned when he answered, "Hell, no. I'm English." I always wondered if the people in Boston knew that.

Then when he was running for the presidency, he volunteered that he had some Jewish blood running through his veins, as well. I guess that's almost mandatory for candidates these days (with the exception of Trump).

Bob Monks: Bill has gone through life with the infinite advantage of a beautiful, redheaded Irish mother.

Jed Lyons: Let's talk about Elliot Richardson. Bill Webster reminded us that you brought Elliot Richardson into the Cohen campaign and Elliot came up and campaigned with us during the walk. We were all astounded by his verbal skills and his intellect. How did you get to know Elliot Richardson, Bob, and how did you get him involved in your campaign and in Bill's campaign?

Bob Monks: Elliot was the leader of the moderate Republican Party. I always viewed him as my mentor and first met him in 1956 in the campaign for governor of Massachusetts. It was a losing campaign, but Elliot was there all the time writing the papers and helping everyone. I have a photograph of Elliot with my wife, Milly, a week before he died. He was a lovely man and I miss him.

Bill Cohen: I got to know him quite well during the Watergate crisis, and when he left office I used to drive him to his law office every morning.

If you listened to him, you would see how brilliant he was. But he took a long time to say things, and he would say them in a way that was grammatically brilliant, but politically ineffective. From my perspective, when you're trying to give a speech, you can't take a long time to convey the message. How he spoke was all very beautifully worded and connected, but his message was lost in the elegance of the words.

Jed Lyons: Bob, would you share with us your impressions of how the Republican Party changed from 1972 to the present?

Bob Monks: Today I am considered a RINO (Republican in name only). I have been a Republican all of my life starting with Wendell Willkie's campaign for president in 1940 but I haven't been able to vote for a Republican with a few local exceptions for the past 15 years. But I continue to call myself a Republican and in my own way try to contribute to the future of the party.

Jed Lyons: What future do you see for the party in Maine?

Bob Monks: If Governor LePage runs for re-election, he will have to reply to the question as to whether he thinks that Biden is the legally elected president of the United States. Senator Rick Bennett, who has been a very moderate and intelligent leader in the legislature for a number of years, managed to keep the party and the governor on compatible terms. At the presidential level, I could imagine that a combination of the Democratic Party and the never-Trumpers could produce electoral victory from top to bottom for the Democratic Party—almost a recollection of 1912. If you simply substitute Trump for Teddy Roosevelt coming in the side and people like me who simply will not vote for him and are content to associate with a Democratic Party, I think there would not be enough votes for the Republican Party to carry the election.

Jed Lyons: Do you have recollections of meeting Susan Collins, Jock McKernan, and Olympia Snowe? All of them worked on Bill's campaign in 1972 and perhaps also worked on your campaign for the Senate in '72.

Bob Monks: I have great admiration for Bill Cohen and his great generosity as a party leader. There are a lot of people who get elected to office, but very few of them have at least two of their employees succeed them as U.S. Senators. Senator Collins was an incredibly competent staff person, and as a result today it is hard to imagine a more prepared and professional senator. Senator Olympia Snowe also worked for Bill and benefited enormously from the support and confidence that Bill gave her.

Jed Lyons: Bill, we'd love to hear from you on the subject of those three individuals: Susan Collins, Jock McKernan, and Olympia Snowe. Tell us how you met them. We know that Olivia, for example, was married to Peter Snowe. She was not in office at the time. He was a State Senator. I believe he died in a car accident in a snowstorm in 1973.

Bill Cohen: I didn't know Olympia other than through Peter at that time. I had met him, and he was obviously pretty active in the Republican Party in the state legislature. I met Olympia only casually when she was helping on the campaign, but I didn't really get to know her. I would say Susan had more of an impact on my campaign than either Jock or Olympia. I met Susan through meeting her father in Caribou. Don Collins was a popular State Senator and was well liked by the Franco-American population up in the Valley. He spoke fluent French. And he took me around by the hand. I went to people's camps and sat down and drank with them during the night. Don had a pretty thriving lumber business. His brother, Sam, was also a State Senator. Don's sons were active too, and Susan drove one of the cars that helped protect me on the walk. So that's how I met her. They became a big help to me in Aroostook County and I stayed in their home in Caribou whenever I campaigned in the area. Don put himself out for me and I think it made a big difference.

Jed Lyons: Chris, how about you, what are your recollections.

Chris Potholm: Well, I just want to ask Bob something. We talked earlier about Don Collins, Joe Sewall, and Harry Richardson. I've always thought they were early supporters of you, and they represented the more progressive wing of the Republican Party. They saw you and Bill coming from the same ideological open part of the party and I wondered if Don Collins was as prominent as Harry Richardson and Joe Sewall in supporting you?

Bob Monks: On the day I announced my first candidacy for the Senate in Augusta, there was Joe Sewall, the Senate President, sitting in the front row. Most Republicans were scared to death—in the manner of Republican officeholders today, they didn't want to upset the senior

Senator, who was known to have sharp elbows. But Joe Sewall gave me the ultimate legitimacy as a candidate. The whole Collins family were wonderful supporters. Susan's father was a State Senator for many years, as was his father; and Sam Collins was a very distinguished member of the Supreme Court for many years. Harry Richardson represented a more liberal wing of the party than did his primary opponent, Jim Erwin.

Chris Potholm: And Dave Huber.

Bob Monks: He was less comfortable being a partisan politically.

Chris Potholm: Ah, yes.

Jed Lyons: Bob, is there anything in particular you wanted to say that we haven't covered?

Bob Monks: I'd like to describe the single event about Bill Cohen that is perhaps my most poignant experience in politics. It took place at a motel at the base of Capitol Hill on a hot day. I was waiting for Bill at the bottom of the escalator and as he comes down, he appears to be distraught, which is not the way he usually looks. So I simply said, "Oh" and he looked at me and he said "You know, I've just thrown away my political career." Bill that day had voted in favor of selling the AWACS surveillance aircraft to the Saudis. Clearly this was not congenial to Israel. Sometime after that he said another memorable thing: "I just can't stand Howard Baker insisting on treating me like a child and saying that I've got to join the party line and back this thing." Bill was and is a person of conscience and will vote what he considers to be in the public interest. Giving away his political career was not his ultimate concern. Getting called by the party leader to be whipped into line probably was one of the reasons that Bill left the Senate after his third term. Of course, Bill's vote as a freshman member of the House Judiciary Committee to vote for the impeachment of President Nixon stands as one of the most courageous political acts of anyone's political career and of course is in marked contrast to the Republican members of Congress in 2000 and 2001. When he was in the Department of Defense in the Pentagon, he had a group of business people come in every once in a while and talk to him. I was one of them, and I was the last one out the door one time. As we were leaving the secretary's office, Bill turns around and he looks at me with a smile as big as all out of doors and said "Bob, this is the best job I've ever had." I can add that he was one of the most applauded secretaries that the Department of Defense has ever had.

Bill Cohen: There's a story behind the AWACS vote. I was way out front in opposing the sale to the Saudis and I got a call from a British friend of mine who I assumed was an Israeli intelligence agent. He said, "You need to come to London to meet the Israeli Ambassador to Great Britain." I asked, "Why?" He said, "You just have to come." So I flew to London; I had a private meeting with the Israeli Ambassador, Shlomo Argov, and he said, "Look, the politics of this thing has gotten way beyond what the Israelis really want. They are not as opposed to the AWACS sale as is being said publicly. But they're worried that AIPAC is making the sale a political test of loyalty to Israel."

And then he said what they really want are these ten things that are far more important to their security than the AWACS, and he recited a list of ten things Israel wanted. He said I should have a meeting with the Israeli Ambassador in Washington. I flew back to Washington and called the Israeli Embassy to ask the Ambassador, Ephraim Evron, to come to my office. He came immediately. I never disclosed to him that I had met with Shlomo Argov but I assumed that he knew. I asked him whether there were any security items that the Israelis wanted. He reiterated that Israel was firmly opposed to the AWACS sale but . . . that there were some things that were of great importance to Israel. He pulled out a sheet of paper from his suit pocket that contained many of the same items that Ambassador Argov had discussed. It became very clear what had happened. The Israelis initially let it be known that they were absolutely opposed to the sale to the Saudis. Then AIPAC (American Israeli Public Affairs Committee) took the lead and ran all the way to Capitol Hill, calling on all of Israel's supporters to defeat the sale. But the Israelis worried that if the Senate defeated Ronald Reagan's strong support for the sale, the Israelis would pay a price for his defeat. So, to turn a victory that might be a defeat for them long term, they decided to use the leverage they had to extract some more arrows from America's vast quiver which would in fact give them far greater security than the threat posed by AWACS. I received a call from the White House that President Reagan wanted to see me. They needed my support for the sale.

I said, in essence, only if you will provide these ten things to the Israelis.

Jim Baker looked at the list and after a few minutes said, "We could do six, possibly seven, but not ten." I said, "Well, okay, let me think about that when I get back to the Hill." I thought about it and called back. I said, "This is too hard for me."

The vote was scheduled to take place in the next hour or two. So, I called the White House and said I want a meeting one on one with Reagan himself, nobody else in the room. I went to the White House and said to the President, "Mr. President, you told me in front of Jim Baker and others that you would be prepared to provide the Israelis with six or seven of the items the Israelis need. And I said I need your word that you will meet every one of these things. He said that I had his word and we shook hands.

So, I went back up to the Hill and I said to Howard Baker that I needed time to speak on the floor of the Senate to explain my vote. Howard said, "You've got ten minutes." I said, "No, I need at least a half hour, maybe longer to explain the reason why I'm about to change my public statements against the sale and vote for it."

I didn't do it for Howard Baker or even for President Reagan. It was because the Israelis found themselves in a bind of their own creation in which they were about to defeat the sale of the AWACS but lose all the other things that mattered far more to their security. The problem was that I was never able to explain that and my role, publicly. I never was able to say that publicly. I'm saying it here now for the first time.

The next day, the journalist, Mary McGrory, wrote a headline story that read, "With Friends Like Cohen, Israel Doesn't Need Enemies." The political fallout was pretty devastating. Many in the Jewish community, to this day, believe I allowed Israel's quantitative or qualitative edge to be eroded. A classic case of "No good deed goes unpunished."

Jed Lyons: Bob, before you go is there anything else you'd like to say.

Bob Monks: No, thank you, I am thrilled to have the occasion to participate. I am delighted that Bill's career is being written about because the timing is perfect and the subject matter couldn't be better. Thank you, Bill, for your friendship and public service.

CHAPTER XII

Oral History Discussion
with Mike Harkins

August 4, 2021

Jed Lyons: Mike Harkins, great to have you on. The first thing I want to tell you is that I have a classic photo of you flipping me the bird in 1972. I don't remember the circumstances, but I'm sure it was well deserved. So tell us what you're up to these days and how you got involved in the campaign in '72.

Mike Harkins: I'm still in Wilmington, Delaware. Helen and I are still married after 57 years. It was all because I just kept saying "YES." We have six grandkids, one of which has Pop Pop's genes—he went to Richmond and is press secretary for Senator Joni Ernst from Iowa. Three more are still in college. I'm retired but doing some consulting to stay out of trouble. All my Republican friends are pissed off at my lifelong friend, Joe Biden. As Bill knows, Joe and I went to high school together. I was with him the day his first wife was killed. We went through a lot of stuff as personal friends—Beau's death, weddings, birthdays, golf matches, and more. Although we don't agree on all his policies, despite all my Republican friends, I remain friends because this is Delaware. That's the way it works here. Since you're asking about the things that we remember from the 1972 campaign, one event sticks out. Two weeks after the election, Bill and Diane came down to Delaware because Maine played Delaware, and they stayed at our house. We went to the game, and I introduced Bill to Joe Biden. It became the beginning of a relationship that continued all the way through their careers.

Bill Cohen: I think I met him before that. There was a parade that I came down to watch. I didn't meet Senator Caleb Boggs who Joe beat at that time, I didn't meet Joe that time, but I was there.

Mike Harkins: It's called "Returns Day." Delaware is the only state that still does this. All the candidates go to Georgetown, which is the county seat in the lower part of the state—Sussex County. The winners and the losers ride together in a parade. And then the two Party State Chairmen bury the hatchet at the public ceremony. Then there is a big pig roast. But the first substantive meeting was at the Delaware/Maine football game (Delaware won) that started the Cohen-Biden relationship.

Jed Lyons: So were you running Joe Biden's first campaign for Congress in '72?

Mike Harkins: No. This is funny. I ran for office (state representative) only once on a bet. I was staff for the Republican State Committee. We flipped the legislature in 1966 and won more seats in 1968. In 1970, the Republican incumbent quit the State Representative seat where I lived. I was meeting with incumbent representatives who I had helped to get elected in '66, '68, and '70. At the meeting, they all said, "Harkins—you can't do what you make us do." I said, "Yeah, I can." So I bet them and I ended up running on a bet.

As it turned out, Joe ran for his first time for a New Castle County Council seat. The council seat and the state representative seats over-lapped. In those days every local candidate had to appear at every local platform—churches, social clubs, Rotary, you name it. So, Joe and I would appear at these events with our opponents. Both of our oppo-nents would read their speeches and leave. That left Joe and I standing there to answer questions—he running for council, me running for the legislature. The day after the election, I called him and I said every damn sewer problem (county responsibility) I'm sending to you. Joe countered with every pothole complaint (state responsibility) I'm sending to you. I served one term. That was enough. That same year (1970) I started The Agency with Chris Perry.

In 1972, when I first did Bill's campaign, I also did Caldwell Butler from Virginia (he also was a Republican on the Judiciary Committee who voted for Nixon's impeachment) and the congressional campaign against John Kerry in Massachusetts—Paul Cronin. They all won.

In 1971–1972, Delaware had a fiscal crisis. I was the freshman member of the Finance Committee which determines the state budget. I was coming back and forth to Dover three days a week and then to Maine, Massachusetts, or Virginia the other four. I finally came home one day and said to Helen, "I'm going to quit Dover. I'm not doing this anymore. Behind the scenes is what I like." How I got involved with Bill is that a guy by the name of Evan Dobelle had worked as a consultant in 1968 for the Delaware Republican candidate for governor, Russ Peterson. After the election, Evan stayed in Delaware for a while and then went back to Massachusetts and worked for Senator Brooke. When I was looking for business, Evan introduced me to Bob Monks's consultant, Bill Webster.

He was running Bob Monks's campaign against Senator Smith. He was looking for candidates to run for the two House seats in Maine. He asked if I wanted to talk to this candidate about the campaign—I said sure. I went up and met with Bill and Chris. The funny thing about the meeting was that Chris had this whole list of questions, several of which asked how we were going to attack Ed Muskie. I'm thinking to myself, these guys are nuts. Muskie was the most popular public official in Maine at the time and they want to start the campaign by attacking him? So, after the meeting, Webster said, "Well, if you want to work on the campaign, we will pay the consulting fee." That's how it all started. I don't think it's in writing, but we came up with this: "**The man the people found.**" And we would add in-house and Dead River finance. We produced this five-minute TV film (they would run them on television in those days). After the campaign, we could never find a copy. One day, in order to edit it, I was in Bangor and had to go to Augusta. (Joe Sewall had airplanes for his mapping company that Bill used. That's how Bill got all over the district.) So I called up and got a plane to go to Augusta. Bill was campaigning in Aroostook County using another plane and Diane was using a third one to go to an event down the coast. Joe Sewall shows up to go somewhere on business and all his planes are gone with the Cohen campaign. That was the end of the Cohen campaign air force. We were then told that Bill was the only person allowed to use them.

The other funny story is the whole walking part of the general election. We did not invent a brilliant campaign strategy. Lawton Chiles running for governor had done it first in Florida. Starting the general election, we were broke. We figured out that you can go from Lewiston to the Canadian border as the summer project. If you look back at the newspaper clippings and coverage for the campaign, the primary was about one third of it and in the general election the walk dominated our coverage. Potholm recruited Jed and Rob Witsil (Bowdoin students) to organize and they were the campaign staff with Bill on the walk. Their assignment was to go each day to the next town to find a place to stay that night (free) and put some voter event together. It worked. Bill doing this different campaign approach forever left a reputation that he was a different kind of Republican. He was viewed by the people in Maine as somebody who cared about the average person.

The other incident that I will never forget, which occurred after he was in Congress, to me represents his approach to important issues that set up his reputation forever—the Nixon impeachment. The hearing and witness testimony were behind closed doors. Bill kept meticulous notes and had a dozen notebooks on individual testimony. He put all the various testimony together into one book. At that time, I was consulting for the 1974 election for Harry Richardson who was running for governor in Maine. Bill calls me up and he says, "I'm going to be in Portland tonight, can we meet?" So we meet and Cohen hands me this notebook. He had indexed everything from the investigation. "Will you read this?" So I read it that night past midnight. The next day we sat down for breakfast, and he said, "Well, what's your conclusion?" I said, "You're going to vote to impeach the President," because he had meticulously put together what I don't think anyone else had done in this thoughtful and thorough way. It is a moment in politics that I'll never forget.

The other great, unique story after the campaign was it led to Bill being named to serve on the Judiciary Committee. As usual, we were in debt and had no political money. So we're in Washington going through orientation. Thanks to Gerald Ford (who was Republican leader at the time) our assignment was to the Judiciary Committee. We were thinking about Maine so we made a strong pitch to Ford for Armed Services. But the Junior Member just does not get there out of the box. Ford thought Judiciary was a good assignment and the rest is history. But he did offer to help on a fundraiser. We had a dandy. Everybody was there. Very rare for a freshman—Jerry Ford, Elliot Richardson, and Chuck Percy. Everybody who was anybody came to this fundraiser including a freshman Democrat congressman from Louisiana. The press had taken a liking to Bill and there was a column that week, I think by Mary McGrory, about how politics was different and friendly.

Bill Cohen: So I have to say, number one, Mike Harkins, I've been under the false impression for years that you were doing Joe's campaign, as well, because I associated you flying back to Delaware, and a couple of times you told me you were meeting with Joe so I assumed that you were doing his campaign as well. I've told the media that you had handled both. The other thing that you mentioned about "the man the people found" and Dead River finance, there's a story behind that that Bob Monks was just telling us, one of the reasons that he was attracted to me, was because I had gained a reputation in Bangor. I had brought a lawsuit against Merrill Trust Company, the state of Maine Recreational Authority and Curtis Hutchins who was the chairman of the Dead River Company. His son, Christopher Hutchins, was one of my closest friends. So in suing his father and his company and the bank and a guy named Louis Hilton of the Hilton family, I brought a suit against all of them because I had been asked by the Supreme Court Justice to be a guardian *ad litem* because they had a conflict of interest on the bank. And that ended up in court for several years, bringing in a former Supreme Court Justice, but the key was I had sued Curtis Hutchins, probably the most powerful man in Bangor. The firm that was representing him, Merrill Trust, the attorney, John Conti, said to me, you have pissed everybody off in this city, you will never practice law in the city again for having brought suit against Dead River and the bank, so they didn't finance me at all. Curtis may have been nice, but they weren't financing me.

Mike Harkins: But that was not my home birth.

Chris Potholm: The problem was that you didn't like being called "The Littlest Gunslinger." Absolutely, I thought it would be very clever that you were "The Man, The Man the People Found" but it never really caught on. It didn't have a rhythm to it, but I've got this in the back of my mind that you and I went to a meeting on our own with only Monks and Webster. We had a whole bunch of things we wanted them to do. And it was the first time I'd ever heard this phrase, but I've used it ever since. At the end of that meeting, we got in the car and you said, "We got the whole schmear." I never heard "the whole schmear" before, but apparently whatever it was they signed off on it, and we were very happy.

Mike Harkins: Yeah, that's right, Chris.

Chris Potholm: We were talking about the walk, trying to figure out the night before the walk ended who stayed where, but I remember the walk was over and the old Sewall air force was no longer part of our repertoire and our car died in Patton, Maine. It just disintegrated; it wouldn't go any farther. You got in a car and went up to Patton, Maine, and picked up Dick Morgan and me. We were standing by the side of the road, and you picked us up and brought us home. Do you remember that?

Mike Harkins: Yes, I do remember a car.

Chris Potholm: What were you doing in Augusta? Do you remember what that was all about?

Mike Harkins: It must have been with the Augusta ad agency we used, I met with them three or four times.

Chris Potholm: Well, that brings us to the second of Jed's obsessions. What was the relationship of Mark Harroff to the 1972 campaign?

Mike Harkins: When Bill asked me to be chief of staff, I came to DC to interview for the position. The reason I happened to be with Joe Biden that day (that was the day his wife was killed) was because we came down together on the train. We walked up to the Senate Office Building. I was using Senator Boggs's office (Delaware) to interview staff. It was different in those days. If you were elected, you didn't have assigned office space. Joe and I parted. He was going someplace to interview and find some office to use. I said, "I'll see you back home." We had talked about getting our wives together. The Bidens were going to get a place in Georgetown and have Helen come down some weekend. I did interviews, one of the guys I interviewed was Mark Harroff. I went back on the train mid-afternoon to Wilmington. A whole bunch of people were looking for me because Joe had gone off to somebody's office and nobody knew where. Somebody called Hale Boggs's office looking for Joe. Boggs's secretary said I don't know where Biden is but Mike Harkins was with him. Where is Harkins? He is on the train back to Wilmington. (No cells.) When I went to the bar across from my house in Wilmington, I was greeted by the owner saying the "western world is looking for you." At some point, Joe called his law office in Wilmington and that's how he found out that his wife and daughter were killed. I hired Mark. He eventually teamed up with Jay Smith in the firm of Smith and Harroff. Smith worked for Congressman Rhodes and then John McCain.

Bill Cohen: They were alike.

Jed Lyons: When did Tom Daffron get involved?

Mike Harkins: Well, my deal with Bill was that I wasn't going to stay permanently. I would hire the staff and get the office started, but I wanted to go back to business and home. Tom Daffron was a reporter for the *Wilmington News Journal* who had left the *News Journal* and hooked up with

Senator Chuck Percy. So I caught up to him when I was looking for experienced staff leads. I said I would not be there permanently. We're looking for a chief of staff. Tom said he might be interested. I got him over to see Bill. So Tom succeeded me and was there forever. One other event that came out of this was Senator Percy agreed to come to Maine for a fundraiser for Bill. He was going to stay at Bob Monks's house. Tom asked because Senator Percy liked to swim every day. Was there someplace in Portland where he could? Of course, it was in the middle of winter. Bob Monks's home was out on a point facing the ocean. I said I didn't know but I'll see what I can find. I called Monks's housekeeper for an idea. I said, "You know that Senator Percy is staying for a Cohen fundraiser and he likes to swim every day. Do you have any idea where we could go?" I'll never forget to this day, she replied, "salt or fresh water?" (Monks had two indoor pools). When I called Daffron back, he thought I was pulling his leg. The night we arrived at Monks's house we were all standing in the kitchen saying hello and Percy opens up the icebox and starts making himself a sandwich.

The other thing Bill might remember that is interesting is that when we first hired staff in those days you didn't have the money for staff that they have today. We could not pay a lot. And in those days, I guess it's still true, but all the organizations from the various states each threw a big event in Washington and usually invited the whole delegation. So you'd have five or six of these every night. What we used to do is have Bill go to the most important one, I went to the next most important one, then the young staffers in the office who needed dinner covered the balance. Their instructions were simple; to pick up Bill's name card, say thanks and don't drink too much. So at least they got fed.

Bill Cohen: The campaign we ran in '72, there was a filming that took place down in Northeast Harbor.

Mike Harkins: Right.

Bill Cohen: We had both my sons, Kevin and Chris, there and it was one of the most poignant moments for me. I don't know who was running the film but he was talking to Kevin and the two of them were together.

We're looking out over the Nelson Rockefeller place and Kevin said, "Dad, if you do get elected, will you still have time to play with us?" They caught that on film and they ran with that for much of the campaign.

Mike Harkins: It was a local film crew from Augusta. Somebody recommended them. That's where I went down to edit. So I don't remember. But I remember that line.

Bill Cohen: Well, the significance was that wherever I went following that ad, running into people who would say, are you going to take time to play with your kids—that was such an emotional thing coming from two kids saying we don't want to lose you.

Mike Harkins: In those days you could have five minutes of TV coverage at the beginning of the hour. That moment and the walk are the two things that best illustrated Bill and made the campaign.

Jed Lyons: Chris, what questions do you have for Mike Harkins with regard to the campaign? You were the campaign chair. Mike, you were the hired consultant. How did you two work together?

Chris Potholm: I remember, we had just a great relationship, we had a lot of fun, we kidded each other. We tried to always put Bill's interests first, ahead of the Republican Party, ahead of Monks, ahead of anybody else. As a result, we kind of stepped on a lot of toes. I remember that we were always apologizing for this or that, not meaning that, but there was a central focus on what was good for Bill. We also had a lot of fun driving around. You know, Mike Harkins would fly in with his briefcase with his underwear and game plans from other places, and he might show up at the Bangor office. It was like a tornado, you know, he came in and swirled around and gave orders, did this and got on the phone, asked me about something that happened just two hours ago.

Bill Cohen: Like that time when Mike lost his briefcase back in Delaware, full of all the documents.

Mike Harkins: That was not the first game plan. It was the second. Remember, Chris, I forget the reporter who actually took it.

Chris Potholm: Yes.

Mike Harkins: It was the governor campaign plan for Harry Richardson or as we called him "Harry the Horse."

Chris Potholm: Mike Harkins never learned the lesson that you can't live out of a briefcase and out would come the underwear and various pill bottles and all kinds of stuff. Then there was an idea like, "You guys haven't thought of using the weekly newspapers"—and we hadn't, so that turned out to be a very important thing. I think that the ads that you did in the primary in the various weekly newspapers, people talked about those as well. I just remember that we had a lot of fun, and we had a central purpose and that's what propelled us through months of the campaign.

Jed Lyons: Do you happen to have a copy of the map of the walk?

Mike Harkins: No, I think it was straight up from Lewiston to the border. I haven't looked at my boxes in a long time and seen what's in there. I do have framed in the basement the large blow-up picture of Bill from the walk.

Bill Cohen: Jed, there was something a couple of years ago, maybe five years or more now, where there was kind of a reenactment of the walk. Some folks went out to try and demonstrate taking the Cohen campaign on the road as a kind of things remembered from the past. But it may be at the University of Maine, I don't know, it may be a copy, but I know exactly where I went and could redraw it, but if you're looking for the original map I don't know where it is.

Jed Lyons: Well, it'd be helpful if you could take a map of Maine and redraw the walk with a highlighted pen or pencil because we will want that for the book.

Chris Potholm: I am certain I sent at least one copy up to the library because I remember sending some papers up there, so somewhere it's in the University of Maine library. The important thing is the book has to have a town-by-town map.

Mike Harkins: Okay, and I think you and Rob would have the real stories, all of the stories which I think are amazing.

Jed Lyons: We have a lot of stories, but we don't want to tell them all.

Mike Harkins: What Chris said about walking the tightrope in the primary, we had the problem with Monks and Senator Margaret Smith. Being asked who is this guy running against Abbott Green? All the real conservatives wanting to know exactly where we stood. We had to walk the walk in the primary. I remember we had county chairmen on the coast we had to duck.

Chris Potholm: Washington County, yeah.

Mike Harkins: Washington, that we had to finance.

Chris Potholm: Well, I think that's right, but several people have, without prompting, mentioned how disliked Abbott Green was by a lot of people in the Republican Party. So I don't remember having a problem finding a town or a county chair against Abbott Green. He expected to be the party choice. He ran against Neil Bishop for the State Senate, but he did not have a lot of support. And I do remember wherever we were we always found somebody who would be against Green in the primary. We just never had any problem finding somebody that would be for Bill against Green.

Mike Harkins: I think the other thing that came out of the whole election, when you think about it, was the future leaders in Maine. Many started with Bill. Bob McKernan, Jock's younger brother, was the driver. Jock was the coordinator in Bangor. Olympia and her husband, who later died in a tragic car accident, ran Lewiston, and Susan Collins's father helped in Aroostook.

Jed Lyons: Don Collins.

Mike Harkins: Yeah, Don Collins, so you figure out where all those people and his daughter ended up, that became the heart of Maine's Republican leaders.

Jed Lyons: It's an amazing story and we've talked a lot about that. Do you have anything you want to say about how the 1972 campaign wound up spawning so many political careers?

Mike Harkins: I don't know how it happened, but I don't think you could find too many campaigns where all the people who played a role in the campaign ended up playing major elected roles in their state. That just doesn't happen normally.

This is my favorite Jock story. He had his tough run for governor (second time reelection). Delaware Governor Mike Castle and Jock had become friends as governors. I was Castle's Secretary of State and Castle had me set up a fundraiser in Delaware. Jock and Olympia came down. We did a fundraiser and we raised $80,000 in Delaware. We got Sununu there, as well. He was Bush's chief of staff at the time. Jock won in November after trailing most of the campaign. The day after the election, Castle and I are in his office and on the speaker phone with Jock. I'm saying congratulations, you got through it. Of course, smart ass me also says yeah and you almost took Olympia down with you. From the back of the room on the phone comes this voice "Yeah, he almost did."

Jed Lyons: Bill, do you have any last questions for Mike Harkins? There's one last question I have for you that actually came up with Rob Witsil. That is the role that Nixon played. Chris, you can explain that better than I can.

Chris Potholm: You remember this point. We shied away. We shied away from Nixon because we were trying to get votes in the Democratic areas, but Nixon actually ran ahead of us in the state, so it was one of those. We had to go one way in order to accomplish our mission, but the way in which we did it, Nixon was more popular than we were when all was said and done.

Bill Cohen: Just let me add a quick footnote here. I think I may have tossed it away, but when Nixon came back to Maine, it would have been in '71. I think he came back from the Middle East, stopped at Loring Air Force Base, and flew down to Bangor. I was on the city council, I may have been mayor at that time, and there was a rally held for him. A lot of protesters came out, they were holding up signs. "Stop the war, stop the war" and the Secret Service went through several hundred people and ripped up their signs and said that they were obstructing the Secret Service's view. So what I ended up doing is writing to complain about it publicly. I wrote to the city manager and said I wanted a full investigation as to why the city police cooperated with the Secret Service and basically took down protest signs that were anti-Nixon and not at all interfering with the line of sight. I had about a three-page legal document of me at my best and worst saying why this is a violation of the first amendment, and that should have been on the radar of the Nixon people, and they would have seen that document that went to the city manager. I had called publicly for an investigation into Nixon and the Secret Service.

Mike Harkins: Well, you got even, Bill. As a big guy go-to.

Bill Cohen: The guy being hope.

Chapter XIII

Oral History Discussion with Severin Beliveau

August 18, 2021

Jed Lyons: Good morning, Severin. Here we are, gathered again 50 years later. It's great to have you here.

Severin Beliveau: Believe me, it's great to be here.

Jed Lyons: You have had a legendary career in Maine politics, almost 60 years, I think.

Severin Beliveau: Almost. I had my 65th high school reunion Saturday.

Jed Lyons: What high school was that?

Severin Beliveau: Stephens High School in Rumford, Maine. And it was kind of uplifting because only the healthy survive, but the balance is changing. Usually there are more—historically there've been more of us alive than dead, and I think we've turned the corner this year. So I raced back home. We spent most of our time in Rangeley. So I'm up here hiding in Rangeley.

Jed Lyons: Oh, is that where you are now?

Severin Beliveau: Yes.

Jed Lyons: Tucker Carlson's up there, I think.

Severin Beliveau: Oh, I know it well. As a matter of fact, I was invited to go fishing with him last year. A friend of mine hosts him. He said, "Do you want to go fishing with him?" And I said, "Are you kidding? Do you think I want to spend any time with Tucker Carlson?" You know, he's up here a week or ten days fishing. He lives in Bryant Pond in the summertime and spends a lot of time in the Rangeley region.

Jed Lyons: Rangeley is a beautiful place.

Severin Beliveau: Yes, it's a lovely place.

Bill Cohen: The last town to give up crank telephones was Bryant Pond.

Severin Beliveau: That's right. Yup. That's right.

Jed Lyons: I wonder if you would take a moment to introduce yourself?

Severin Beliveau: I was born and raised in Rumford, Maine, and went to local schools, Georgetown University undergraduate, Georgetown Law School, and served on the U.S. Capitol Police for a year. If we'd been on the force on January 6, I don't think any of that would have happened. But, in any event, I returned to Maine, became Oxford County Attorney, served a term there, then I served one term in the State House of Representatives and one term in the Senate, Democratic Party Chairman for five or six years, and served on the Democratic National Committee for several years. I then retired from elective office and developed a law firm in Rumford with my father and brother and eventually with offices in Augusta, Portland, Boston, and Concord, New Hampshire. Now we have a pretty good-sized law firm. I married later in life and we have four boys who are now scattered around the country. We live on Munjoy Hill in Portland and spend most of our free time at our home in Rangeley. I've been involved with most, if not all, Democratic campaigns since the early '70s in various roles. I'm happy to be here.

Jed Lyons: How would you describe Maine politics in 1972 in terms of the Republicans and Democrats in the state? How did they split in terms of the percentage of voters who were Republican versus Democrat? How's it changed from 1972 to now?

Severin Beliveau: Well, I think that it changed dramatically, because up until that time there was what I call the "Muskie Revolution" that started in 1954 when Muskie was elected governor. From '54 to '72, the Democrats gained strength annually, controlling both congressional houses and the legislature for several terms. In Maine, 1972 marked the change and the redirection of the two-party system. There were a number of factors that contributed to it. Prior to that time, the Republican enrollment exceeded that of the Democrats, and then in the '60s and '70s, as a result of a major effort by the Democratic Party, the enrollment of Republicans and Democrats became somewhat equal—I think it was almost a third, and a third with independents. In '72 there was a dramatic change, and a number of factors contributed to it. One, I think, was the role of Bob Monks who ran against Margaret Chase Smith in '72. He spent a great deal of money, I think a quarter of a million dollars, campaigning all over the state. Margaret Chase Smith spent $10,000 and campaigned only on weekends and she won. The other factor was the Big Box (straight ticket voting) that Democrats really capitalized on and benefited from. And as a result of an effort by Bob Monks, the Republicans and the League of Women Voters initiated a petition and had a very successful drive to remove the Big Box from the ballot, and that resulted in a lawsuit which I think was kind of defining and led to meetings at the Blaine House with Governor Curtis, Congressman Hathaway, Elmer Violette, and a few of us, to discuss what would happen. Following the successful petition drive, the governor had the choice of when to schedule the election. He could have chosen either the primary in June or the general election in November. Bill Hathaway was urging him to delay it to November, so he'd have the benefit of the

Big Box, as did I and others. And as a result of that, a lawsuit ensued. So John Kelly, who we all know was an active Republican at the time, sued Governor Curtis to get the court to order him to schedule the election for June and not November. That case went up to the Law Court. I argued the case before the court, which ruled that it wasn't up to them to make the decision; it was solely at the discretion of the governor. So we were concerned at that time that the governor would schedule it for June which, in fact, he did. The primary election vote in June eliminated the Big Box. There was a number of other things, including Billy Cohen's campaign, which obviously redefined the way campaigns were run in Maine. Elmer Violette ran a traditional campaign, a low-key campaign. And there was a number of factors that were helpful to Billy and very harmful to Elmer. One is that he really neglected Androscoggin County, which, at that time, was a treasure trove for Democrats. I think that Bill and his people did a great job of focusing on Penobscot and Androscoggin counties, traditional Democratic counties. Elmer went to the convention in Miami, while Bill ignored the Republican Convention to continue campaigning. He stayed in Maine to campaign during that time, and he ran a really transformational campaign, particularly his 600-mile walk from Bethel to Fort Kent, and then focusing a great deal of time in Androscoggin County. Elmer, ironically, did not spend much time in Androscoggin County. He took it for granted that the votes were there. What he failed to do was to spend time with people like Louis Jalbert, who we all know was a very colorful Democratic leader and who felt neglected by Violette and his campaign and made no real effort to assist him at that time, nor did the local union leader Denny Blais, who was the executive director of the local textiles union. They made very little effort. The last couple of weeks of the campaign, as I recall, Elmer spent his time in Aroostook County while Bill and his people were focused on Androscoggin and Penobscot counties. The result was that Bill won because he kept the historic margin in Androscoggin County from about 25,000 votes to 5,000 votes.

Jed Lyons: Let's stop there and see if Bill or Chris have any questions for you.

Chris Potholm: I think Severin just said something that rings very true. He said Elmer ran a low-key campaign and I remember, being campaign manager, I was always on the lookout, like what were they doing, and I was astonished at how little he actually campaigned, what little news he actually made. I agree with Severin that he's going to the convention while Bill stayed at home working the state, which was a turning point, I think.

Severin Beliveau: As I mentioned to you, Elmer Violette's campaign manager was Frank Murray, who later became my brother-in-law. I spoke to Frank last night and asked him that very question because, as I recall, at that time I was trying to get Elmer energized. Elmer was not a good campaigner and didn't engage very well with people. He felt very uncomfortable in that environment. And so, he thought by using mailings and the traditional way of working with the unions, the farmers, and people like that, that he would prevail. He ran against Margaret Chase Smith and lost. He later became a State Senator, but, no, I think there's nothing there, and Frank Murray told me last night that his biggest problem was trying to encourage Elmer to campaign. And I said, "Why did you guys neglect Androscoggin County to the extent you did?" And another thing I heard, maybe you know about this, is that he ran a television ad in Bangor in French, which kind of offended the Irish in Bangor more than anything else. There is a very small French population in that part of the state, and that seemed to backfire on him. And the other factor here was that Hathaway's campaign diverted many of the resources. People would invest in Hathaway's campaign and not Elmer's campaign. Frank said they didn't have a hell of a lot of money to run the campaign. And Chuck Cianchette, who was the treasurer at the time, was desperately trying to raise money for a media campaign, but they weren't able to raise that type of money, which I believe Bill and his campaign succeeded in doing.

Bill Cohen: Severin, you just touched upon a point that I've always wondered about. When I was first deciding to run, a number of people said a guy named Cohen can't win in Maine. Basically, anti-Semitism was strong enough as an undercurrent that it would be enough to discourage me. But I felt that because I looked more Irish than Jewish, it wouldn't be an obstacle. And I was wondering if the opposite of that was true as far as Elmer was concerned. Do you think because of his Franco-American ethnicity, and the fact that he spoke with a Franco-American accent, that was a liability for him? That he was less inclined to be a TV personality for fear that they would say we like him and he's a nice fellow, but well . . . no one's ever expressed that publicly. I really liked him, and I thought he was one of the most decent people I've ever met. He was easy to campaign against because there were no rough edges. There were no attacks on me in any way and I always felt that he was self-conscious being Franco- American from the St. John Valley. Once the Big Box voting was eliminated, I don't think he had it in his heart to go out there and try to mix with people either in person or on TV. That was my sentiment, and I don't know if it's true or not.

Severin Beliveau: Bill, that's the exact question I asked Frank Murray last night, and I believe Elmer was self-conscious about his accent. His principal language as a child, and throughout his life, was French. He and his wife spoke French to each other at home, and his son Paul would say that they all went to French schools, and even French high school back then. That was a fact. And, secondly, the accent issue was there, but it wasn't one of those things you could define or quantify very easily, and some of the Francos were saying to themselves, "Do we want someone with an accent serving in the Congress?" It deals with the historic insecurities of the French-Catholic community, which was a factor. I think he was very reluctant to campaign to begin with. That wasn't his nature, and he felt much more comfortable in the Valley, and the fact that he was there the last two weeks or 10 days of the campaign says it all. Also, and I was thinking about it this morning, the French-Catholic community is really comprised of two types: the Acadians and the Quebecois. Elmer's family, and most of the people in the St. John Valley, are Acadians; our family is Acadian. But the Lewiston crowd, for the most part, are Quebecoise. And that created a little tension between the two areas (not so much today, but back then). They didn't feel that they had that much in common with Elmer. The fact that he neglected them, and for the reasons you suggested, I think, contributed significantly. Plus, the other factor that carried a lot of weight was your title as mayor of Bangor, which played well in Lewiston, because in Lewiston to become mayor, you really had to work at it. You ran citywide for office. It wasn't like in Bangor where you were appointed. So people gave you a lot of credit for "this guy must have worked his ass off to become mayor of Bangor, therefore, he must be a pretty good guy." And that carried a lot of weight.

Jed Lyons: What about anti-Semitism in Maine in 1972? Do you see it as a factor in politics back then?

Severin Beliveau: Yes, I do. Not so much today. I think it was there to a degree. I think beneath that veneer in the '30s, '40s, and '50s, there was a lot of anti-immigration feeling in this state, and it applied to Catholics and Jews. I don't believe it was there during the '72 campaign. I believe that Bill's straightforward description of his family was very helpful in dealing with this issue. I don't think the anti-Semitism was as serious back then as some of the anti-Franco and anti-Catholic feelings that existed in the '20s and '30s. In 1928 and 1930 my father ran for Congress and experienced it all over the 2nd District, but we've improved greatly since that time. But to just see what's happening in Maine now, look at the Trump success in the 2nd District where there are white supremacists who are anti-everything. They're not overtly anti-Semitic and maybe anti-Catholic, for that matter, but that's another issue for another time.

Jed Lyons: How about Joe Sewall's role in the 1972 campaign and Louis Jalbert who apparently went to a sporting camp owned by Sewall that neutralized Jalbert?

Severin Beliveau: Louis Jalbert was a great self-promoter. He viewed himself as the leader of the Democratic Party, and was the self-appointed, self-anointed Mr. Democrat. And I know that he did not assist Elmer in the campaign. He felt that he should have been the candidate. Throughout his life, Louis always undercut any promising Franco politician. He and Joe Sewall and Ken MacLeod were close friends. And he loved being entertained by that crowd up at Joe Sewall's camp. There is no question that Louis was compromised in this whole process, and, in great part, was responsible for the textile workers union not making the effort that they had done historically.

Chris Potholm: Severin, I wonder if you could give us a little background about how you met your wife during this campaign? This campaign obviously had a big impact on you as it resulted in your lovely wife and children.

Severin Beliveau: Yes, so this occurred in '72. There was a fundraiser event for Elmer in Bangor coordinated by Frank. I was party chairman and a speaker, so I showed up there with a girlfriend and Cynthia was there completing name tags for Frank. Cynthia was one of the hostesses and I noticed her and observed, "Well, there's a very attractive young lady." I was in my thirties at the time. I called her brother the next day and said, "How do I reach your sister?" He said, "Why?" And I said, "I'd like to chat with her." In the meantime, the night before that we all went out and had a beer somewhere in Bangor. I was with my girlfriend and, Billy, you'll appreciate this, Cynthia was with Marshall Stern. That was enough to make me upset, you know. Marshall Stern was a very colorful lawyer in Bangor and active in Democratic politics. His father later became a Superior Court judge. He was very close to George Mitchell. When Mitchell was a U.S. District Court judge in Bangor, he and Marshall were very close. And Marshall was kind of a man about town, and, as I said, a good criminal trial lawyer. He died in an automobile accident at a young age. But, in any event, that's how it happened. I called Cynthia the next day and invited her to dinner. She was a hostess. I was a speaker. I had a girlfriend. She wouldn't talk to me that night because she thought I was with this girl and, in any event, from then on. . . . We were married a year later and have four boys. The rest is history.

Chris Potholm: What role did Neil Rolde play in the campaign? I know he came to Bowdoin to negotiate with me about the various debates they were going to have. I could have sworn he said he was the campaign manager.

Severin Beliveau: I think that just confirms what we're saying. Frank Murray was the campaign manager. There's no question about that. Neil played a major role. He wrote a lot of material for Elmer, most of his position papers, and a few of his speeches, but Frank was responsible for the day-to-day management of the campaign. That just shows the state of the campaign. Frank, who was really a novice at this, did it because Elmer and he were good friends. Although he had not been involved in a congressional campaign, at the time he was serving in the State House of Representatives. Neil was quite active, but he wasn't the technician. He did a lot of the substantive work, but I think Frank was responsible for the day-to-day operations of the campaign.

Jed Lyons: When you first heard that Bill was going on a 650-mile walk across the 2nd District, what was your impression? Did you think this is a gimmick or did you think it was a good idea? What was your opinion?

Severin Beliveau: I think it was both. It was a gimmick and a good idea. It succeeded because Bill was unknown and Elmer was better known, but not much better, and it changed the traditional way of campaigning. I think he added a whole new dimension to the campaign, and the contrast was very dramatic. Billy came across as a young, attractive, and energized candidate. Elmer was the traditional, almost a backroom politician with a three-piece suit, dependent upon the conventional, traditional way of campaigning. So Bill broke the stereotype and added this whole new dimension. And then, Billy, weren't you hospitalized a couple of times because of alleged foot problems? You received as much credit in the press on your treatment as you did on the issues.

Bill Cohen: They didn't keep me overnight, they simply lanced the blisters I had on my feet because they were filled with so much fluid I couldn't get my shoes on. But they just kind of cut those open, wrapped my feet, and sent me back out on the highway. So that was my heroism for the day. We tried to capitalize and show how tough I was and could bear any burden, in JFK's phrase, to achieve success. So it was that kind of spirit that I tried to convey. I guess, as you say, it probably gave me some votes and some visibility. I helped the shoe industry because I kept donating all my shoes in every little town. They'd be having a local fund-raiser and I kept donating my boots.

Jed Lyons: Will you reflect for a moment on your views in 1972 of the Democrats who you were going to be competing against in the campaign? Severin shared his views. Tell us yours.

Bill Cohen: Well, number one, if anyone was a novice at the game, it was me. I had no real experience, other than being elected to the city council, appointed to the school board, and serving as the assistant county attorney. I had a lot of things going on in Bangor but nothing beyond the city. When I was on the city council, I ran against Bob Baldacci. The Baldacci family was close to mine because my dad used to make all the rolls for his restaurant. I grew up as a five- or six-year-old going to Baldacci's Italian restaurant (originally called The Baltimore) with my father and holding some of the bags of rolls. So it was a little more challenging to consider running against Bob. I thought, when the time came, I was going to try to be chairman or mayor. But beyond that I had no political skill. When I first went back to Bangor after law school, I was asked to be Howard Foley's campaign manager because they couldn't find anyone else. Howard was running against Bill Hathaway in the 2nd District. Howard was the former Penobscot county attorney and a really gifted trial lawyer. But he was really stubborn. He insisted that he was going to stand on the Dickey Lincoln Dam, if it was ever built, and raise a toast to the people of Maine. I tried to persuade him not to take that issue as it was very popular, but he was absolutely opposed to what would have been a huge public works program that created hundreds of jobs in the area that really needed them. I didn't view the Democrats in any negative way. I was probably closer to their philosophy in terms of the role that the government had an obligation to help people who couldn't help themselves. I thought myself to be pretty moderate, pretty conservative on fiscal issues. I was appointed to be chairman of the finance committee when I was on the city council. And then, as chairman of the committee, they put me on the school board to control the school board's finances.

That didn't go down well and in fact the members of the school board boycotted the first three meetings. School board meetings at that time were very controversial because they had the previous year voted for the concept of open classrooms. But, in addition to the concept being controversial, they initiated it in high school and not at the first-grade level. Students were told that they could take their exams when they were ready rather than on a fixed date. The students took advantage of this policy and deferred taking their exams until well into their final year. As a result, many of them were not granted entry into college because of having incomplete grades. So I was put in charge of overseeing the school board's budget which the city council normally would simply approve. But the city council had the responsibility to raise the property taxes to pay for the school board's budget. Anyway, that was my focus on the fiscal side of things. I was always more concerned about finances and how much we're spending. Coming from my dad being a really small businessman, I felt the need to be more fiscally conservative. I've always been sort of in the middle and I really didn't see the Democrats as the enemy or in a negative way. I knew I had a problem in Lewiston and the St. John Valley. Severin, you mentioned how bizarre it was for Elmer to run ads in Bangor in French. I really think he was trying to copy what we did in Lewiston. Thanks to Chris Potholm, we were running ads both in English and in French and all of our literature was double sided. I think he saw that and the impact it was having. Well, what's good for Cohen in Lewiston should be good for the Franco-Americans in Bangor. When I finally got to Washington I found myself right in the firing line with Republicans. How come you're not attacking the Democrats? They are sons of bitches who do everything to screw the Republicans. They are our enemies! So almost from the very beginning, I found myself an outsider. That's been kind of my life, of being on the outside. I enjoyed what I was doing politically as mayor of the city, as a city councilman, as a school board member, I really enjoyed that rather than the practice of law.

Severin Beliveau: Who was the county attorney then, Bill, when you were the assistant?

Bill Cohen: Errol Paine, my partner.

Severin Beliveau: Oh, yeah, that's right. Yes, I remember meeting you in Errol's office. Errol invited me to Bangor for a meeting of the county attorneys, and I recall passing through your office. You had a small office with a manual typewriter, and you were working on a brief; that's my recollection. That night Errol and Marshall Stern took me to a bar in Bangor where a kid from Rumford was exposed to the wild Bangor nightlife.

Bill Cohen: Errol was a brilliant lawyer and he won election as county attorney. There were two assistant county attorney slots open, but no one wanted either position. They took a lot of time so Errol appointed me to both positions. I took both assistant county positions and that's how I got my trial experience.

Severin Beliveau: You're right. He had a huge retail practice, didn't he? I mean, as you say, District Court, Municipal Court, Superior Court, and so forth.

Jed Lyons: Chris, you were going to say something?

Chris Potholm: Severin might get a kick out of this. Not only in this campaign, but subsequent to all the congressional campaigns and in the Senate campaign, I had no recollection of Bill or I ever knowing what was in the party platform, let alone following it. I also appreciated the genius of Joe Sewall, who as President of the State Senate, scheduled an open bar at the time of the platform discussions. Pure genius. Nobody who mattered wanted to miss the free drinks so only a handful went and yakked and passed something or other. We never paid any attention to it. Not then. Not later.

Bill Cohen: I was on a fundraising mission to Northeast Harbor. Brooke Astor, a wealthy socialite and philanthropist from New York, held a fundraiser for me. She was among those like the Rockefellers who had summer mansions in Maine who were quite liberal. I also went to meet

Roger Milliken. He invited me to join him out alongside his saltwater pool. I told him I was running for Congress and would like to have his support. He then asked me, "How do you feel about Social Security? I said, "You mean the cost-of-living increases that are being discussed in Washington? "No, I mean what is your position on the need for the Social Security program?" I said that I favored it and he then said, "Well, if that's your position, this conversation is over."

Severin Beliveau: And it hasn't changed with some of those people, you know? It hasn't changed. I remember Milliken. The other part of it was that Billy was not viewed as a partisan Republican back in those days. The whole political climate was far different than what we see today, and that made a huge difference. And I don't want to overemphasize it, but the fact that he identified himself as mayor of Bangor was very effective in Androscoggin County, because voters supported their politicians because they worked hard to be elected to office. To become mayor of Bangor, you ran for and served on the council for a while, then were appointed mayor, so I think that everything that Bill said is correct. It's sad that we don't see that stuff here today, but that's where we are.

Jed Lyons: So the major industries back in 1972 in the state were paper making, including in Rumford. You had lots of shoe manufacturing, of course, farming, some industry. Severin, which of those industries still has a foothold.

Severin Beliveau: Well, back then, you're right, we had shoe, textile, and pulp and paper mills.

Bill Cohen: Bath Iron Works.

Severin Beliveau: BIW, I see BIW as an extension of the Pentagon.

Jed Lyons: The Bath Iron Works.

Severin Beliveau: Yes, I think you're right. Bath Iron Works, and the Navy shipyard in Kittery. As an example, my hometown of Rumford, when I was a kid there were 3,300 people who worked at the mill at that time. Today there are 600. That mill and the Old Town mill are owned by Nine Dragons, a Chinese company owned by the wealthiest woman in China. And so what's happened in Maine is that over the past 30 years there has been a dramatic decline in the pulp and paper industry. I think four or five paper companies have closed. The remaining ones are struggling to survive, and what we see with Rumford and Old Town is what's happening, I think, internationally. They are producing pulp in Old Town and Rumford, shipping it to Boston and then by freighter to China, where it's then processed by their own paper companies into the final product, and then delivered back to the States for sale. The textile industry is gone, the shoe industry is practically gone—there are a few remnants in Lewiston—and the paper industry is struggling to survive. So our economy is in tough shape with the exception of two counties. We've had no growth in 12 of the 16 counties in the past 50 years. Population growth in Maine in the last 10 years is around 36,000. But for immigrants, we would have a declining population.

Jed Lyons: Do you see any industries on the horizon that are growing in Maine?

Severin Beliveau: No. There's a real attempt in Millinocket and northern Maine to do something with biofuels. That's becoming fairly attractive. The wholesale of carbon credits which has some appeal to the owners of the approximately 17 million acres of forestlands. Forty years ago, the paper companies dominated the state's economy. They owned most of the forests, the 17 million acres that we have right now. Today paper companies don't own one acre of land; it's all owned by developers. So we really are and continue to be a tourism state. The biggest employer in Maine today is healthcare—110,000 people dependent upon healthcare for employment—that is, nursing homes, hospitals, and so forth. The second largest employer in Maine is government. That's kind of frightening. And the third is tourism. So that's where we are, and every governor and every politician in North America is always promising to improve our economy, but it's really tough because we're in a very difficult place geographically. It's difficult to reach us up here.

Jed Lyons: Who are the immigrants, Severin?

Severin Beliveau: West Africans, primarily, who have settled in Lewiston and Portland. When they came here 20 years ago, they came from North Carolina and Georgia because of our social programs, and, as you know, there was a lot of resistance at first. As a matter of fact, the mayor of Lewiston was asked to resign because he publicly discouraged their movement to Maine. Now they've turned out to be a positive economic force. But for the immigrants in Lewiston, its population would have declined by, I think, about 6,000 or 7,000. And then in the Portland area, you have a lot of the African countries, particularly from the French-speaking African countries. One projection I saw is that by 2025 our population, which is now about 1.3 million, will remain at that figure only because of the immigrants. We have a huge migration from West Africa. Unfortunately, we have, in terms of live births in Maine, a declining population, and we are still the oldest state in the country.

Bill Cohen: What's the reaction to the West African population?

Severin Beliveau: They've been absorbed. Cynthia and I support a couple families from Burundi and have been deeply involved with the Burundi community. They are very proud. Most of them are well educated in their home countries. They had to flee, for a variety of reasons, all of which are legitimate, and they emphasize education. They want to work; they don't want to depend upon the government for support, and they really have emerged as a major force in the state. For instance, two members of the city council of Lewiston are African Americans, and that seems to be the case in Portland as well. At one time we were the whitest state in the country—I think 5 percent of our population, or 4 percent was nonwhite. Now we're about 7 or 8 percent, with Hispanics being number one, African Americans number two, and then a scattering of others after that.

Jed Lyons: Let's get back to 1972. Severin, you mentioned Bob Monks earlier. Bob was running against Margaret Chase Smith in the primary in 1972. He lost that election. Can you give us any insight as a Democrat into why Bob Monks lost that election?

Severin Beliveau: At the outset of his campaign, he was identified as an outsider. As I recall, there was a photograph taken when he was leaving his condo in Boston to travel to Maine to campaign, which portrayed him as a nonresident, as a person who was trying to utilize his wealth to buy an election in Maine. He married into a very wealthy family. He was not viewed as a Mainer. I think that was a real issue. He's a Democrat today (true, ask Monks), ironically, but back then he was an active and high-profile Republican. Billy, I'm sure he talked to you and probably tried to encourage you to run as well. That's one of the things he did, and I give him a lot of credit. He raised a lot of money and traveled around the state encouraging young Republicans to run for office. He built up quite an organization back then. He ran three times for office, and lost all three elections, but in each case, he contributed, at least from an organizational perspective, a great deal to the party.

Jed Lyons: Has it struck you how many of Maine's future Republican leaders emerged in 1972 in the Cohen campaign? Susan Collins was a volunteer, Jock McKernan worked on the campaign, Olympia Snowe, Tom Daffron. Tom didn't get involved until later. What are your views on that?

Severin Beliveau: Well, obviously, I wasn't all that familiar with their role. Of course, I knew the people, and you're right. They were building their bench at that point. Our bench was Ken Curtis, and he had attracted a lot of young people to the party at the time, a lot of guys my age who were involved. As time passed, our base load I guess wasn't as extensive as the Republican, particularly with McKernan and Olympia Snowe. I would like Billy's perspective on this, that 75 percent of a candidate's appeal is based upon his or her appearance. You can talk about policy and issues all you want, but if you don't project well, you don't look good, and you're not somewhat articulate, you lose your appeal to the voters. Billy's strength is that he possessed all of those qualities and he came across that way, and that wasn't the case with some of our candidates. No, I'm not at all surprised, back to those days, because the Democrats were pretty secure. Think about it. In '54 we dominated

Maine politics. We had both congressional seats and one Senate seat. Young John Martin, who later became the longest-serving Speaker in the history of the state, together with Ken Curtis, became leaders in the party. Regrettably, Louis Jalbert and the Franco leaders discouraged others—people like myself and others—from really advancing in the party. Whatever we accomplished, we did despite them.

Jed Lyons: Did you ever consider running yourself?

Severin Beliveau: Yes, I ran for governor in '86. I lost to Jim Tierney in the Democratic primary.

Jed Lyons: Chris and Bill, do you have any other questions for Severin before we wrap it up?

Chris Potholm: I think it's been a terrific session. I've learned a lot and I really think that, Severin, all kidding aside, your career was just astonishing and you were a major player when we stumbled onto the scene and after we stumbled off it there you are still today and every single governor has had to deal with you in one way or another, so thank you for sharing your many stories.

Severin Beliveau: One other suggestion. You may want to read Doug Rooks's book on the history of the Democratic Party. It came out about two years ago. He comments on the '72 campaign and the rise of the Republicans and all the factors that contributed to their success.

Jed Lyons: Is there anybody else that you think we should talk to?

Severin Beliveau: Ken Curtis is in his early '90s, is well, and lives in a retirement home in Scarborough. You may want to chat with him. He was deeply involved in the growth and success of the Democratic Party in the '60s and '70s, because, as I said earlier, he's the one who convened that meeting at the Blaine House when we made the decision regarding the Big Box. The Law Court's decision redefined Maine politics.

Jed Lyons: All right, we'll follow up on that. I have one last question for you. I've been close to the Delahanty family from Lewiston for 50 years. Unfortunately, two of the three brothers just passed away this year. John and Tom. Kevin is still alive. Did you know the judge, their father?

Severin Beliveau: My first jury trial was before Judge Delahanty at the Superior Court in Rumford, with my father as co-counsel. My father had just retired from the Law Court, and he and I tried the case. Delahanty declared a mistrial and my father got so upset that he ran up to the bench and said, "You can't do that. That was an improper ruling." I had to contain him. I know the Delahanty and the Clifford families very well. We're very close to them. Because Delahanty, the judge, was very close to Muskie, he was later appointed to the Superior Court and, ultimately, to the Law Court.

Bill Cohen: I argued cases before him in the Supreme Judicial Court. How many people are in your law firm, Severin?

Severin Beliveau: 101. It's a long way and a long time from Rumford where my brother and I began our legal careers. I am overwhelmed by the nature of law practice today, and I am certain that my grandfather, Mathew McCarthy, who graduated from the first University of Maine Law School in 1900, and my father, who graduated from the Law School in 1915, would have difficulty understanding how a two- or three-person law firm in Rumford is now a 100-person law firm.

Bill Cohen: Well, thanks, Severin. This has been great, and feel free to slash and burn anything.

Severin Beliveau: When Chris called me about this, I said, "This could be fun." So I just dug up some of the data that I have shared with you this morning, and it brought back all these great memories, particularly Marshall Stern, that whole Bangor scene that you're familiar with. Some of the stories about George Mitchell and Marshall Stern will be left for another time.

CHAPTER XIV

Oral History Discussion
with David Emery

October 14, 2021

Jed Lyons: Thank you for joining us. Where are you today?

David Emery: I'm in Tenants Harbor, Maine. It's a beautiful morning here; the temperature is already around 68 degrees.

Jed Lyons: Would you mind sharing some background information about yourself?

David Emery: Sure. I was born in Rockland, Maine, on September 1, 1948. My mother was a nurse and my father was a hospital accountant. After graduating from Rockland District High School in 1966, I went to Worcester Polytechnic Institute, earning a bachelor of science degree in electronic engineering. But rather than continue on the career path of being an electrical engineer, in 1970, I decided to run for the state legislature, was elected and served two four-year terms representing the city of Rockland. I decided to run for Congress in 1974. Being a young man, my future was at a fork in the road. I was either going to stay in government and make a career out of it or I had to get a job as an electronic engineer before my degree became too stale. So I ran in the improbable year of 1974 against Peter Kyros, who was the incumbent congressman, a Democrat, in Maine's 1st Congressional District.

Jed Lyons: Chris reminded me that you are the youngest person ever elected to the Maine legislature. Is that correct?

David Emery: I don't think I was the youngest ever elected, but I was certainly one of the youngest, and I was the youngest Republican at the time I was elected. That same year, Frank Murray from Bangor, a Democrat, was elected, and I think Frank was younger than me, but, if so, not by much.

Jed Lyons: How old were you?

David Emery: I was 21 when I won the primary and 22 when I was actually elected that November.

Jed Lyons: You joined a legislature that must have been significantly older. What would you say the average age would have been?

David Emery: Well, I don't know what the average age was, but when you're only 22 years old, by definition, the whole legislature is older. The legislature at that time was certainly a mixture of ages, and there were a significant number of women elected. I remember a legislator by the name of Harry Williams from Hodgdon, in Aroostook County, who must have been in his mid-to-late 80s. He sat behind me and he was I think the oldest person in the House at the time.

And there was a number of young legislators as well, particularly from the Portland area.

Jed Lyons: What are your memories of 1972, the primary that Bill ran in and the race in general in '72.

David Emery: Well, you know, obviously this race looked to those of us who were active in the Republican Party at the time as an opportunity to pick up a congressional seat. If I remember correctly, Bill, you had a primary with Abbott Green from Columbia Falls . . . isn't that right, Bill?

Bill Cohen: Yes, in '72.

David Emery: I think there was some question at that point as to whether Bill Cohen or Abbott Green was likely to win. But Bill had the advantage of being well known in the Bangor area and I think he presented himself as a much more mainstream candidate, so it should really have been no surprise to anyone that Bill won that primary, even though it wasn't obvious to casual observers early on. I think one of the things that stuck out to me was Bill's walk across the state, which I think started in the Oxford County town of Gilead, if I remember correctly. I did pretty well pulling that one out of the cobwebs, didn't I? The walk was inspiring to voters because it showed a commitment to do a heck of a lot of work to earn support, and I think it paid off in spades because the press and most people statewide were curious to know where he was, where did he stay last night, and where is he going next. It just generated a buzz that had never existed before in a congressional campaign. It was a brilliant thing. As I recall, Bill, your walk was preceded by a similar walk by Lawton Chiles in Florida, the first candidate to do so.

Bill Cohen: You really are picking the cobwebs out of the attic there, but yes.

David Emery: Yeah, minutiae, but anyway that was actually inspirational, particularly to young guys like me who were ambitious and wanted to run. It showed that there was a path forward and you didn't necessarily have to have millions of dollars and you didn't have to be a well-known statewide figure, because you could generate a following and some press coverage, as well. That is one of the things that motivated me.

The other thing I remember about that race was the presidential campaign. Richard Nixon was running for reelection in 1972. There was a growing controversy over the Vietnam War and, later on, the Watergate matter began to generate concern. I remember that it was a rather disquieting time because there was so much division in the country which, I guess, we've never completely gotten over. I remember the political environment going back to 1968 when I was in college, at the time that Nixon was elected. I was kind of in the middle of it in '72 as a state representative. It was a difficult time to be in politics.

Jed Lyons: Chris has pointed out that your success really paved the way, along with Bill's, for Jock McKernan, Olympia Snowe, and Susan Collins. And without your campaign in 1974, Bill might have been the only Republican in the Maine delegation and the Republican image may have reverted to a more old-fashioned Republican. What elements in your campaign in '74 were modeled on Bill's?

David Emery: Well, certainly the walk. I also did a walk. It was something that I was able to do easily because I was young, healthy, and strong and it seemed to make sense from the standpoint of the contrast it would project if I expected to beat Peter Kyros. The other thing it did for me since I'm not a naturally gregarious person, was to teach me how to campaign effectively one-on-one and easily interact with strangers. I had to learn how to be a public figure in the sense that I had to learn how to be open, how to greet people warmly and exude self-confidence. I had to learn all those things on the fly because they weren't natural for me. These are all things that I had to learn very quickly as a candidate, so it was a growth experience for me during that campaign. It was certainly a lot easier for me at the end of the campaign than at the beginning.

The other thing was that I didn't have any campaign money. I had no significant personal resources, so we spent, if I remember correctly, about $65,000 on the entire campaign. I think I raised about $45,000 and we spent $65,000. That $20,000 debt would have been a significant burden had I lost. Today, you'd laugh at such a small campaign budget, but that's all we had to work with. So I had to invent things that generated a following, interest, and press. I was able to do that pretty well, actually, and I think that I had a very good relationship with the press during that campaign.

I also remember that there wasn't a soul who thought I was going to win until the votes were being counted on election night. An interesting story, however: there was a young fellow by the name of Peter Burr who was a volunteer on my campaign. There is another tragic story involving Peter, but we won't get into that. Peter was very bright, and he decided that his contribution to the campaign would be to set up a polling operation. So we came up with a system by which we'd make a dozen calls in one town, a dozen calls in another town, and a dozen calls in a third town, and so forth. We used an algorithm to compare the results through a mathematical formula that I devised that attempted to relate towns that performed in a predictable way, one versus the other, and district wide. We had numbers two nights before the election that showed that I was about half a point behind Kyros. I remember going into the statehouse late in the afternoon the day before the election. In those days, the press was up on the fourth floor so I went in with these numbers in an envelope and gave them to a wire service reporter.

And I said, "You're not going to believe this, but we've got numbers that show that this is a dead even race. I can't predict what's going to happen, but I feel really good about this."

He kind of rolled his eyes and said something like, "Well, you worked at this race."

Well, after the election, I held a news conference at the statehouse about 10:30 Wednesday morning. I had had no sleep, nor had some of the press reporters, I'm certain. That wire service reporter was there, and he asked me afterward, "How did you know? How did you do it?" I told him, "Two thirds hard work, one third blind luck."

Jed Lyons: In 1970, think about the Republican Party in the state of Maine. Was it changing the face of the party? You had the old Yankees in different parts of the state, different kinds of Republicans, how would you characterize it back in 1972?

David Emery: Then, as now, there were strong Republican areas that consistently voted more than two to one Republican, such as western Penobscot County, Piscataquis County, and southern Aroostook County. But you also had more moderate Republicans along the coast and in southern Maine, in places like York, Cape Elizabeth, Falmouth, Yarmouth, and Camden. In those days, they were Republican strongholds, but more moderate. But on occasion they would grit their teeth, question one position or another, and you could see the beginnings of the schism that we're now familiar with. You could see differentiation in the legislature between, for example, Dave Huber, a moderate/liberal state representative from Falmouth; and Lowell Henley, the very conservative state representative from the town of Norway in Oxford County. They were worlds apart philosophically, but yet they were both Republicans.

One particular difference is that in those days, a Republican might get 15 percent of the vote in Lewiston or Biddeford and be very happy to do even marginally better than that. The Franco-American vote was monolithically Democrat and that was all there was to it. A Republican candidate knew that he had to get enough of a vote in suburban areas outside of those old industrial cities to overcome what you knew was going to be an overwhelming Democratic vote.

One of the things that Bill did was to make a breakthrough in Lewiston and various other places where he got a substantially better vote than recent Republicans had done. This success was, I think, based on the fact that you showed up, you showed interest, you paid attention and listened to people, and not surprisingly, people responded to that.

Jed Lyons: Thank you. Bill, what are your thoughts? In light of what Dave just said, what were your thoughts about these tectonic plates shifting or was it not that dramatic?

Bill Cohen: Well, I'm going to say something about David. The one thing that really stood out about you, David, was the word authenticity. I was going to ask you how your accent, which played well from Rockland all the way up the coast to the north, how it played in Portland? Even though you had a moderate element of Republicans in Portland and the Falmouth area, the fact is that you had to win a general election against a guy who was pretty liberal, very liberal. So I was just curious how you were able to win in those areas? I think the difference was that people saw you were a young, strong, vibrant candidate with a great Maine accent. In fact, in Washington they used to ask me, "What the hell happened to your Maine accent? David Emery, he's a real Mainer. I don't know where you're from, Cohen, but you ain't from Maine." So I think you seemed very authentic to Maine people at that time and I think your accent was a great advantage to you as opposed to Kyros who seemed like he came from Boston. And you had that element of innocence that conveyed a sense of "What the hell am I doing here? I don't have any money, I've never done this before. I'm just going to count on sheer luck to get myself through." Frankly I didn't think you had much of a chance knowing who and what you were up against. You are quite right that at the time, the Republican Party held a moderate to conservative philosophy. But the Democratic Party was pretty liberal. You had to campaign in Portland, and I was wondering how difficult that was for you and the reaction you got from the Democrats. Or did you just try to appeal to the Republicans in the 1st District?

David Emery: No, I jumped into that with some enthusiasm and I spent three days walking through Portland during that first campaign. And that included the West End, Munjoy Hill, all places that Republicans weren't ever seen. I don't remember the exact numbers, but as I recall, I think I got around 43 or 44 percent in Portland. And I carried Portland twice, in '78 and '80 and lost it fairly narrowly in '74 and '76. In that first race, I was able to carry Cumberland County by about 3,500 votes.

Chris Potholm: Dave, didn't Biddeford turn out to be your Lewiston?

David Emery: Oh, great story there. I spent a lot of time in Biddeford and Saco. I spent quite a bit of time in Sanford as well, but Biddeford and Saco both responded very well. There's a substantial Greek community in that area, the Droggitis family in particular comes to mind. I remember going into the Wonderbar Restaurant in Biddeford which was a place where local Democrats gathered. I just went in with some campaign workers for a bite to eat, and after a few minutes, one of the owners came over and introduced himself. Alex Droggitis, as I recall. He ran the place with his three brothers. "You're Emery, aren't you?" he asked.

And I said yes, introduced myself, and he sat down. Then he asked me to tell him a little bit about myself, so I talked with him for a few minutes, and he said, "You know, there are a lot of Greeks in this area, and some of us are not happy with your opponent. He hasn't paid enough attention to us, and some people here feel disrespected. We've been watching your campaign, and I think you're going to do pretty well."

As you can imagine, I was pretty excited because it's not what you expect to hear in Biddeford. Then he said, "Let me take you around and introduce you to a few people."

So he took me around the restaurant and into the kitchen and introduced me to his employees and some of the customers. And he said, "Next time you're in town we will do this again." So that was kind of the Good Housekeeping Seal of Approval in Biddeford, and a similar thing happened in Saco.

Jed Lyons: You really made my day because Spiros Droggitis, the nephew of Alex and the son of Charles who owned the Wonderbar with two other brothers, is one of my closest Bowdoin friends. We were roommates at Bowdoin. We're still very close. He lives in Biddeford now. He'll love that story.

David Emery: They're an absolutely wonderful family, and anytime I was within 25 miles of Biddeford, I would always go in, even if it was just a cup of coffee, so they knew that I hadn't forgotten.

Jed Lyons: Tell us about Saco.

David Emery: There was a state senator from Saco named Peter Danton also a Greek-American, who ran a restaurant called the Hitching Post. Peter never said if he voted for me or not (he was a very strong Democrat), but he always showed me around and introduced me to people whenever I went into his restaurant. So I think there was an opening there. But as a candidate, you have to be willing to open the door; I mean, you can't just assume that one group is for you and another is against you. You have to make the effort, you've got to show interest. So I always followed up and tried to maintain those contacts and the good will.

There is another story from my unsuccessful Senate race in 1982. There was a Democratic legislator from Lewiston by the name of Albert Cote, who was very heavy—so heavy, in fact, that he had an extra-wide chair and sat on the aisle in the Maine House. It was my impression that some legislators didn't pay too much attention to Albert, but since he was on the Legal Affairs Committee with me, I got to know him and liked him. I was house chairman of the committee in my second term, so in that capacity, Albert came to me one day and told me that he had introduced a bill to allow Lewiston snowshoe clubs to raise money through "Lucky Sevens" drawings. This seemed to me to be a simple and reasonable request, so I agreed to support his bill when it came to our committee. And it passed. I forgot all about it, but when I ran for the U.S. Senate in 1982, I ran into Albert while campaigning in Lewiston and he said, "I'm supporting you because you were always ready to help me."

Albert was as good as his word and showed me around several of the Lewiston snowshoe clubs one evening—places that probably hadn't seen a Republican in decades! In the end, I didn't get that much of a vote in Lewiston but I did a little better than I would have done otherwise. That's another example of why it's important to help people whenever you can; it made no difference to me or to my own constituents whether Albert's bill passed or not, but it was helpful to his constituents, and he appreciated it.

Jed Lyons: Chris, what do you have for Dave?

Chris Potholm: Well, I actually have a couple of questions. I'm very interested in the connection that George Smith had with the Cohen campaign in '72 and then working on your '74 campaign. What did he bring from the Cohen campaign that was useful in your campaign?

David Emery: Well, I knew George and Gordon, his brother, through Republican politics. At the time I decided to run for Congress, George was working at a bank in Rockland, so we got together a couple of times to discuss politics. George was very anti-Nixon, primarily due to the Vietnam War, but he separated that issue from other political matters and remained an active Republican. I told him that I was thinking about running and, like everyone else, he thought I was crazy, but that it might be fun. He signed on as campaign manager. It was quite a Quixotic undertaking: I mean we had no money, we had no formal organization, the National Republican Campaign Committee didn't take the race seriously; I was just a ticket filler. Our campaign organization was a bunch of young people, many from the University of Maine campus in Gorham, as it was at the time. Another key volunteer was Charlie Smith from Stockton Springs. Waldo County was in the 1st District at that point, so he was responsible for that end of the district. The campaign strategy basically amounted to just going around and seeing people, plus coordinating my 600-mile walk. After I won, both George and Charlie came onto my congressional staff; George remained with me until I left Congress.

Bill Cohen: David, the Collins family was very helpful to me in Aroostook County. How was your relationship with Sam Collins?

David Emery: We were very close. I have been very close to the Collins family throughout my political career. Sam was a strong supporter of mine. He was my state senator at the time, helped to raise some money for me locally. His children were a little younger than me, but we all knew each other from school and through mutual friends. Sam's son Ed, now deceased, worked both in my Washington congressional office and also as a campaign volunteer. We remained friends until his death. The Collinses are a wonderful Maine family. I served in the legislature with Senator Susan Collins's father, Don, and Susan was a campaign volunteer during my 1982 Senate race. So the Collins family was always very supportive and I have always been proud to have been associated with them.

Jed Lyons: Do you happen to remember where their hunting camp was located?

David Emery: I never went to it, so I don't.

Jed Lyons: Chris got sick drinking the water there.

Chris Potholm: There was beaver shit in it, I think.

David Emery: I doubt that it was water.

Jed Lyons: How important to you, David, was the support of people like Richardson, Sewall, Huber, and MaCleod?

David Emery: Well, it would have been helpful, had I had it. But they were not inclined to be very helpful, and were known to be skeptical of my chances, and probably felt that I was not equipped to run or to serve. Now that changed later on, but when I initially ran, they were not big supporters.

Jed Lyons: Did you intersect with Bob Monks? Was he supportive of you?

David Emery: Yes, he was. He contributed. That's interesting, because in 1972, I was a big Margaret Chase Smith supporter. You will remember that he ran against her in the primary that year and, in many circles, is credited with having given Bill Hathaway an opening that led to his upset election victory that fall. But he offered to help during my first campaign, made a substantial contribution for which I was very grateful, and we were good friends thereafter.

Bill Cohen: Did you campaign with him when he was running?

David Emery: I did. That was an interesting question because he ran against Susan, as I recall, in the primary. That caused a bit of angst in my mind, because I'd always been so close to the Collins family. But I had signed on with Bob Monks before Susan decided to run, and I didn't feel it would have been ethical for me to go back on my word to him.

Chris Potholm: You might have worked for him and supported him when he ran against Muskie for the Senate.

David Emery: Oh, definitely then, absolutely. We were both on the ballot in 1976.

Jed Lyons: So, Chris, you were the campaign manager for Bill's campaign in 1972 and you did some very useful analysis of voting counts not just by county, but by towns, that turned out to be remarkably accurate on election day. What are your insights into what Dave just described to us and his successful effort to predict his own race?

Chris Potholm: Well, I do think that his system with Peter Burr became the gold or platinum standard for how you do predictive polling and it was way, way ahead of its time. I always thought, as Bill said, whatever Dave did in 1974 had authenticity and Dave was not wanting to be put off by different people once he got into this world. And I do think the Saco-Biddeford thing was a huge contributor because he shaved the margin a lot for Kyros in those areas.

David Emery: Nothing succeeds like success. That was, indeed, a huge factor, particularly since I won that first race by only 432 votes after a recount. Charlie Cragin was my recount attorney, and he did a fabulous job protecting that razor-thin lead. That was quite an experience, going through a congressional recount at 26 six years of age and knowing that your future was in the balance. At that point, the state and national party organizations pitched in to help. The whole party did at that point.

Chris Potholm: And how about Mert Henry? He was linked to Bill, to you, then Jock, then Olympia, then Susan: he was a kind of a fairy god-father for everybody in the Republican world.

David Emery: He was fabulous. I was close to Mert and had a great deal of respect for both Mert and Harriet who, in their own respects, were prominent, sophisticated, very able and accomplished people. Mert was on board right from the beginning and was very helpful and supportive.

Chris Potholm: And he was the head of youth for Margaret Chase Smith, I mean he really spans three, almost four generations of Republicans and, if you don't mind me saying so, the right kind of Republicans. Inclusive, not exclusive. Caring, not uncaring.

David Emery: Absolutely right.

Jed Lyons: What about the Delahanty family up in Lewiston? Were they helpful? They were Democrats, of course.

David Emery: The first time I had any significant experience campaigning in Lewiston was when I ran for the Senate in 1982. They were very much in George Mitchell's camp that year, unsurprisingly.

Bill Cohen: How about the Bath Iron Works employees who lived in Lewiston?

David Emery: Certainly, there were some, but the union supported Mitchell in the '82 race. I didn't carry Bath in the first campaign or in '82, but did very well there in '76, '78, and '80. My primary supporters in Bath were the Small family.

Jed Lyons: Which family was that? The Smalls?

David Emery: Mary Small was in the State House of Representatives and in the State Senate for many years. Her father had been mayor of Bath some years before, but I never knew him because he was deceased by the time I was active in politics.

Bill Cohen: You had the support of the management, Bill Haggett.

David Emery: Yes, Bill was always very supportive, as were other BIW management personnel, including John Sullivan.

Bill Cohen: How about Buzzy Fitzgerald? Was he a supporter of yours?

David Emery: He was, but he didn't support me when I ran for the Senate, as I recall.

Bill Cohen: Well, you would have the support of the management, but typically the labor force would be with the Democrats.

David Emery: That's true, but I broke into that pretty well. I lost Bath narrowly in '74 and then the other three times I carried it quite handily. I had a lot of support in the union membership. At that point I was on an Armed Services Committee, and I had the ability to relate to a lot of the working people there. It was good chemistry. At the same time, I always did well in Kittery and always supported the Kittery-Portsmouth Naval Shipyard.

Jed Lyons: Do you have any stories from the 1970s about families like Rockefeller, Millken, some of the wealthy out-of-state families that may or may not have participated in your campaigns in some way?

David Emery: Well, the Rockefellers always helped me, but their base was in Northeast Harbor, Hancock County, which was not part of my district. The other family that was always very supportive was the Paysons: Charles Shipman Payson and Mary Payson. Mary was in the state legislature with me.

Most of those well-known wealthy Republican families were helpful in terms of having functions for me or providing campaign contributions, but that was not the focus of my campaign. I didn't spend a lot of time trying to ingratiate myself or to win over wealthy or prominent families; I spent most of my time in places that I knew would vote for me if I made the effort, but not necessarily places that would provide a lot of money, and I think that's one of the reasons I did well. I ran up huge totals in Knox, Lincoln, and Waldo counties in those days. It's quite different now because the political ground has shifted to the left along the coast. I would get 75 or 80 percent of the vote in the most of those small, rural communities. When you come out of those three counties with a 3 to 1 lead over your opponent, it doesn't really matter a lot what happens in Democratic strongholds like Brunswick, because you've pretty well neutralized them.

Bill Cohen: David, what were the defining issues for you and your campaign? You had the Watergate investigation underway which had Nixon on the ropes, but you had Republicans who were really solid Nixon supporters until he resigned. Was there a lingering resentment toward Republicans, as far as you were concerned?

David Emery: It's interesting. I think that campaign did not turn so much on issues and positions as it did on personality and personal qualities. I talked about spending and I talked about energy, whatever issues I was asked about, but people were looking for a fresh face and, I think, character. My standard answer regarding Watergate was that I had always supported the president, but when he was shown to have been culpable, I couldn't condone that behavior. I always said that I could not overlook or condone the Watergate break-in and demanded accountability, but it really wasn't the big issue.

The big issue, to the degree that there *was* a big issue, was, of all things, a megavitamin bill before the Commerce Committee on which Peter Kyros served. This particular bill, as I recall, would have allowed expanded sale and reduced regulation of megavitamins and certain health foods. A pro-megavitamin group contacted me, and specifically criticized Kyros for his votes as being anti-consumer, in that he opposed these health foods and megavitamins. This group held a news conference, where they accused Kyros of switching his vote in exchange for campaign contributions. That accusation caused a tremendous uproar. The pro-vitamin group supported me, but it became a little uncomfortable because I didn't know whether they were telling the truth or not. So I was suddenly on the opposite side of that issue from Kyros, which provided a contrast. I think that made a huge difference in the campaign because there were a lot of people who just didn't trust him anyway, and true or untrue, it didn't seem like such a stretch to some that he would take campaign money in exchange for a vote. This controversy clearly hurt him badly.

Bill Cohen: So you're saying that really it came down to personality.

David Emery: I think so, definitely. We had substantive differences of opinion on certain spending bills and other issues, but I think perceptions of personality and character were what made the difference in the race.

There was the question of supporting the war, and there was horrible stagflation at the time that badly hurt people in the pocketbook. I took the usual Republican position of cutting spending and not raising taxes. I managed to raise money for TV ads during the last three weeks of the campaign, a pathetically meager amount of money, but it was nevertheless effective. But you know, for all the issues that we may have discussed in the press, as I have said, I don't think they had as much impact as the contrast of personality and the appearance of a fresh young face.

Bill Cohen: Well, I had two years of serving with him and one thing that always stands out in my mind was his cruelty. Each year, a group of Maine people would come down to D.C. We arranged to host a breakfast and the four of us would spread out and sit at the various tables. We wanted to show that whatever our political differences, we stood in solidarity on issues affecting Maine citizens.

At the beginning of the breakfast, I was standing in the middle of six or seven Mainers and Kyros said, "Bill, God, I hope you don't have a hangover after the way you were drinking last night." I was stunned! He made it look as if I was a drunk coming in after a night of heavy drinking. It was just so stunning to me that he would make such a statement and never tried to portray it as a joke. He said it seriously and that changed my attitude toward working with Kyros. That was my first encounter with him. And it set the table for me. I didn't want to be near this guy or work with him and form any relationship.

David Emery: Well, there is another good story from when I was campaigning in Portland. Sounds like I spent most of my time campaigning in restaurants, but I went into Tony DeMillo's restaurant; it was on the inland side of Commercial Street in those days, when he was just starting out. I sat down for lunch with a campaign staffer and Tony came over and introduced himself. Then he says, "You're campaigning in Portland today?"

I said something like, "Oh yeah, wow. It's a tough area. Peter Kyros always does really well here. But I'll just have to work hard and do the best I can." Then he says, "You're welcome to come into my restaurant anytime you want, but you got to pay for your meals. I'm not giving free meals to politicians."

That was more than a little strange and I said, "Of course. Naturally, I expect to pay."

Then he says, "Well, your opponent likes to stick me with the bill." "How does that work?" I asked. "He comes in here, grabs a seat in the middle of the dining room, wants a telephone, and causes a fuss that disturbs my other customers. Then sometimes he leaves without paying the bill."

So it's the same story as I previously related. Tony took me around the restaurant and introduced me to everyone, as well as to his kitchen staff. He became a very strong supporter of mine.

As I began to learn, Peter left a trail of destruction throughout the district. I think it was a case of critical mass, in a year when typical politicians were out of favor. People were looking for new faces. I think there were any number of votes that I got for that reason alone, not based on any particular qualification or positions on issues.

Jed Lyons: Do you have any stories about Graziano's in Lisbon Falls where we used to go?

Bill Cohen: Oh yes, but let me say that Tony DeMillo never suggested that I stuck him with the bill. Number one, I never campaigned in Portland when I was in the 2nd District and number two, if ever he was stuck with a bill, Chris was supposed to have paid it!

David Emery: Certainly not you . . . Peter Kyros. If I misspoke, I apologize. I was talking about Kyros.

Bill Cohen: As far as the Grazianos, they were big fight fans. You walk into that restaurant and you could see all of the old fighters, Jake LaMotta and just about everybody on the wall. I used to watch a lot of fights with my dad. He took me to these clubhouse fights in downtown Bangor when I was just a kid. I established this relationship with the Graziano family and they treated me just like one of their family members. So it was a great place to campaign. I knew a lot about the boxers on the walls from my dad talking about them all the way from Joe Louis to Sugar Ray Robinson, but it was just a great experience to go into the restaurant, sit down with these guys, and have a beer and talk about the great fights.

Jed Lyons: And the best Italian food, as I remember. They loved seeing you. How about you, Dave, did you go there?

David Emery: That was not far out of Brunswick so we'd go for dinner once in a while. It wasn't my district so I had no reason to campaign there. But yeah, I'd go have dinner there once in a while, just because it was a fun place to go and the food was great. The last time I was there, which was not recently, my photo was still on the wall.

Jed Lyons: When you were representing the 1st District, Dave, was the Bowdoin community supportive of your campaigns?

David Emery: No, but I had contacts with Bowdoin students. I spoke there, certainly. Chris, I probably addressed your classes at one point or another.

Chris Potholm: Yes, and the Morrells, Bob and Dick, they were huge supporters of yours.

David Emery: That's not necessarily a Bowdoin connection, but the Morrells were certainly supporters. Dick's daughter, Sandy, worked on my congressional staff.

Chris Potholm: They both were Bowdoin graduates and very, very respected, not only in Brunswick, but around the state.

David Emery: The Morrells were huge supporters, Bob and his brother both. As a matter of fact, Dick's son-in-law built my house here in Tenants Harbor; he was in residential construction for a while, then I think he went into boat building.

Bill Cohen: And the Hancock family?

David Emery: Not so much, I mean I wasn't close to them particularly, but they've contributed and supported me over the years.

Bill Cohen: Did you serve with Dave Hancock in the legislature?

David Emery: No, he must have served after I left the legislature.

Jed Lyons: Dave, do you have any funny stories about your walk? Bill had plenty of funny stories about his.

David Emery: Well, there was one particularly funny story: I was in Waterboro in York County on my walk, and it was a beautiful sunny day. I came upon a marvelous old Maine farmhouse with a large barn, all perfectly manicured. I saw a man working in his huge garden, so I went over to talk to him. I introduced myself, and as we were talking, all of a sudden he says, "Hold on a minute. I'll be right back."

Well, he came out of his barn with a shotgun, and he says, "Look over on the far side of the garden; that goddamn woodchuck has eaten my lettuce and my spinach and now I'm finally going to get him!" Blam! Sure enough, he fired the shotgun and killed the woodchuck. I don't know what he was using for shot, but he couldn't have cut down more vegetables if he'd been using a lawn mower; his shot plowed a swath through the vegetables that the woodchuck couldn't have eaten in a month! So I said, "Good shot. Guess you got him." And off I went on my next adventure.

Bill Cohen: Did you have any encounters with André the Seal? The famous seal?

David Emery: Oh yes, of course. Paula, one of the Goodridge daughters, worked for me on my congressional staff. So you know there were always photographs with Harry and Andre the Seal, which was great fun for kids visiting the office; they'd see the photographs of Harry, Andre, and me. Oh yes, it was great fun.

Bill Cohen: Well, I was not very fond of Andre. I was in a boat with him and he bit me in the ass!

David Emery: Seal of approval, Bill! But you know there were all kinds of stories about fishermen in Rockport that hated Andre because Andre wasn't afraid of anyone in a boat, so on several occasions, a lobsterman would be in his skiff on his way to or from his lobster boat and all of a sudden this 300-pound seal would try to jump in looking for a fish to eat. More than one lobsterman went for a cold water swim thanks to Andre the Seal.

Bill Cohen: It's good that your fisherman friend didn't have a shotgun around.

David Emery: Yeah, I know, exactly! I've never forgotten that incident. As I said, I couldn't cut more vegetables with a lawn mower than what he blew away!

Jed Lyons: Chris, any final questions for Dave?

Chris Potholm: Just a footwear question—Bill blew through a lot of shoes and boots. How about you?

David Emery: Oh, I wore running shoes, but I remember the first couple of weeks was torture. The bottom of my foot was just raw with blisters. My feet toughened up after a while, but I probably went through five or six pairs of running shoes; they just fall apart after a while. I never tried heavy shoes or boots; Bill advised me not to, as I remember.

Another thing I remember, Bill. One time we were walking together in York County during your '78 Senate race. It was a hot day, and I remember that by the end of that walk I felt like I had been through the ringer: I was hot, tired, hungry, and thirsty with sweat pouring down my face and back. I must have looked like I had crawled out of a sewer pipe. And you looked like you had just changed your clothes! I never figured out how to do that, but it was very impressive.

Bill Cohen: I just went into a telephone booth, spun around, and came out.

David Emery: I think you did. That's right! Superman vs. Sewerman!

Bill Cohen: It's been great talking to you, David and catching up. It's fun to pick out all of these old stories from the cobwebs.

David Emery: Yeah, it really is. It was a different time. We were there at a time when people generally were respectful and were glad to see you as a candidate. Differences of opinion didn't spill over into acrimony. This is a very difficult time.

Bill Cohen: We're on the edge of watching democracy becoming unraveled. I don't think we can reverse it in the short term.

David Emery: Yes, it's a very worrisome thing. I wish there was an easy answer to it but I don't know what we do with Trump. His antics are disgraceful, not just for the Republican Party, but a danger to liberal democracy as it exists.

Bill Cohen: The sad thing is that Trump could have been, not a great, but effective president because he was right on a number of issues. He was right in dealing with China, saying you've taken advantage of an unlevel playing field. He was right in telling the NATO countries you've got to pay more. The manner in which he did it was so demeaning and disgraceful, appealing to the core base, which has now become so Trumpified that anyone who speaks with reason and reflection is ridiculed and attacked physically, as well. So it's really a very difficult time for this country, at a time when his base is so solid and Democrats do what they normally do in terms of eating their young. Biden, who's basically a slightly left of center Democrat, is being pulled to the left and I think it's pretty clear what's going to happen over the next two years and next three years. Anyway, that's another story.

David Emery: Well, this has been a lot of fun, Bill, it's good to catch up. It's been a long time since we've had a conversation.

Bill Cohen: One final question: what was your favorite restaurant in the 1st District?

David Emery: Oh well . . . let me think about that.

Bill Cohen: We had Helen's restaurant in Machias in the 2nd District.

Jed Lyons: The best apple pie I ever had.

David Emery: Obviously you've never had mine, but that's another story.

Jaed Lyons: Their blueberry pie was good, too.

David Emery: That's a tough one. I made the rounds throughout the district in order to cement contacts where it really mattered, like DeMillo's. Peter Ott's Tavern in Camden comes to mind. And in Portland, F. Parker Reity's and the Roma. Remember the Roma on Congress Street?

Bill Cohen: I do.

Jed Lyons: Still there?

David Emery: It actually closed for a number of years, but I believe it's reopened, and I don't know whether it's completely new ownership or a relative of previous ownership. Carol and I have not been there yet, but we should do that sometime soon.

Jed Lyons: What was it called?

David Emery: F. Parker Reity's in the Old Port. Parker always wore a red scarf and a cowboy hat.

Chris Potholm: It's been a lot of fun to see Bill and Dave together and it's just that dynamism of youth, of taking over the Republican Party and all the contributions you guys made and how the others followed you. I think it's just really great. I really enjoyed listening to the reminiscences. I've always been struck by how important Dave's victory in 1974 was to Bill's legacy. Bill's approach to politics, his brand of Republicanism, his youth and his dynamism could have ended up being unique, but you carried it on and paved the way for Jock and Olympia and Susan. You were the link that institutionalized the Cohen counterrevolution, bringing the Republican Party back from the abyss. A very important contribution to the history of the Republican Party in Maine. Maine owes you a lot, Dave, not just for that but the way you represented the state so well in Congress and the Arms Control Agency.

INDEX

Kelly v. Curtis, 135–36, 142
Kendrick, Nate, 33–35, 40
Kennedy, Robert, 57, 113
Kerry, John, 163–64, 173
King, Angus, 111, 142–43
Kissinger, Henry, 53–54
Koelln, Fritz, 35
Kyros, Peter, 72, 120, 124; Emery and,
202–3, 205–6, 208, 213, 216–18

Lahey, Patrick, 113
Lambert, Thomas F., Jr., 43, 48, 51,
107
League of Women Voters, 186
Lee Kuan Yew, 54
Leonard, Ralph, 56–57
LePage, Paul, 143, 165
Lewis, Bill, xiii, 69–71, 101–2, 104,
117, 119
Lewiston, Maine, 87, 107, 112–13,
128–29; Cohen, B., campaign in,
81–83, 145, 147, 151, 190, 194,
p7; Delahanty family in, 214;
Emery in, 210; Monks, B., in,
163; West African immigrants
in, 198
liberal Republicans, 45, 101–2, 104,
107, 167
Lindsay, John, 98
Linnell, Jack, 96
Linsky, Marty, 139
Lippmann, Harvey, 155
Lisbon, Maine, *p5*
Loeb, Bob, xiii, xix; at Bowdoin,
125–26, 131; children of,
131–32; in Cohen, B., 1972
campaign for Congress, 125–30;
early life, 125; law career, 130;

in Maine referenda campaigns,
132; Potholm and, 125, 151;
The Walk and, 77–78, 127–29,
140–41, 146, *p7*; Watson-Welch
and, 150–51
Longley, James B., 97
Look Homeward Angel (Wolfe) 16
Loscutoff, Jim, 32
Lupus, Peter, 72
Lyons, Jed, 1–2; at Bowdoin College,
16, 36–37; in Cohen, B., 1972
campaign for Congress, 74; early
life and school years of, 15–16;
Potholm and, 37, 147; on The
Walk, 64, 77, 92, 102–3, *p7*
Lyons, Jim, 15

MacLeod, Ken, 45, 52, 54–56, 97,
103, 190
Maine Democratic Party, xiii–xiv,
45, 57, 128, 199–200; Beliveau
in, 185–87, 190; Cohen, B., on,
193–94, 208; Maine Republican
Party and, changes since 1972,
186
Maine referenda campaigns, 132
Maine Republican Party, x, xiii–xiv,
xvi, xx, 45, 52–53, 57; college
Republicans, 108, 112; Collins
family in, 128; Emery and,
203–4, 206–7; ethnic and
age demographics of, 1972,
136, 162; on Green, 181;
Harrington in, 101; Henry in,
118; Hildreth in, 122; LePage
in, 143; Maine Democrats
and, changes since 1972, 186;
Monks, B., and, 120, 137, 158–

About the Contributors

Severin Beliveau is a graduate of Georgetown and Georgetown Law and a longtime political candidate, activist, lobbyist, and founding partner of the Preti Flaherty law firm. Having served in the Maine House, the Maine Senate, and running for governor, he advised Democratic candidates from city councilors to presidents for over 50 years. The year 1972 was a watershed year for this longtime political savant. Although his candidate for Congress, Elmer Violette, lost, Beliveau met his future wife, Cynthia Murray, thanks to her brother, Frank Murray, who was Violette's campaign manager at the time. He also served as the Honorary French Consul in Maine.

William Sebastian Cohen is the former mayor of Bangor, Maine. In 1972, he was elected to serve as a U.S. Congressman for the 2nd Congressional District of Maine and served three consecutive terms in that capacity before being elected to serve for three terms in the U.S. Senate. Following his retirement from the Senate in 1996, former President Bill Clinton asked Cohen to serve as his Secretary of Defense. At the end of his term in January 2001, he founded The Cohen Group, an international business consulting firm. Cohen is an honors graduate of Bowdoin College and Boston University Law School. He is the author of fourteen books, consisting of seven novels and seven nonfiction books that include two books of poetry. Cohen was named to the Maine All-State high school and college basketball teams, to the New England All-Star Hall of Fame Team in 1962, and to the National Association of Basketball Coaches (NABC) Silver Anniversary Basketball team in 1985. In 2000, the NABC presented him with its highest award, the Theodore Roosevelt Trophy.

Dave Emery is a graduate of Worcester Polytechnic Institute and was a member of the Maine House. His subsequent upset of Congressman Peter Kyros in 1974 made him the youngest Maine congressman since at least the Civil War. He would go on to serve four terms in Congress, rising in leadership to become Chief Deputy Republican Whip. Later appointed by President Reagan to serve as the Deputy Director of the United States Arms Control and Disarmament Agency, he also represented the United States at the UN. Upon his return to Maine in 1989, Emery served as interim president of Thomas College and founded Scientific Marketing and Analysis, which soon became the premier political polling firm in the state. He has also lectured at Bowdoin College on numerous occasions.

Mike Harkins is the founder of the political advertising and consulting company "The Agency," and he remains prominent in Republican circles for his moderate and bipartisan political beliefs and his perspicuity in action on behalf of many national Republican candidates. In addition to helping elect Bill Cohen in 1972, some of his other clients include Congressmen Caldwell Butler, Paul Cronin, Tom Kean, Tom Petri, Senator William Roth, Governor Michael Castle, Governor Pierre du Pont, and many other down ballot officials.

Jim Harrington graduated from the University of Maine in Orono and Suffolk University Law School and practiced law in Winthrop, Maine, from 1975 until the present. Active in Maine Republican political circles since high school, he was a major youth supporter of Margaret Chase Smith. In addition to his contributions to Bill Cohen, he worked on the Maine campaigns of Neil Bishop, Harry Richardson, and Joc McKernan as well as the presidential campaigns of Pete McCloskey and John Anderson. He has had a long career of public service including as a lifetime member of Winthrop Lions Club, board member of the Maine State Golf Association, Trustee of the Winthrop Utilities District, member chair of the Maine Harness Racing Commission and National Council of Alcoholism.

Robert Loeb is a graduate of Bowdoin College and DePaul University College of Law. He prosecuted major felonies in the Office of the State's Attorney of Cook County (Chicago, IL) and was the supervisor of the Election Law Unit of that office. He has taught trial advocacy for over thirty years at DePaul's law school and for twenty years at the National Institute of Trial Advocacy. Mr. Loeb also serves as the chairman of the Illinois Supreme Court Committee on Pattern Criminal Jury Instructions and is the co-author of the book *Blackjack and the Law*.

Jed Lyons was one of Bill Cohen's advance men during the 1972 walk. He helped organize four counties, including Androscoggin, a Democratic stronghold. Jed worked in Bill's Washington office in 1973. In 1975, he cofounded the precursor to Rowman & Littlefield, the publisher of this book. He currently serves as its CEO and president. He is a member of the Council on Foreign Affairs.

Bob Monks, a graduate of Harvard and Harvard Law School, is the author or co-author of ten books on corporate governance and economics and was President Reagan's selection to direct the United States Synthetic Fuels Corporation and a founding Trustee of the Federal Employees' Retirement System. He played a pivotal role in the rise of the Republican Party in Maine from 1972 to 1990 and led the successful fight to eliminate the Big Box from Maine politics. Politically fearless, Bob also ran for the U.S. Senate against Margaret Chase Smith, Ed Muskie, and Susan Collins. Bob is currently recognized as a powerful force behind the shareholder activist movement that demands that corporate leaders establish and maintain high governance standards and accountability.

Christian P. Potholm II is the author of five books on Maine politics including *"An Insider's Guide to Maine Politics," "This Splendid Game: Maine Politics 1950-2002," "The Delights of Democracy," "Just Do It! Politics in the 1990's," "Maine: An Annotated Bibliography,"* and a work of fiction on "the Maine beyond the street lights" titled *"Tall Tales from the Tall*

Pines." He taught politics for 51 years at Bowdoin College and was Bill Cohen's campaign manager in 1972.

Cindy Watson-Welch is a graduate of Bowdoin (and one of its pioneering female cohorts when the college went coed). After obtaining her political education on the Cohen walk, working in the field and on the road, she worked at the Department of Conservation in Augusta and the Land Use Regulation Commission. Later she and her husband, Tucker Welch, went into the real estate business, and seven years ago she joined LandVest /Christies International as project manager for the Berkshires. When she looks back on the 1972 campaign, Cindy says "it was a highlight of my life."

Bill Webster, a graduate of Amherst College and Harvard Law School, was campaign manager for the Monks for Senate campaign in 1972. Previously, he served as the traveling aide to Governor John A. Volpe's 1964 campaign. Subsequently, he served in Volpe's administration and re-election campaign and was active in John Sears's mayoralty race in Boston. Webster became a principal in the Becker polling firm and an advisor to Campaigns for Congress. He remains active in various entrepreneurial businesses and on an avocational basis continues to consult on Maine Republican political campaigns.

Peter B. Webster graduated from Bowdoin College and Cornell Law School. He practiced law at the Portland firm of Verrill Dana for 56 years. A Silver Sword Honor Graduate of the Maine Military Academy and second lieutenant, he served as Bowdoin College Counsel for 39 years and was a trusted advisor to five Bowdoin presidents. Webster has been very active in community and professional activities, serving on the board and as president of the Community Counseling Center, North Yarmouth Academy, the Board of Overseers of the Bar and its Grievance Commission, the Commission of Governmental Ethics and Election Practices, and the Lawyers' Fund for Client Protection. He also was moderator for the town of Yarmouth and has been an adjunct professor at the University of Maine Law School.

Rob Witsil graduated from Bowdoin College and Delaware Law School. He credits The Walk for changing his major to government and legal studies after meeting so many political figures. Witsil's law career has focused on representing political entities. He has served as a deputy attorney general for the State of Delaware in the Criminal Prosecution Division, then as attorney for the Sussex County Council in southern Delaware. Later he was attorney and general counsel for many towns and community governments during his 40 years (and counting) of general practice and zoning and real estate law in and around Rehoboth Beach, Delaware. Witsil has long enjoyed interacting with people in his avocations of ski patrolman and lifeguard.

Christian P. Potholm II
Professor Emeritus
Bowdoin College, Maine
Campaign Manager of the 1972 Cohen for Congress Campaign